Preface Books

A se.... of scholar **IN SIXTH FORM COL** intended
for those needing mod. rough the
characteristic difficulties of their work to reach an intelligent understanding and enjoyment of it.

General Editor: MAURICE HUSSEY

A Preface to Wordsworth   JOHN PURKIS
A Preface to Donne   JAMES WINNY
A Preface to Milton   LOIS POTTER
A Preface to Coleridge   ALLAN GRANT
A Preface to Jane Austen   CHRISTOPHER GILLIE
A Preface to Yeats   EDWARD MALINS
A Preface to Pope   I. R. F. GORDON
A Preface to Hardy   MERRYN WILLIAMS
A Preface to Dryden   DAVID WYKES
A Preface to Spenser   HELENA SHIRE
A Preface to James Joyce   SYDNEY BOLT
A Preface to Hopkins   GRAHAM STOREY
A Preface to Conrad   CEDRIC WATTS
A Preface to Lawrence   GĀMINI SALGĀDO

A Preface to Conrad

Cedric Watts

Longman, London and New York

LONGMAN GROUP LIMITED
Longman House
Burnt Mill, Harlow, Essex CM20 2JE, England

Published in the United States of America by Longman Inc., New York
©Longman Group Limited 1982

First published 1982
British Library Cataloguing in Publication Data
Watts, Cedric Thomas
  A Preface to Conrad.—(Preface books).
  1. Conrad, Joseph—Criticism and interpretation
  I. Title II. Series
  823'.9'12   PR6005.04Z/
  ISBN 0 582 35273 8 cased
  ISBN 0 582 35274 6 paperback

Set in 10/11pt Baskerville
by Pearl Island Filmsetters (HK) Ltd

Printed in Hong Kong
by Wilture Enterprise (International) Ltd

CEDRIC WATTS served in the Royal Navy, took a first in English and a doctorate at Cambridge, and since 1965 has taught at Sussex University, where he is a Reader in English. He is author of *Conrad's 'Heart of Darkness': A Critical and Contextual Discussion* (Mursia, Milan, 1977) and co-author of *Cunninghame Graham: A Critical Biography* (Cambridge University Press, 1979); he has edited *Joseph Conrad's Letters to R. B. Cunninghame Graham* (Cambridge University Press, 1969) and *The English Novel* (Sussex Books, 1976). Dr Watts was a founder of the Joseph Conrad Society, UK.

Contents

LIST OF ILLUSTRATIONS   vii
FOREWORD   ix
ACKNOWLEDGEMENTS AND EDITORIAL NOTES   x
ABBREVIATIONS   xii

PART ONE: THE WRITER AND HIS SETTING

Chronological table   2

1   *Biographical background*   7
The double man   7
Poland   8
Marseilles   18
England and the Merchant Navy   21
The Congo and its aftermath   27
The second career: Conrad the novelist   30

2   *Cultural background*   46
The tensions   46
Conrad's pessimism   48
Religious matters   51
Poland and Conrad's political outlook   54
Imperialism   59
Science and determinism   66
The Superfluous Man   68
The Hamlet/Don Quixote dichotomy   70
Anti-rational primitivism   77
Determinism and solipsism   82
Darkness and the dying sun   86
Darwinism   88
Darwinism and psychology   91
Atavism and doubles   93
Evolution, aestheticism and sex   95
Literary influences   102

PART TWO: THE ART OF CONRAD

3   *Conrad on his art*   112

4   *The pressure towards paradox*   115

5   *The covert plot: two examples*   118
The conspiracy against Kurtz in *Heart of Darkness*   118
The attempt to defraud the hero in *The Shadow-Line*   118

6   *Textual commentaries*   120
The opening of *Almayer's Folly*, 1895   120
The ending of 'An Outpost of Progress', 1897   122
A passage from *Heart of Darkness*, 1899   123
Jim's jump: *Lord Jim*, 1900   127
Three Conradian cruces   129

7   *Nostromo*   135
Genesis and production   135
Sources   138
Nostromo and the meanings of its techniques   144
Chronological tables and maps for *Nostromo*   158

8   *The Conradian Hero*   166
Misgivings   166
A typology   167

9   *Conrad's place in literary history*   171

PART THREE: REFERENCE SECTION

A list of symbolic or allegoric names in Conrad's fiction   176
Biographical list   180
Gazetteer   185
Further reading   187

INDEXES

General Index   190
Index to Conrad's Works   192

List of illustrations

Detail from *The Snake Charmer* by Henri Rousseau, le Douanier, 1907 — cover
Joseph Conrad in 1904 — frontispiece
Map showing the partitions of Poland — 10
Bydgoszcz, Poland, September 1939 — 11
The last days of the Warsaw Uprising, 1944 — 13
Warsaw, 1944 — 14
Conrad as a young man — 19
Agreement and account of the crew of the *Skimmer of the Sea* — 22–3
The *Torrens* — 25
The *Roi des Belges* — 28
Edward Garnett with his son, David, in 1897 — 32
R. B. Cunninghame Graham — 36
Pent Farm — 37
Ford Madox Ford — 39
Conrad in old age — 42
Oswalds — 43
Conrad's grave — 44
Somewhere in the Pacific by Max Beerbohm — 49
Don Quixote by William Nicholson — 71
The Second Sally by William Strang — 73
Drawing by Conrad: Woman with Serpent — 99
Drawing by Conrad: The Diffident Suitor — 100
The beginning of the manuscript of *Nostromo* — 136–7
Map of Costaguana'a occidental province — 164
Map of part of the town of Sulaco — 165

Foreword

This authoritative volume sets forth both informed personal response and academic knowledge in the service of the student of the novels of Joseph Conrad. The views that this Polish novelist held constituted a unique aristocratic and artistic reading of human nature and its aims and philosophy: they have to some degree been heard from other Europeans or Americans in our century but before Conrad hardly at all in England. Cedric Watts, offering an account of his subject's beliefs and literary output, furnishes the reader at the same time with an introduction to much early twentieth-century thought and culture also.

The earlier sections that constitute Part One, whose rationale is explained on pp. 7–8, should be read as varied modes of access to Conrad's own writings. They govern the highly effective discussion of his art following in Part Two. Here, after a close commentary upon a number of passages from the novels in order to accustom the reader to the linguistic development and modernist overtones of a writer who came to English out of Polish and through French as his second language, follows a substantial essay on *Nostromo*. I know no more thorough and yet imaginative discussion of this novel than forms the crown of the whole Preface. How Conrad's varied experiences prepared him for writing that masterpiece is one of the principal purposes and accomplishments of Dr Watts's contribution to the series. This he does most helpfully after an extensive and intimate awareness of everything that Conrad left us, through which he speaks most powerfully to us today.

MAURICE HUSSEY General Editor

Acknowledgements and editorial notes

Quotations from Conrad's novels, tales, essays and autobiographical works are from the Dent Collected Edition, London, 1946–55, unless otherwise specified (the Collected Edition does not include all Conrad's works).

In any quotation, a row of five dots (.....) indicates an elision that I have made, whereas a row of three dots indicates an ellipsis already present in the original text.

When discussing *Nostromo* I correct the novel's accentuation of Spanish names.

In preparing Part One of this book, I was helped by Jocelyn Baines's *Joseph Conrad: A Critical Biography* and by Norman Sherry's *Conrad and His World*. In Parts One and Two I have drawn on my previous writings about Conrad, particularly *Conrad's 'Heart of Darkness': A Critical and Contextual Discussion*. I consulted so many commentators that sometimes I had difficulty in stepping over the piles of books that surrounded my chair; but I have made every effort to acknowledge local debts in my text, and if there are any inadvertent oversights I express my sincere regret now for them.

Hans van Marle of Amsterdam, who in matters of scholarly documentation is one of the most indefatigable and accurate Conradians in the world, kindly scrutinised my chronologies and maps for *Nostromo*. I have revised and corrected them in the light of his advice; any errors that remain are mine alone. I am again indebted to Alan Sinfield for his encouragement. Maurice Hussey was admirably stoical, sharp and lively, as occasion required. Professor R. A. Foakes and Mr M. B. Hrynkiewicz-Moczulski gave helpful advice.

This book was written in 1978 and 1979.

The author and publisher are grateful to the following for permission to quote copyright material:

Duke University Press for extracts from *Joseph Conrad: Letters To William Blackwood and David S. Meldrum*, edited by William Blackburn, Copyright 1958 Duke University Press; the author's agent and Simon & Schuster Inc. for an extract from *A Sort of Life* by Graham Greene, published by The Bodley Head; Yale University Press for extracts from *Letters of Joseph Conrad to Marguerite Poradowska* translated and edited by John A. Gee and Paul J. Sturm, published by Yale University Press.

We are grateful to the following for permission to reproduce photographs and illustrations:

BBC Hulton Picture Library, pages ii, 14, 39 and 42; Henry W. and Albert A. Berg Collection, The New York Public Library, Astor, Lenox and Tilden Foundations and the Trustees of the Joseph Conrad Estate, page 99; British Library, London, page 73; Camera Press, page 11; David Garnett, page 32; Humanities Research Center, The University of Texas at Austin, page 44; Lilly Library, Indiana University, Bloomington, Indiana, page 100; Mansell Collection, page 19; National Maritime Museum, London, page 25; Prasa Agency, Warsaw, page 13; Public Record Office, London, pages 22–3; Mrs Eva Reichmann, page 49 (photo: Bodleian Library, Oxford); Miss M. Rishworth, pages 37 and 43; from the Collection of the Rosenbach Museum and Library, Philadelphia, pages 136–7; Scala/Vision International, cover (Louvre, Paris); Thames and Hudson Ltd., London, from *Conrad and His World* by Norman Sherry, page 28; Victoria and Albert Museum, London, page 71; Cedric Watts, pages 36, 164–5.

Abbreviations

With a few clearly-indicated exceptions, the quotations from Conrad's novels, tales, essays and autobiographical works are from the Dent Collected Edition, London, 1946–55.

AF	Joseph Conrad: *Almayer's Folly*. London: Dent, 1947.
Baines	Jocelyn Baines: *Joseph Conrad: A Critical Biography*. London: Weidenfeld and Nicolson, 1960.
BB	*Joseph Conrad: Letters to William Blackwood and David S. Meldrum*, edited by William Blackburn. Durham, N.C.: Duke University Press, 1958.
CN	Albert Guerard: *Conrad the Novelist*. Cambridge, Mass.: Harvard University Press, 1958.
CP	Avrom Fleishman: *Conrad's Politics*. Baltimore, Maryland: The Johns Hopkins Press, 1967.
CWW	Norman Sherry: *Conrad's Western World*. London: Cambridge University Press, 1971.
EG	*Letters from Conrad, 1895 to 1924*, edited by Edward Garnett. London: Nonesuch Press, n.d.
HD	Joseph Conrad: *Heart of Darkness*.
KRZ	*Joseph Conrad: Centennial Essays*, edited by Ludwik Krzyzanowski. New York: Polish Institute of Arts and Sciences, 1960.
LCG	*Joseph Conrad's Letters to R. B. Cunninghame Graham*, edited by Cedric Watts. London: Cambridge University Press, 1969.
LE	Joseph Conrad: *Last Essays*. London: Dent, 1955.
LL	*Joseph Conrad: Life and Letters*, edited by G. Jean-Aubry; 2 vols. London: Heinemann, 1927.
LMP	*Letters of Joseph Conrad to Marguerite Poradowska, 1890–1920*, translated and edited by J. A. Gee and P. J. Sturm. New Haven: Yale University Press, 1940.
MPL	*Lettres de Joseph Conrad à Marguerite Poradowska*, edited by René Rapin. Geneva: Librairie Droz, 1966.
N	Joseph Conrad: *Nostromo*. London: Dent, 1947.
Najder	*Conrad's Polish Background*, edited by Zdzisław Najder. London: Oxford University Press, 1964.
NLL	Joseph Conrad: *Notes on Life and Letters*. London: Dent, 1949.
NN	Joseph Conrad: *The Nigger of the 'Narcissus'*. London: Dent, 1950.
PR	Joseph Conrad: *A Personal Record*. London: Dent, 1946.
R	Joseph Conrad: *The Rescue*. London: Dent, 1949.

SL	Joseph Conrad: *The Shadow-Line*. London: Dent, 1950.
TH	Joseph Conrad: *Tales of Hearsay*. London: Dent, 1955.
TLAS	Joseph Conrad: *'Twixt Land and Sea: Three Tales*. London: Dent, 1947.
TU	Joseph Conrad: *Tales of Unrest*. London: Dent, 1947.
UWE	Joseph Conrad: *Under Western Eyes*. London: Dent, 1947.
V	Joseph Conrad: *Victory*. London: Dent, 1948.
Y	Joseph Conrad: *'Youth', 'Heart of Darkness' and 'The End of the Tether'*. London: Dent, 1946.

The only legitimate basis of creative work lies in the courageous recognition of all the irreconcilable antagonisms that make our life so enigmatic, so burdensome, so fascinating, so dangerous – so full of hope.

Joseph Conrad, Letter to the *New York Times*, 2 August 1901.

Part One
The Writer and His Setting

Chronological table

CONRAD'S LIFE

OTHER EVENTS

1854–55 Crimean War.

1856 Freud born.

1857 Conrad born at Berdyczów
(Ukrainian: Berdichev) in
partitioned Poland.

1857 Flaubert's *Madame Bovary*
published.

1859 Darwin's *Origin of Species*;
Dickens's *A Tale of Two
Cities*.

1861 Conrad's father, Apollo
Korzeniowski, arrested.

1862 Apollo and his wife sent
into exile: Conrad with
them.

1863 Polish uprising.

1865 Conrad's mother dies.

1865 Kipling born.

1866 Dostoyevsky's *Crime and
Punishment*.

1869 Apollo dies.

1869 Tolstoy's *War and Peace*.

1870 Dickens dies; Lenin born.

1872 George Eliot's
Middlemarch; Bertrand
Russell born.

1874 Conrad travels to
Marseilles to become a
seaman.

1878 Suicide attempt. Later enters British Merchant Navy.	
	1879 Stalin born.
1880 Qualifies as second mate.	
1883 Shipwrecked.	1883 Marx dies; Mussolini born.
1884 Qualifies as first mate.	
	1885 D. H. Lawrence born.
1886 Becomes a British subject; qualifies as master.	1886 Greenwich bomb outrage; Cunninghame Graham becomes MP.
1887 First mate of barque *Highland Forest*.	1887 'Bloody Sunday': Cunninghame Graham arrested and subsequently jailed.
1888 His first command: the barque *Otago*.	1888 T. S. Eliot born; Graham becomes founder-president of first Labour Party in Britain.
1889 Begins *Almayer's Folly*.	1889 Hitler born.
1890 The Congo journey.	
1891 First mate of clipper *Torrens*; meets Galsworthy on board.	
1893 Second mate of steamship *Adowa*.	
1894 Tadeusz Bobrowski dies; Conrad inherits about £1,600; *Almayer's Folly* accepted for publication.	1894 Robert Louis Stevenson dies.

1895 *Almayer's Folly* published; reviews vary but include high praise.	1895 Engels dies; Wells's *Time Machine*; Kipling's *Captains Courageous*; Hardy's *Jude the Obscure*; Crane's *Red Badge of Courage*.
1896 *An Outcast of the Islands* published; Conrad marries.	
1897 *The Nigger of the 'Narcissus'*; Conrad meets Graham and Crane.	1897 Queen Victoria's Diamond Jubilee.
1898 *Tales of Unrest*; birth of son, Borys; Conrad meets Hueffer (Ford), Wells and James.	1898 War between Spain and USA.
1899 *Heart of Darkness* serialised in *Blackwood's Magazine*.	1899–1902 Boer War.
1900 *Lord Jim* serialised and published as book.	
1901 *The Inheritors* (with Hueffer as co-author).	1901 Queen Victoria dies; Graham's *A Vanished Arcadia*
1902 *Youth*.	
1903 *Typhoon* volume; *Romance* (with Hueffer).	1903 Panamá secedes from Colombia.
1904 *Nostromo* serialised in *T.P.'s Weekly* and published as book.	1904–5 Russo-Japanese War (won by Japan).
1905 *One Day More* staged.	
1906 *The Mirror of the Sea*; second son (John) born.	1906 Samuel Beckett born.
1907 *The Secret Agent*.	
1908 *A Set of Six*.	

1909 'The Nature of a Crime' (with Hueffer) in *The English Review*.	
1910 'The Secret Sharer'. Conrad has breakdown after completing *Under Western Eyes*.	1910 Freud becomes internationally famous around this time.
1911 *Under Western Eyes* published.	1911 William Golding born.
1912 *A Personal Record*; *'Twixt Land and Sea*; *Chance* serialised.	
1913 Book of *Chance*. Conrad meets Russell.	1913 Lawrence's *Sons and Lovers*.
1914 *Chance* becomes a best-seller; Conrad re-visits Poland.	1914–18 First World War.
1915 *Within the Tides*; *Victory*.	
1916 *The Shadow-Line* serialised.	
1917 *The Shadow-Line* (book).	1917 Russian Revolution.
	1918 Poland reborn as independent republic; fights Russia.
1919 *The Arrow of Gold*.	
1920 *Laughing Anne* (play) written; *The Rescue* published, 22 years after its commencement.	1920 Poles rout the Russian invaders. Lawrence's *Women in Love*.
1921 Corsica; *Notes on Life and Letters*.	

5

1922	Play of *The Secret Agent* fails.	1922	Eliot's *The Waste Land*; Joyce's *Ulysses*; Mussolini takes power in Italy.
1923	*The Rover*; visit to USA, giving readings.		
1924	Conrad declines knighthood. Dies on 3 August; buried at Canterbury. *The Nature of a Crime* published as book.	1924	Ramsay MacDonald heads first Labour Government of Great Britain.
1925	*Tales of Hearsay*; *Suspense*.		
1926	*Last Essays*.		

I Biographical background

The double man

Since August 1924, Conrad's body has been rotting beneath the granite chippings in a public cemetery at Canterbury. 'As to the soul', he once remarked, 'You and I, cher ami, are too honest to talk of what we know nothing about.' His imagination, however, can be said to be more effectively alive than ever before, as more and more readers have come to enjoy and respect his works; and one of the main reasons for this continuing vitality is that he was a double man.

'Homo duplex has in my case more than one meaning', he wrote to a Polish friend. 'Homo duplex': the double man. The phrase will serve as a theme for this book. Sometimes it seems to me that if any god presides over Conrad's best work, it is the god Janus. Janus is the two-headed god: he looks in opposite ways at the same time; he presides over paradox; and he is the patron of janiform texts.

Let us imagine that we could travel back in time to call on Conrad in 1903, when he was writing *Nostromo*. We would see a middle-aged man of barely average height; square-shouldered, almost stocky in build; dark hair neatly brushed back, a dark beard tidily trimmed; high cheek-bones, with penetrating eyes somewhat hooded at the corners by drooping lids. Expecting visitors, he has taken care to dress in formal gentlemanly style: a smart suit, waistcoat, stiffly starched collar and cuffs, a monocle. His manner would be elaborately courteous, yet at the same time reserved and watchful; outwardly composed, yet sensitive, touchy: a tactless political or literary reference could draw a cold stare of rage or a snarl of exasperation. He could be capable, too, if we won his trust, of impetuous, passionate agreement, seizing our hands in his to make his point, speaking rapidly in a fluent English with a marked Polish accent, misplacing stresses on words so that 'success' would become '*suc*cess', for example, adding the occasional phrase in French when the English did not come rapidly enough, and happy to reminisce about his many years of voyaging.

Already some meanings of that phrase 'homo duplex' would suggest themselves. Conrad was a patriotic Pole who became a British citizen. He was 'a Polish nobleman cased in British tar'. He was a seaman who laboriously rose to the peak of his career as a captain in the merchant navy, yet abandoned that career to try his luck as a creative writer. His manner retained both an aristocratic air of command and the neurotic intensity of a ruthlessly-dedicated

7

artist. To his Uncle Tadeusz, he was a mixture of dreamer and practical man; to Cunninghame Graham, his mind seemed 'a strange compact of the conflicting qualities'; and to Edward Garnett, he seemed 'masculinely keen yet femininely sensitive'.

A survey of his career from its Polish origins will help us to understand the duplicity of his nature and the janiformity of his works.

Poland

'..... We had once more to murmur "*Væ Victis*" and count the cost in sorrow. Not that we were ever very good at calculating, either, in prosperity or in adversity. That's a lesson we could never learn, to the great exasperation of our enemies who have bestowed upon us the epithet of Incorrigible ...'

The speaker was of Polish nationality, that nationality not so much alive as surviving, which persists in thinking, breathing, speaking, hoping, and suffering in its grave, railed in by a million of bayonets and triple-sealed with the seals of three great empires .....

Patriotism [is] a somewhat discredited sentiment, because the delicacy of our humanitarians regards it as a relic of barbarism.
Joseph Conrad, 'Prince Roman' in *Tales of Hearsay*.

Poland was and is a proudly patriotic country: its people pride themselves on the nation's liberal traditions, its cultural riches, and their heroism down the ages in defence of their homeland. To the western imagination, there is something romantic, tragic and also quixotic about Poland. Romantic, for it is the birthplace of Chopin and of celebrated defiant patriots like Prince Roman Sanguszko, the poet Mickiewicz and the warrior Kościuszko; quixotic and tragic, because its patriotism has burnt all the more brightly for its oppression by stronger, more powerful neighbours.

A few years ago, on a visit to Poland, I spoke to a lady who had lived through the Second World War and who spoke of the time when Poland might be a free nation once more. 'And when will that be?' I asked. 'Who knows?' she replied; 'We outlived the German barbarians, and we will outlive the Russian barbarians too.' A scholar told me the apocryphal story of a noted atheist who had recently been seen, apparently at prayer, in one of the Roman Catholic churches. When a neighbour said, 'What are *you* doing here?', the man replied fiercely: 'I may be an atheist, but I am also a Pole.' On another occasion there, a student reminded me in an undertone that for many years after the war, for all Conrad's popularity in Poland, certain of his works were unavailable in Polish – notably *Under Western Eyes* and 'Autocracy and War', which had prophesied that a Russian revolution could be followed by further tyranny. At night, the police patrolling the streets of Warsaw carried guns. Every so often, as I walked down the main streets, I could see candles glimmering by plaques on walls; and the plaques commemorated the patriots who had been executed there or who had died fighting at those places during the uprising of 1944.

If Conrad could re-visit Poland today, he would find wearisomely familiar the fact that Poland is part of the Russian empire; but he would also find encouragingly familiar the stubborn spirit of independence and the hunger for individual and national freedom which is still alive among many of its people. His essays 'The Crime of Partition' and 'Autocracy and War' (both in *Notes on Life and Letters*) celebrate that spirit and condemn sardonically the nation's oppressors – a condemnation that prior and subsequent events so fully vindicate.

In the late eighteenth century, Poland was one of the more liberal of the European nations, having an elective monarchy and a loosely federal administration. But in 1772, at the instigation of Frederick the Great, one-third of Poland was seized and divided by Prussia, Austria and Russia. A second 'Partition' followed in 1793: Russia seized more land. Then Tadeusz Kościuszko, who had once fought for the American Army in the War of Independence, organised an insurrection: under his leadership the Poles rose against the Russians and defeated them at Racławice; but eventually the insurrection was crushed and Kościuszko captured. In the Third Partition (1795), the whole of the country was engulfed by the three autocracies: Poland vanished from the map of Europe, though its patriots kept up resistance and led revolts in 1830 and 1863. After German defeat in the First World War, and in the wake of the Russian Revolution, an independent Poland was re-established in 1918. The Polish Republic, however, was short-lived. In 1939, following the signing of the Molotov–Ribbentrop pact whereby the USSR gave support to Hitler's Germany, the Germans carried out their *Blitzkrieg* against Poland with tanks, Stukas and paratroops. The ill-equipped Polish troops fought bravely but in vain: poignant spotty newsreels of the time show Polish cavalry charging – and being mown down by – the invaders' tanks; and while the Germans thus engulfed most of Poland from the west, the Russian army, in compliance with the pact with Hitler, seized territory in the east. Many of the defeated Poles made their way to England, where in the RAF, the Navy and the Army they continued their struggle, fighting and dying at Tobruk, Monte Cassino, Arnhem; and in conquered Warsaw there were heroic but doomed uprisings: the Ghetto uprising, by the Jews against their exterminators in 1943, and the general uprising of 1944, when for two months, contesting every street, every block of houses, the men and women of the Polish resistance withstood the might of German tanks, dive-bombers and heavy artillery. By the

The partitions of Poland

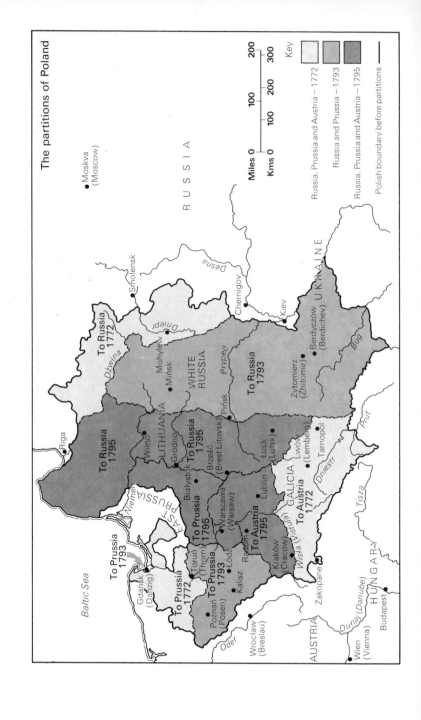

Key

Russia, Prussia and Austria – 1772

Russia and Prussia – 1793

Russia, Prussia and Austria – 1795

Polish boundary before partitions

Miles 0 — 100 — 200

Kms 0 — 100 — 200 — 300

Baltic Sea

Moskva (Moscow)

RUSSIA

Smolensk

Desna

Dniepr

Dźwina

To Russia 1772

Mohylew

Mińsk

WHITE RUSSIA

Prypeć

To Russia 1793

Chernigov

Kiev

Berdyczów (Berdichev)

UKRAINE

Zytomierz (Zhitomir)

Bug

Riga

Wilno

LITHUANIA

Grodno

To Russia 1795

Brześć (Brest Litovsk)

Pińsk

Łuck (Lutsk)

Lwów (Lemberg)

Tarnopol

GALICIA To Austria 1772

Dniestr

Prut

Białystok

Lublin

To Russia 1795

Niemen

EAST PRUSSIA

To Prussia 1793

Gdańsk (Danzig)

To Prussia 1772

Toruń (Thorn)

To Prussia 1795

Warszawa (Warsaw)

Łódź

Radom

To Austria 1795

Kraków (Cracow)

Wisła (Vistula)

To Prussia 1793

Poznań (Posen)

Kalisz

Wrocław (Breslau)

Oder

Zakopane

AUSTRIA

Wien (Vienna)

Dunaj (Danube)

Tisza

HUNGARY

Budapest

above *Bydgoszcz, Poland, September 1939. German soldiers contemplate the corpses of Polish residents whom they have 'executed'.*

In 1905, Conrad wrote: 'Germany . . . . . is a powerful and voracious organisation, full of unscrupulous self-confidence . . . . . The era of wars so eloquently denounced by the old Republicans as the peculiar blood guilt of dynastic ambitions is by no means over yet. They will be fought out differently, with lesser frequency, with an increased bitterness and the savage tooth-and-claw obstinacy of a struggle for existence.' (NLL, *104–5.)*

left *Among writers of fiction, Conrad was the most incisive commentator on imperialism. This map suggests one of the reasons for his preoccupation.*

'As an act of mere conquest the best excuse for the partition lay simply in the fact that it happened to be possible; there was the plunder and there was the opportunity to get hold of it.' (NLL, *115.)*

end of that second uprising, much of Warsaw was in ruins, its palaces and churches reduced to rubble. Hitler ordered that the whole city should be totally destroyed, and with dynamite and fire the troops systematically obliterated street after street. On the defeat of Germany, Poland became part of the Russian empire, controlled by a nominally communist government subservient to Moscow and unfettered by such inconveniences as democratic elections. However, massive reconstruction has taken place: with the aid of old prints, maps and photographs, Warsaw was slowly rebuilt: even the Old City, with its alleys and market-square and steeply-roofed houses, was restored as an exact visual replica of the ancient centre the Nazis had destroyed; even the Royal Palace has been reconstructed stone by stone. The city of Warsaw as it now stands can be seen as a monument both to human inconsistency and to human indomitability.

An ex-resistance man told me that during the war Conrad's *Lord Jim* was regarded almost as a Bible, a moral support, by some of the Polish combatants. After the war, Conrad was officially out of favour with the régime: Jan Kott and other critics attacked his work for being negative, reactionary, defeatist. In the 1970s, with the official translation of his collected works into Polish, the régime seemed to have bestowed its blessing; but there were tell-tale omissions. The omissions were 'The Crime of Partition', 'Autocracy and War', 'A Note on the Polish Problem', the 'Author's Note' to *Under Western Eyes*, part of the 'Author's Note' to *Notes on Life and Letters*, and 'The Censor of Plays'. Among these writings Conrad claims that post-revolutionary Russia will be as tyrannical as pre-revolutionary Russia and that censorship is a contemptible weapon of tyranny. By censoring his claims, the eastern authorities have elegantly verified them.

Even without the régime's blessing, Conrad's work would continue to be widely remembered and respected in Poland; and the visitor to that country will find that Conrad's father, Apollo Korzeniowski, is also alive in memory, as a patriot.

Apollo Korzeniowski was a member of the land-owning gentry. He had little aptitude for practical, business matters, though he worked for a time as an estate manager; his real interests were literature and Polish politics. He wrote comedies, mystically patriotic poems, and translated works by Shakespeare, Dickens, Victor Hugo and de Vigny. In 1856 he married Ewelina (Eva) Bobrowska, a young woman of another prosperous land-owning family, and their only child, Józef Teodor Konrad Nałęcz Korzeniowski, was born in December of the following year. There is no doubt that Konrad – the name by which Conrad's father referred to him, and which, anglicised, was to serve as the novelist's pseudonym – was a patriotically-chosen Christian name. It brings to mind the hero of

The last days of the Warsaw Uprising, 1944. The wounded Poles often lacked food, water and medical attention.

  *While the Germans suppressed the uprising, the Russian Army halted on the outskirts of Warsaw. In 1919 Conrad had prophesied of Germany and Russia: 'The old partners in "the Crime [of Partition]" are not likely to forgive their victim its inconvenient and almost shocking obstinacy in keeping alive.' (*NLL, *121.*)

Cracow Market, Warsaw, at the time of the 1944 uprising. A statue faces the burning telephone exchange.

Conrad wrote in 1905: 'Civilization has done its little best by our sensibilities for whose growth it is responsible. It has managed to remove the sights and sounds of battlefields away from our doorsteps. But it cannot be expected to achieve the feat always and under every variety of cicumstance. Some day it must fail, and we shall have then a wealth of appallingly unpleasant sensations brought home to us with painful intimacy......Germany's attitude proves that no peace for the earth can be found in the expansion of material interests......' (NLL, 110, 113.)

Mickiewicz's drama *Dziady* (*Forefathers' Eve*, 1832), who, awakening to a mystical sense of his power to free Poland from Muscovite tyranny, declares that his old private self, Gustavus, is dead: 'Hic natus est Conradus' – 'Here Conrad is born'. It would also have been linked in Apollo's mind with Mickiewicz's poem of historic legend, *Konrad Wallenrod* (1828), in which the leader of the Teutonic Crusaders proves to be a Lithuanian Pole who had cunningly obtained that leadership so as to be able to take the German troops on a completely disastrous campaign. (This poem stresses a theme that would later preoccupy Joseph Conrad – the seeming paradox that loyalty often entails betrayal. Here loyalty to one's native land is seen by Mickiewicz as justifying treachery to one's trusting followers.) To commemorate his son's baptism, Apollo Korzeniowski composed a poem which is dated 'in the 85th year of Russian tyranny' and ends thus:

My child, my son – tell yourself that you are without land, without love, without homeland, without humanity – so long as Poland, our Mother, is enslaved.

In Warsaw, Apollo became one of the leaders of the 'Reds', the more extreme of the two main patriotic parties: it advocated the liberation of the serfs as well as national independence. On his initiative was formed the underground committee which was eventually to launch the bloodily-suppressed insurrection of 1863. But in 1861 Apollo himself was arrested and imprisoned; both he and Eva were sentenced to exile for their subversive activities, and the four-year-old Conrad accompanied them on the bitter journey to the far-off Russian province of Vologda. This period of exile sapped Eva's health: after her return, ailing with advanced tuberculosis, she died in 1865 at the age of 32.

Understandably, Apollo became a brooding, melancholy figure, possessed by a rather morbid religiosity. He wrote:

I have kept my eyes fixed on the Cross and by that means fortified my fainting soul and reeling brain. The sacred days of agony have passed, and I resume my ordinary life, a little more broken but with breath still in me, still alive. But the little orphan is always at my side, and I never forget my anxiety for him . . . . . He grows up as though in a monastic cell. For the *memento mori* we have the grave of our dear one . . . . .

(*LL*, I, 16)

And even before then, at the age of five, that 'little orphan' had acquired a proudly self-conscious sense of social and political destiny, to judge from Conrad's earliest extant piece of writing, an inscription on the back of a photograph:

To my beloved Grandma who helped me send cakes to my poor
Daddy in prison – grandson, Pole, Catholic, nobleman – 6 July
1863 – Konrad.

(Najder, 8)

After Eva's death, Apollo attempted to undertake Conrad's education himself, teaching him some French, for example; and Conrad
came to know his father's work as a translator into Polish of Hugo's
Les Travailleurs de la mer and of Shakespeare's *Two Gentlemen of
Verona*. But eventually the dispirited father, stricken with tuberculosis as Eva had been, was prostrate, confined to a sickroom,
attended by nuns. Many years later Conrad recalled the atmosphere:

> The air around me was all piety, resignation, and silence.
>
> I don't know what would have become of me if I had not been
> a reading boy. My prep finished I would have had nothing to do
> but sit and watch the awful stillness of the sick room flow out
> through the closed door and coldly enfold my scared heart. I
> suppose that in a futile childish way I would have gone crazy.
> But I was a reading boy.

(NLL, 168)

On 23 May 1869 Apollo died, and Conrad was thus an eleven-year-
old orphan. He followed his father's coffin in the funeral processio.
through the streets of Cracow – a procession that was also a huge
national demonstration.

> What I saw with my own eyes was the public funeral, the cleared
> streets, the hushed crowds; but I understood perfectly well that
> this was a manifestation of the national spirit seizing a worthy
> occasion. That bare-headed mass of work people, youths of the
> University, women at the windows, school-boys on the pavement,
> could have known nothing positive about him except the fame of
> his fidelity to the one guiding emotion in their hearts.

(PR, viii)

So already, by the age of eleven, Conrad knew bitterly well many
of the themes which were later to be so prominent in his writings.
The theme of loneliness; of tragic death; of Polish nationalism;
of self-sacrifice for a noble cause; of beleaguered solidarity. And he
could also have sensed some paradoxes, too: that loyalty may entail
subversion or betrayal; that there may be conflicts between the claims
of honour, the claims of the law and the claims of affection; and that
works of literature may awaken us to reality, yet also offer us an
escape and refuge from it. He knew the power of words over flesh
and blood: their power to heal or kill.

Conrad's uncle, Tadeusz Bobrowski, now became his guardian.
Bobrowski was wealthy, astute, and unfailingly conscientious in his

guardianship, which virtually extended until his death a quarter of a century later; for in letter after letter, even after Conrad had long left Poland, he was to be a source of detailed advice and exhortation, always trying to steer Conrad towards the path of diligent, steady work and practical attainment, and away from introspection, inconsistency, speculative schemes. Initially, he provided Conrad with a tutor and enrolled the boy in a Cracow school. Gradually the young Conrad became stubbornly determined to go to sea; and in 1872 the pupil and the tutor, Adam Pulman, went on a long tour of Switzerland, during which Pulman was charged with the task of dissuading Conrad from his ambition to become a sailor. The climax of the argument, as Conrad recalled it many years later, was strangely oblique:

> We sat down by the side of the road to continue the argument begun half a mile or so before. I am certain it was an argument because I remember perfectly how my tutor argued and how without the power of reply I listened with my eyes fixed obstinately on the ground. A stir on the road made me look up – and then I saw my unforgettable Englishman.....He marched rapidly towards the east (attended by a hang-dog Swiss guide) with the mien of an ardent and fearless traveller.....His calves exposed to the public gaze and to the tonic air of high altitudes, dazzled the beholder by the splendour of their marble-like condition and their rich tones of young ivory. He was the leader of a small caravan. The light of a headlong, exalted satisfaction with the world of men and the scenery of mountains illuminated his clean-cut, very red face, his short, silver-white whiskers, his innocently eager and triumphant eyes. In passing he cast a glance of kindly curiosity and a friendly gleam of big, sound, shiny teeth towards the man and the boy sitting like dusty tramps by the roadside, with a modest knapsack lying at their feet. His white calves twinkled sturdily, the uncouth Swiss guide with a surly mouth stalked like an unwilling bear at his elbow; a small train of three mules followed in single file the lead of this inspiring enthusiast.....
>
> The enthusiastic old Englishman had passed – and the argument went on. What reward could I expect from such a life at the end of my years, either in ambition, honour or conscience? An un-answerable question. But I felt no longer crushed. Then our eyes met and a genuine emotion was visible in his as well as in mine. The end came all at once. He picked up the knapsack and got on to his feet.
>
> 'You are an incorrigible, hopeless Don Quixote. That's what you are.'

(PR, 40–1, 43–4)

17

This passage is taken from *A Personal Record*. Conrad is recalling events of long ago; his memory, like anyone else's, is fallible; and like any imaginative writer he is giving to his recollections a dramatic heightening and an increase in thematic order. It is admirably vivid writing, with a gently ironic humour and an eye for the quietly absurd or mildly ridiculous, and with a characteristic deviousness about the narrative sequence. The argument over Conrad's apparently quixotic determination to go to sea is clinched not so much by logic as by the incursion of an English reincarnation of Don Quixote – almost as though a tutelary deity in disguise had crossed the scene. And indeed there may have been something quixotically arbitrary or irrational about Conrad's choice of career. His country lacked a navy; there were no naval connections in his family; and in those days of sailing ships, when vessels were so commonly lost at sea in storms and gales, to choose a career which promised hard knocks and mortal risks could well seem foolhardy. But there's nothing uncommon about a youthful desire to travel the world and see exotic places, and Conrad had probably been influenced by his youthful reading, which included the maritime adventure-tales by Captain Marryat and Fenimore Cooper as well as travel-books like McClintock's *Voyage of the 'Fox'*; and Poland could have seemed psychologically oppressive after his bitter childhood experiences. It was also the case that as he was legally a Russian citizen and the son of a political convict, Conrad was liable to conscription in the Russian Army for up to twenty-five years. There is no certain explanation for his ambition, and as he himself remarks, 'The part of the inexplicable should be allowed for in appraising the conduct of men in a world where no explanation is final.' (*PR*, 35.) Whatever the reason, in October 1874 his uncle and his weeping grandmother saw the sixteen-year-old Conrad board the train, alone, for Marseilles: the start of a journey to the Mediterranean, and thence to the oceans of the world; to England, and after many years to a plot of earth at Canterbury.

Marseilles

After the sombre, death-haunted years in Poland came the utter contrast of southern France with its long hot summers and the crowded colourful streets: Conrad's four years in Marseilles were probably the most varied and adventurous of his whole career, though death hovered even in this crowded Arcadia. Marseilles in the 1870s was both a bustling, thriving port and a cosmopolitan city, with its theatres, operas and salons, its fashionable or bohemian restaurants, its waterfront taverns. Conrad received a generous financial allowance from his uncle, but he repeatedly over-spent it wildly on a very full social life. It was here, almost certainly, that

Conrad as a young man, around the time of his departure for Marseilles.

he came to know the plays of Scribe and Sardou, the operas of Meyer-beer and Offenbach; later writings indicate that he had an intense love-affair, and at his age it would be surprising if he had not; and he certainly made friends easily, being popular with aristocrats and artists, sea-captains and pilots.

> The very first whole day I ever spent on salt water was by invita-tion, in a big half-decked pilot-boat, cruising under close reefs on the lookout, in misty, blowing weather, for the sails of ships and the smoke of steamers rising out there, beyond the slim and tall Planier lighthouse cutting the line of the windswept horizon with a white perpendicular stroke. They were hospitable souls, these sturdy Provençal seamen.....Their sea-tanned faces, whiskered or shaved, lean or full, with the intent wrinkled sea-eyes of the pilot-breed, and here and there a thin gold loop at the lobe of a hairy ear, bent over my sea-infancy ..... And I have been invited to sit in more than one tall, dark house of the old town at their hospitable board, had the *bouillabaisse* ladled out into a thick plate by their high-voiced, broad-browed wives, talked to their daughters – thickset girls, with pure profiles, glorious masses of black hair arranged with complicated art, dark eyes, and dazzlingly white teeth.
>
> (*PR*, 123–4)

Conrad's love of the sea stood him in good stead with these pilots, and in course of time he was in demand as a pilot himself; and his aristocratic 'drawing-room manner' gave him entry to the salons of the wealthy and fashionable – of Monsieur Delestang, for example, 'a frozen, mummified Royalist', and Delestang's imperious wife, who reminded Conrad of Dickens's Lady Dedlock; and more bohemian companions included Frétigny the sculptor, who later appeared as Prax in *The Arrow of Gold*, and Clovis Hugues, a left-wing journalist and poet who had shot and killed a political opponent in a duel. Many of the experiences of these years were to find their way – sometimes deceptively transformed – into the pages not only of the late novel, *Arrow of Gold*, but also the autobiographical *Personal Record* and *The Mirror of the Sea*, while sunny Provence and the Mediterranean provided the location for *The Rover*.

It is certain that during this period Conrad made his first ocean-going voyages on sailing-ships: at first as a passenger, then as an apprentice, then as a steward. He voyaged to the West Indies in the *Mont-Blanc* ('She leaked fully, generously, over-flowingly, all over – like a basket', he remarked later) and subsequently in the *Saint-Antoine*. While he was a steward with the *Saint-Antoine* he had his sole glimpse of South America, probably going ashore for a few days at Venezuela; and it is possible that (as he darkly hinted) the ship was engaged in smuggling arms to the conservative side in a South American civil war. The first mate was Dominic Cervoni, bold, broad-chested and vain – 'His thick black moustaches, curled every morning with hot tongs by the barber at the corner of the quay, seemed to hide a perpetual smile' – and later to be reincarnated as the fictional Nostromo and as the Dominic of *Arrow of Gold*. In *The Mirror of the Sea*, Conrad says that he had joined Dominic Cervoni in a syndicate which smuggled arms from Marseilles along the coast to Spanish Carlists, the Royalists who supported the Pretender, Don Carlos. According to Conrad, the syndicate was betrayed to the authorities by Dominic's nephew César; their vessel, the *Tremolino*, was pursued by coastguards; the crew wrecked her to escape the pursuers, and during the crisis Dominic hurled his nephew (who happened to be weighted with stolen gold) to death in the sea. As common sense rightly warns us, this last part of the yarn is pure invention; but there is ample evidence that Conrad was indeed involved in a smuggling venture that ended disastrously during a run of bad luck which, we now know, culminated in his attempt at suicide.

His long-suffering Uncle Tadeusz wrote to a Polish friend:

I was absolutely certain that he was already somewhere in the Antipodes, when suddenly, amidst all the business at the Kiev Fair in 1878, I received a telegram: 'Conrad blessé envoyez argent – arrivez' ['Conrad wounded send money – come'].

(Najder, 176)

Conrad's troubles had begun when he had found that as an alien he was barred by law from French ships; nor did he have a consular permit for service at the port.

While still in possession of the 3,000 francs sent to him for the voyage, he met his former Captain, Mr Duteil, who persuaded him to participate in some enterprise on the coasts of Spain – some kind of contraband! He invested 1,000 francs in it and made over 400 which pleased them greatly so that on the second occasion he put in all he had – and lost the lot.

Heavily in debt, he borrowed a further 800 francs from a friend, went to Villefranche to try to join an American squadron, failed; and finally in desperation gambled away the 800 francs at Monte Carlo.

Having managed his affairs so excellently he returns to Marseilles and one fine evening invites his friend the creditor to tea, and before his arrival attempts to take his life with a revolver. (Let this detail remain between us, as I have been telling everyone that he was wounded in a duel.....) The bullet goes durch und durch [through and through] near his heart without damaging any vital organ.

Bobrowski paid the debts, 'influenced by considerations of our national honour' as well as by family loyalty, while Conrad recovered from the deep wound in the chest.

My study of the Individual has convinced me that he is not a bad boy, only one who is extremely sensitive, conceited, reserved, and in addition excitable. In short I found in him all the defects of the Nałęcz family. He is able and eloquent.....very popular with his captains and also with the sailors.....In his ideas and discussions he is ardent and original.....and is an imperialist. De gustibus non est disputandum.

(Najder, 176–8)

Finally, it was agreed that Conrad should join the British Merchant Navy ('where there are no such formalities as in France'); and four years after leaving Poland he arrived at Lowestoft on the coal freighter *Mavis*.

England and the Merchant Navy

In his letters to Conrad, Uncle Tadeusz repeatedly offered warnings that Conrad was a double man: an inheritor of a janiform personality. On the father's side, Tadeusz claimed, he had inherited an unstable temperament, changeable, imaginative, impatient, impractical; while on the mother's side, he had inherited powers of patient diligence and steady application. Conrad's career as a seaman was

	SIGNATURES OF CREW	Age	Town or County where born	If to the Reserve, No. of Commission of RNR	Ship in which he last served (Ship's Name and Official No. or Port she belonged to)	Date and Place of signing this Agreement (Year / Date / Place)
1	William Cook (Master to sign first.)	42	Lowestoft	—	Skimmer of Sea 1878	July 11th Lowestoft
2	Arthur W Chandler	28	Pakefield		do	do do do
3	Henry Boom	26	Corton do		do	do do do
4	William Munning	29	?		do	do do do
5	Alfred Goldspink	34	Pakefield		do	do do do
6	Conrad K Korzeniowski	20	Poland	—	do	1878 July 11th Lowestoft
7	Albert Barham	17	Lowestoft		do	do do do
8	Ernest George Sturgeon	16	Lowestoft	—	Thomas Lord do	do August Lowestoft

Agreement and account of the crew of the Skimmer of the Sea.

Conrad, who signed himself there 'Conrad de Korzeniowski', looked back with affection on this humble coaster. '*My teachers had been the sailors of the Norfolk shore; coast men, with steady eyes, mighty limbs, and gentle voice; men of very few words, which at least were never bare of meaning.*' (NLL, 155.) The Skimmer *is mentioned as 'a smart craft' in the tale 'To-morrow'.*

to illustrate this duplicity. He never stayed on any vessel for long, sometimes because of quarrels with his captains, sometimes for no evident reason (and to the disappointment of the owners); yet, on the other hand, his zealous efforts took him to the pinnacle of a naval career by the age of thirty.

His beginnings in England could not have been more humble. He obtained a berth on a small coaster, the barquentine *Skimmer of the Sea* (also known as *Skimmer of the Seas*), which, belying her romantic name, carried coal from Newcastle to Lowestoft; and I find that Conrad's wage was recorded as one shilling per month when even the ship's boy received £1 5s 0d. Two and a half years after Conrad left her, she sank at sea, drowning some of his former shipmates; and in one of his letters he was to look back nostalgically:

Skimmer of the Seas what a pretty name! But she is gone and took a whole lot of good fellows away with her into the other world. Comme c'est vieux tout ça! [How long ago it all seems!] In that craft I began to learn English from East Coast chaps each built as though to last for ever, and coloured like a Christmas card.

Ship *Skimmer of the Sea* AGREEMENT No. 73112

In what Capacity engaged and if Master, Mate, or Engineer No. of Certificate (if any)	Amount of Wages per Week Calendar Month, Share, or Voyage	Time at which he is to be on board	Amount of Wages advanced on entry	Signature of Superintendent of Mercantile Marine, H.M. Consul, or other Witness to the Engagement	Date and Place of Commencement of Service on board.		Date, Place, and Cause of leaving this Ship, or of Death.			Report of Character		Reference No.
					Date.	Place.	Date.	Place.	Cause.	For General Conduct.	For Ability in Seamanship.	
Master	6		*Will. Robt. Williams*	8/5 *Lowestoft*					*Remand*	G	G	1
Mate 1854	74·5·0	a R W		11th July a						G	G	2
Seaman	4·0·0	a R W		do						G	G	3
a-	3·15·0	a R W		do	a					G	G	4
	3·0·0	or R W		do	a					G	G	5
Ordinary	1·0·0	or R W		9 July Lowestoft	23 do Lowestoft					G	6
Boy	·5·0	or R W		11 July Lowestoft	3 Aug Lowestoft		Do	G	W	7
do	1·10·0	or R W		6 Aug Lowestoft					*Remand*	G	W	8
												9

Tan and pink — gold hair and blue eyes with that Northern straight-away-there look! Twenty two years ago!

(*LCG*, 74-5)

After *Skimmer*, he soon found a berth as an ordinary seaman on the wool clipper *Duke of Sutherland*, which plied between London and Sydney; and gradually, over the subsequent sixteen years, with numerous voyages on ships ranging from elegant three-masters to rusty tramp-steamers, rose in rank — third mate, second mate, skipper. Repeatedly on the great ocean-going sailing-ships he made the run between England, Bombay and Australia; gradually, struggling with the wayward English language, he learned the rules of seamanship and passed the successive inquisitorial examinations; and in 1886, he not only gained his master's certificate but also took British nationality. Bobrowski was delighted by the double achievement: he had long urged his nephew to relinquish Russian citizenship and become 'a free citizen of a free country'. Ford Madox Ford, subsequently Conrad's literary collaborator, emphasises Britain's reputation in Europe as a land of liberty:

During the last century if you went down to Tilbury Dock you would see families of Jewish-Poland emigrants landing. As soon as they landed they fell on their hands and knees and kissed the soil of the land of freedom . . . . . England of Conrad's early vision: an immense power standing for liberty and hospitality for refugees; vigilant over a pax Britannica that embraced the world.

(*Joseph Conrad*, 1924, pp. 57-8)

I imagine that if Conrad had ever found himself amid a crowd of soil-kissing immigrants at Tilbury Dock he would have picked his way through the crowd with an expression of patrician distaste at such emotionalism; but there is no doubt that Ford's note of enthusiasm for Britain accorded well enough with Conrad's feelings. Culturally, Conrad's upbringing had been anglophile; as recently as the 1850s, the British at Crimea had fought the Poles' most hated oppressors, the Russians; and intermittently Conrad the writer was to offer warm tributes to that 'liberty, which can only be found under the English flag'. And it was in the service of the 'pax Britannica that embraced the world' that Conrad repeatedly voyaged across the globe: to Bombay, Singapore or Melbourne. This was the last great era of sail, of the full-rigged iron sailing ships like the *Tilkhurst* that carried jute from Calcutta to Dundee (Conrad was her second mate in 1886; she endured until 1923) or of majestic clippers like the *Torrens* that carried wool from Adelaide to London. He came to know the foaming seas and hot sunsets, the storms and calms that later he was to celebrate in his books; he came to know Singapore, Java, Sumatra and Borneo, regions which provide settings for *Lord Jim* and the early novels; he came to know those borderline areas of human experience where the civilised meets the primitive and the familiar meets the alien. He also came to have an intimate knowledge of work – monotonous, backbreaking, unremitting work as a crewman; the worries of responsibility as mate or captain; the fears of storm and fog at sea.....or even the fear of fear.

Of the risks and frustrations that Conrad encountered, the *Palestine* voyage (on which he was second mate) provides some of the best examples. The *Palestine*, an old and decrepit barque with an appropriate captain, left Newcastle for Bangkok with a cargo of coal, but after three hundred miles she lost her sails in a gale, sprang a leak, and returned to England for repairs, which took eight months. At the second attempt the vessel voyaged from September to March, reaching the Bangka Strait off Sumatra, before disaster struck. In the words of the Court of Inquiry:

> Smoke was discovered issuing from the coals.....Water was thrown over them until the smoke abated, the boats were lowered, water placed in them. On the thirteenth some coals were thrown overboard, about four tons, and more water poured down the hold. On the fourteenth, the hatches being on but not battened down, the decks blew up fore and aft as far as the poop.....About 11 p.m. the vessel was a mass of fire, and all hands got into the boats, three in number.

That was in March 1883. More than fifteen years later, in the tale 'Youth', Conrad's narrator recalls the explosion, thus:

The Torrens, *1892.*

On this ship, Conrad, serving as her first mate, met John Galsworthy and Edward Sanderson, who were travelling as passengers.

He paid tribute to the vessel in Last Essays *(22–3): 'The* Torrens *had a fame which attracted the right kind of sailor, ...for, apart from her more brilliant qualities, such as her speed and her celebrated good looks. . . . ., she was regarded as a "comfortable ship" in a strictly professional sense. . . . .'*

I seemed somehow to be in the air. I heard all round me like a
pent-up breath released – as if a thousand giants simultaneously
had said Phoo! – and felt a dull concussion which made my ribs
ache suddenly. No doubt about it – I was in the air, and my body
was describing a short parabola. . . . . I did not know that I had
no hair, no eyebrows, no eyelashes, that my young moustache
was burnt off, that my face was black. . . . .

(*Y*, 22–3)

And later, as the narrator looks back at the wreck from the lifeboats:

Between the darkness of earth and heaven she was burning fiercely
upon a disc of purple sea shot by the blood-red play of gleams;
upon a disc of water glittering and sinister. A high, clear flame, an
immense and lonely flame, ascended from the ocean, and from its
summit the black smoke poured continuously at the sky. She
burned furiously; mournful and imposing like a funeral pile
kindled in the night, surrounded by the sea, watched over by the
stars. A magnificent death had come like a grace, like a gift, like
a reward to that old ship at the end of her laborious days.

(*Y*, 34–5)

On these voyages he came to encounter so many of the people,
vessels and locations that were to appear in the subsequent works of
fiction. The *Palestine* reappeared in 'Youth' as the *Judea*; the captain
and first mate retain their original names and, it appears, their
original characters. Conrad came to learn about A. P. Williams,
the seaman involved in scandal who tried to make good, and who
became one of the models for Lord Jim. (Williams and the other
European officers had abandoned a crowded pilgrim-ship, the
Jeddah, when they thought it was going to sink, leaving the pilgrims
to their fate. On reaching shore they announced that the ship had
foundered – but the next day she was towed into harbour with the
thousand pilgrims safely on board.) On a voyage to the Berau River
in Borneo, Conrad met Charles Olmeijer, the trader whose fictional
counterpart was the Almayer of *Almayer's Folly*. Then there was
William Lingard, a formidable sea-rover who had fought pirates
and knew the coastal waters better than any other European – the
genitor of the Tom Lingard of *Almayer's Folly*, *An Outcast of the
Islands* and *The Rescue*. At Singapore there was Captain Ellis, the
laconic Master-Attendant of the harbour, who was to make brief
appearances in three novels. And it was at Bangkok in 1888 that
Conrad took charge of his first command – the beautiful *Otago*, a
367-ton three-masted thoroughbred: 'a harmonious creature in the
lines of her fine body, in the proportioned tallness of her spars'.
There was disease (dysentery and cholera) among the crew, and his
first voyage, from Bangkok to Singapore, took three weeks instead

of the usual three days, for she was often becalmed; but out of Conrad's frustrations and anxieties would one day be born one of his finest novels, *The Shadow-Line*.

It was while he was captain of the *Otago* that on a visit to Mauritius he fell in love with a pretty young girl called Eugénie Renouf, and actually announced to the girl's brother that he hoped to marry her – only to discover that she was already engaged. He retreated rapidly to the sanctuary of his cabin. In Australia in March 1889 he resigned his command and returned as a steamship-passenger to England – to furnished rooms at Bessborough Gardens, near Vauxhall Bridge in London; and it was in that riverside setting that at the age of thirty-one, with time on his hands while looking for another command, he 'on an autumn day with an opaline atmosphere' began his first novel, *Almayer's Folly*. The manuscript was to accompany him on his travels for the next five years – a wad to be brooded over, to be forgotten for a while, then to be pulled out for additions and revisions. With Conrad the papers survived even the heart of darkest Africa.

The Congo and its aftermath

In 'Geography and Some Explorers', Conrad writes:

> One day, putting my finger on a spot in the very middle of the then white heart of Africa, I declared that some day I would go there. My chums' chaffing was perfectly justifiable.....Yet it is a fact that, about eighteen years afterwards, a wretched little stern-wheel steamboat I commanded lay moored to the bank of an African river.....The subdued thundering mutter of the Stanley Falls hung in the heavy night air of the last navigable reach of the Upper Congo.....and I said to myself with awe, 'This is the very spot of my boyish boast.'
>
> (*LE*, 16–7)

It was in 1890 that Conrad had gained employment with the Société Anonyme Belge pour le Commerce du Haut-Congo, the company largely responsible for exploiting the resources of the Belgian Congo – that vast tract of central Africa which was the private property of King Leopold II. Conrad expected to be given command of one of the steam-boats that plied up and down the Congo River, because one of the company's captains, Freiesleben, had been killed by natives during a petty quarrel. Part of Conrad's African journey was overland, through dense bush, his European companion sick and the native bearers mutinous; part was upstream in the frail *Roi des Belges*, a wood-burning paddle-steamer that reminded him of a sardine-can or a Huntley & Palmer biscuit-tin; and after a journey of well over a thousand miles he reached the township at Stanley

The Roi des Belges.
On this 'wretched little stern-wheel steamboat' Conrad travelled up the Congo in 1890, on the journey recalled in Heart of Darkness.

Falls, the settlement closest to the heart of the continent. But there, he recalled later, his mood was one not of achievement but of disillusionment:

> A great melancholy descended on me. Yes, this was the very spot. But there was no shadowy friend to stand by my side in the night of the enormous wilderness, no great haunting memory, but only the unholy recollection of a prosaic newspaper 'stunt' and the distasteful knowledge of the vilest scramble for loot that ever disfigured the history of human conscience and geographical exploration.

> (*LE*, 17)

The stunt was the much-publicised 'discovery' of Livingstone, the missionary, by Stanley, the journalist, and Conrad was rightly sceptical of its value, since Livingstone had never actually been lost. The 'vilest scramble for loot' was, of course, the Belgian exploitation of the Congo. Even in his few months in this wilderness, Conrad saw ample evidence of the brutal ways in which the supposed emissaries of European civilisation were plundering the land of rubber and ivory by treating the natives as expendable slave-labour. Conrad noted in his diary:

> Met an off^{er} of the State inspecting. A few minutes afterwards saw at a camp^g place the dead body of a Backongo. Shot? Horrid smell.....

Saw another dead body lying by the path in an attitude of meditative repose . . . . .

On the road to-day passed a skeleton tied up to a post. Also white man's grave – no name – heap of stones in the form of a cross.

(*LE*, 163, 165, 169)

Such horrors, and their implicit comments on the arrogance and hypocrisy of civilisation, were to be incentives to the writing of his most mordant tale, 'An Outpost of Progress', and his most complex novella, *Heart of Darkness*.

Conrad was invalided home to London, having been stricken with dysentery and malaria: malarial gout and feverish ailments were to recur for the rest of his life. After convalescing at Geneva he took a desk job, helping to manage a warehouse in London; and he maintained an ample correspondence with his 'aunt' – really a second cousin – Marguerite Poradowska, who lived at Brussels and was establishing her reputation as a novelist, and who certainly encouraged Conrad to persevere with his literary ambitions. Conrad's letters to her established a pattern that was to recur in others to various later acquaintances, for those letters are often Jeremiads: eloquent, rhythmic, sonorous lamentations about the futility of life and the hopelessness of his situation. Even a letter of consolation becomes almost gloatingly pessimistic:

One must drag the ball and chain of one's selfhood to the end. It is the [price] one pays for the devilish and divine privilege of thought; so that in this life it is only the elect who are convicts – a glorious band which comprehends and groans but which treads the earth amidst a multitude of phantoms with maniacal gestures, with idiotic grimaces. Which would you be: idiot or convict?

(*LMP*, 72)

In 1891 Conrad sailed as first mate in the *Torrens*, one of the most famous and beautiful of the clippers, on the first of two voyages to Australia and back. Long afterwards, in 'The *Torrens*: A Personal Tribute' (*LE*), Conrad wrote:

The *Torrens* had a fame which attracted the right kind of sailor . . . . . for apart from her more brilliant qualities, such as her speed and her celebrated good looks (which by themselves go a long way with a sailor), she was regarded as a 'comfortable ship' in a strictly professional sense, which means that she was known to handle easily and to be a good sea boat in heavy weather . . . . . I can testify that, on every point of sailing, the way that ship had of letting big seas slip under her did one's heart good to watch.

(22–3)

On the final journey, one of the passengers was E. H. Jacques, a young Cambridge man who was the first reader of the manuscript of *Almayer's Folly*.

> 'Is it worth finishing?' . . . . .
> 'Distinctly,' he answered in his sedate veiled voice, and then coughed a little.
> 'Were you interested?' I inquired further, almost in a whisper.
> 'Very much!' . . . . .
> 'Now let me ask you one more thing: Is the story quite clear to you as it stands?'
> He raised his dark, gentle eyes to my face and seemed surprised.
> 'Yes! Perfectly.'

(*PR*, 17–18)

Jacques, who was dying of tuberculosis, did not live to see the end of the story; but by prophetic coincidence, another of the *Torrens* passengers was the young John Galsworthy, who listened avidly to the mate's yarns of 'ships and storms, of Polish revolution, of youthful Carlist gun-running adventure', and who subsequently maintained a friendly correspondence with Conrad through the years when both men achieved fame.

In 1894 there came a lull in Conrad's maritime career when, having joined another ship, the *Adowa*, as second mate, the voyage was cancelled. He learned that his Uncle Tadeusz ('the wisest, the firmest, the most indulgent of guardians') had died. In this period of waiting and melancholy, he continued the slow work on *Almayer's Folly*, and at last, on April 24, he was able to write to Marguerite Poradowska: 'J'ai la douleur de Vous faire part de la mort de M. Kaspar Almayer qui a eu lieu ce matin à 3ʰ' ('I have the sorrowful duty to inform you of the death of Mr Kaspar Almayer which took place at 3 o'clock this morning'). He wrapped the manuscript in two pieces of cardboard and some brown paper, enclosed twelve penny stamps in case of rejection, and sent the book to the publishing house of T. Fisher Unwin.

The second career: Conrad the novelist

Early writings

In October 1894 Fisher Unwin accepted *Almayer's Folly* for publication in the following year, paying Conrad just £20 for the copyright. For this acceptance the publisher's two readers were responsible. One was W. H. Chesson, who was immediately impressed by the book's 'magical melancholy' – 'its note of haunted loneliness called me into isolation, while I read it in the clamorous heart of London'; the other was Edward Garnett, who, equally impressed, was to be an enthusiastic, loyal and keenly intelligent correspondent and

publicist of Conrad for many years to come. Garnett – tall, bespec-
tacled, floppy-haired, careless over matters of dress, forgetful of
fly-buttons, but passionately vigilant to maintain high literary
standards – was probably the most brilliant reader ever to be employed by a publisher. He was man-midwife to the literary offspring
of W. H. Hudson, Galsworthy, W. H. Davies, Cunninghame Graham
and D. H. Lawrence, as well as of Conrad; and the respect and
affection with which he was regarded is well shown in his subsequent
fictional characterisation as Lea in *The Inheritors*, a novel written
jointly by Conrad and Ford Madox Hueffer:

> Lea had helped me a good deal in the old days – he had helped
> everybody, for that matter. You would probably find traces of
> Lea's influence in the beginnings of every writer of about my
> decade; of everybody who ever did anything decent, and of some
> who never got beyond the stage of burgeoning decently. He had
> given me the material help that a publisher's reader could give,
> until his professional reputation was endangered, and he had
> given me the more valuable help that so few can give.....
>
>   He was sprawling angularly on a cane lounge, surrounded by
> whole rubbish heaps of manuscript.....And on the floor, on the
> chairs, on the sideboard, on the unmade bed, the profusion of
> manuscripts.
>
> (*The Inheritors*, Dent, 1923, pp. 46, 47–8)

Garnett was eager to meet the unknown author of *Almayer's Folly*:

> The strangeness of the tropical atmosphere, and the poetic
> 'realism' of this romantic narrative excited my curiosity about
> the author, who I fancied might have eastern blood in his veins.
> (*EG*, vi)

And at their first meeting, it was Conrad's janiformity, his duplicity
of character, that struck the twenty-six-year-old Garnett:

> My memory is of seeing a dark-haired man, short but extremely
> graceful in his nervous gestures, with brilliant eyes, now narrowed
> and penetrating, now soft and warm, with a manner alert yet
> caressing, whose speech was ingratiating, guarded, and brusque
> by turn. I had never seen before a man so masculinely keen yet
> so femininely sensitive.
> (*EG*, vii)

There is no doubt that in recommending the acceptance of
Almayer's Folly, Chesson and Garnett were influenced first and fore-
most by its literary merits rather than by considerations of its commercial profitability. Certainly the book had some of the ingredients
of popular fiction. It had an exotic eastern location – the jungles
and riverbanks of Borneo. It had a tale of long-sought treasure, of

Edward Garnett with his son, David, in 1897.

smuggling, and of the elopement of a Eurasian girl with a brave Balinese prince. But it was also an uncompromisingly original work, difficult in the convolutions and ellipses of its narrative, subversive in its scepticism and cynicism, complex in its interweaving of political and anthropological material with the fortunes of individuals in the foreground: a novel that would have to be read twice before its main ironies would be fully perceived. And a novel that, for all its cumbrously literary descriptions, remained plangent and strange in its emphasis on human isolation, on the inadequacy of communication between people, and on the cracks in the shields of illusion forged by men to ward off hard realities.

Almayer's Folly was widely reviewed, though the reviews were mixed. A few critics were sneering or derisory ('Borneo is a fine field for the study of monkeys, not men'); most spoke of the book with respect modulating to enthusiasm; and some hailed the arrival of a writer of genius. A large number of the reviews emphasised its originality and power (the diffuseness notwithstanding), and the author's skill in establishing an exotic atmosphere. Conrad was frequently compared with Kipling – and even when the reviewer concluded that he was Kipling's inferior, the comparison was still, for the time, a flattering one, given that in the mid-1890s many British reviewers regarded Kipling as the leading contemporary writer. The *Spectator* prophesied that 'Joseph Conrad.....might become the Kipling of the Malay Archipelago', while the *Manchester Guardian* later claimed that he was 'as masculine as Kipling, but without that parade of masculinity which Kipling loves'.

Conrad, who followed the reviews closely, had good grounds for feeling proud of his achievement. After twenty arduous years at sea he had dared to embark on a career which financially was far riskier – that of a full-time novelist; and a novelist, moreover, in an alien and difficult language, English. ('I had to work like a coal miner in his pit quarrying all my English sentences out of a black night,' he said.) His inheritance – eventually of about £1,600 – from Bobrowski's estate may explain the timing of the decision, and the reception of *Almayer's Folly* helped to confirm him in the new course; and though there was to be a phase in 1898 when he attempted to return to sea, he was to remain a writer until his death in 1924. 'But I *won't* live in an attic. I'm past that, you understand? I *won't* live in an attic', he had told Garnett at their first meeting; and his life-style was never poor: he lived the life of an upper-middle-class gentleman, and moved through a succession of ever-larger houses. In 1896 he married Jessie George, a young typist by whom he had two sons; and the Conrad households generally had a servant or two to do the menial work. Nevertheless for years Conrad was living beyond his means, dependent on the generosity of appreciative publishers like William Blackwood, on advances from his trustful literary agent, J. B. Pinker, on loans from various friends, and even on the occasional state grant. In his old age, following the commercial success of *Chance* (published in 1912), he became very rich; but until then he was repeatedly in a state of anguish and sometimes near-madness because of the strain of trying to write uncompromisingly while yet racing against time in order to gain more money or to repay in pages the cash he had already received and spent. Again and again he speaks of his current engagement with a manuscript as a hideous ordeal, his mind blank, the words elusive; repeatedly his completion of a novel was marked by physical and mental breakdown, a combination of gout, exhaustion, depression and mild derangement. Had he known of the repeated ordeals that lay ahead, it is doubtful that he would ever have embarked on *Almayer's Folly*.

However, its sequel, *An Outcast of the Islands*, using the same exotic location and some of the same characters as the previous novel, appeared in 1896, and further consolidated his reputation with the critics. Though there were complaints about the baseness portrayed ('Never did so mean a skunk figure as the hero of a novel') and again about the 'besetting sin of wordiness', comparisons with Kipling – and with Stevenson, another highly-rated novelist – continued to imply that Conrad's work, even though flawed, challenged comparison with the very best of the times.

Then came several false starts. Conrad embarked on *The Sisters*, of which only the opening was ever completed: the story of a sensitive young Slav, an artist who comes to live in Paris. The second start was on *The Rescuer*, a novel which gave Conrad such extreme and agonising difficulty that he took more than twenty years to complete it (eventually, as *The Rescue*, it was serialised in 1919). And in 1896–97 he published in magazines the highly uneven quartet of stories ('Karain', 'The Lagoon', 'The Idiots', and 'An Outpost of Progress') which, with the 'left-handed production' 'The Return', comprise *Tales of Unrest*.

The major phase

Conrad's major phase as a writer extends from 1897 to 1911. It includes *The Nigger of the 'Narcissus'*, 'Youth', *Heart of Darkness*, *Lord Jim*, 'Typhoon', *Nostromo*, *The Secret Agent*, 'The Secret Sharer', *Under Western Eyes* and 'A Smile of Fortune'. This is a period of astonishing richness and majesty: *Heart of Darkness* or *Nostromo* alone would have sufficed to give Conrad an enduring reputation as a major writer; but when to them are added the diverse strengths of the other tales and novels in the list, the effect is to emphasise his stature as one of the half-dozen of the very greatest fiction-writers in English.

34

It is a familiar irony of literary history that during this major phase Conrad's financial struggles were as bitter as ever; but there is no doubt that an increasing majority of the reviewers sensed and respected (even if they could not fully define or comprehend) the stature of Conrad the writer. Garnett noted that *The Nigger of the 'Narcissus'* received 'a general blast of eulogy from a dozen impressive sources'; and Garnett himself seized every opportunity to proclaim Conrad's brilliance in the review columns. Conrad's fame was spreading widely, partly through the prior publication of his works in magazines and journals. It is often forgotten that Conrad was paid twice over for much of his material: even the convoluted novel *Nostromo* appeared in a popular periodical, *T. P.'s Weekly*, as a serial, and all the other works mentioned in the previous paragraph appeared in magazines before being published in book form.

This was also the period during which Conrad came into personal contact with many of the most brilliant writers and personalities of the day. R. B. Cunninghame Graham, the aristocratic socialist and adventurer, became a close friend; Galsworthy kept up a fraternal correspondence; and there was a brief, touching friendship with Stephen Crane, the bright but short-lived young American author of *The Red Badge of Courage*. Conrad met H. G. Wells, who had enthusiastically reviewed *Almayer's Folly* and *An Outcast*; Kipling sent a flattering letter; and Ford Madox Hueffer became a friend and collaborator, subsequently establishing an enduring reputation of his own with the novel *The Good Soldier*. Other contacts were with George Bernard Shaw, who irritated Conrad intensely, and with the magisterial Henry James, whom Conrad addressed in somewhat bleating tones as 'Cher Maître'. (Most of these writers lived or stayed in the south-to-south-east corner of England: Kipling at Rottingdean in Sussex; Hueffer, Crane, Garnett and subsequently Conrad himself at Pent Farm, near Hythe; James at Rye, Wells at Sandgate; and all, thanks to the splendid railway services, were within easy commuting distance of London, where Cunninghame Graham had a flat.) The sense of friendly rivalry with these un-compromisingly innovatory figures must again and again have driven Conrad to reject the second-rate or derivative in his own writing and to strive for the exact truth of feeling and expression.

Meanwhile, Conrad was becoming as domesticated as was possible for so highly-strung and temperamental a person. His proposal of marriage to Jessie had been abrupt and awkward: 'Look here, my dear, we had better get married and out of this. Look at the weather'; and he had assured her mother 'that he hadn't very long to live and that there would be no family'. In spite of the latter assurance, the plump Jessie produced two sons – Borys in 1898 and John in 1906. She claims that when Borys was born, Conrad was wandering vaguely in the kitchen garden, and on hearing the child cry he shouted to

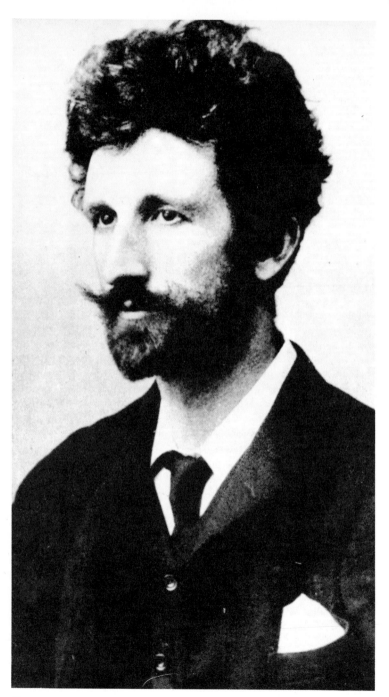

left *R. B Cunninghame Graham*

below *Pent Farm, near Aldington in Kent.*
  Conrad lived here from 1898 to 1907, the period in which he wrote Heart of Darkness, Lord Jim *and* Nostromo.

Rose, the maid: 'Send that child away at once; it will disturb Mrs Conrad!' 'It's your own child, sir', the patient maid replied. On rail journeys with his wife and the baby, Conrad pretended to be a stranger to them if other travellers were in the carriage; 'I hate babies', he told Garnett. Nevertheless he was to be an affectionate (if often sternly awe-inspiring) father to both boys and a loyal husband to Jessie. She, in turn, strove to organise the household so as to guard his privacy and enable him to work as steadily as possible; though her memoirs make quite evident the ripples of resentment and bitterness that she felt when her struggles lacked recognition or appreciation. And there is no doubt that to his pert, buxom but rather naïve young wife, Conrad must often have been an alarming husband. When guests came to dinner, he would absent-mindedly roll pieces of bread into pellets and flick them about the room – 'I have seen them fly into the soup-plates and glasses of our guests. The more excited or irritated he got, the quicker flew the missiles, and those in the line of fire would look apprehensively at their host'. On another occasion, Conrad, suspecting that there was an intruder in the garden, seized his rifle and rushed down the path to the little building (a privy) in which the 'intruder' was concealed. Waving the rifle he boldly burst into the place, shouting 'Come out you – Damn you', and found himself facing his mother-in-law, who never visited him again.

Such social embarrassments were the outer signs of Conrad's long lonely ordeals in his study, wrestling to create a fictional Patusan or Costaguana. He was to say about the writing of *Nostromo*, for example:

> I hesitated, as if warned by the instinct of self-preservation from venturing on a distant and toilsome journey into a land full of intrigues and revolutions. But it had to be done.
>
> It took the best part of the years 1903–4 to do; with many intervals of renewed hesitation, lest I should lose myself in the ever-enlarging vistas opening before me as I progressed deeper in my knowledge of the country.....On my return I found (speaking somewhat in the style of Captain Gulliver) my family all well, my wife heartily glad to learn that the fuss was all over, and our small boy considerably grown during my absence.
>
> (N, x)

Cunninghame Graham noted that Conrad 'almost needed a Caesarian operation of the soul before he was delivered of his masterpieces'; and often the delivery was marked by physical and mental collapse. When Conrad had just finished *Under Western Eyes*, Jessie wrote:

> The novel is finished, but the penalaty [*sic*] has to be paid. Months of nervous strain have ended in a complete nervous

Ford Madox Ford, who published lively reminiscences of his earlier years when, as Ford Madox Hueffer, he had collaborated enthusiastically with Conrad. 'We saw that Life did not narrate, but made impressions on our brains.'

breakdown. . . . . There is the MS complete but uncorrected and his fierce refusal to let even I touch it. It lays on a table at the foot of his bed and he lives mixed up in the scenes and holds converse with the characters.

(*BB*, 192)

Yet, after such deranging efforts, the material rewards could be ludicrously small: in 1909, when Conrad was 51, he said: 'My immortal works (13 in all) have brought me last year something under five pounds in royalties'; and this only served to increase the bitterness of his contempt for the popular, commercial novelists of the day – Grant Allen, Marie Corelli and Hall Caine, for example: 'All three are very popular with the public – and they are also puffed in the press. There are no lasting qualities in their work. The thought is commonplace and the style(?) without any distinction. They are popular because they express the common thought, and the common man is delighted to find himself in accord with people he supposes distinguished.' (Najder, 228.)

He did, however, make some clear attempts at popularity with that wider public. One was by the writing – or rather dictation to a secretary – of *The Mirror of the Sea*, a book of ruminative (and sometimes waffling) reminiscences: 'I've discovered that I can dictate that sort of bosh without effort at the rate of 3,000 words in four hours. Fact. The only thing now is to sell it to a paper and then make a book of the rubbish.' And another way of accelerating the flow of marketable material was collaboration with his eager admirer,

Ford Madox Hueffer (who changed his name to Ford Madox Ford during the First World War). The fruits of this collaboration were *The Inheritors*, 1901, *Romance*, 1903, and 'The Nature of a Crime', 1909. Although Hueffer had definite talents as a novelist, collaboration did no justice to the abilities of either man. *The Inheritors* (a mixture of science fiction, political allegory and topical *roman à clef*) will certainly bear some reconsideration; but 'The Nature of a Crime' is a negligible tale, while *Romance* is a trite and prolix attempt on the Stevenson market for glamorous adventure-narratives set in the picturesque past. Literary collaborations are more fruitful in quarrels than in masterpieces, and by 1909 Conrad was complaining that Ford's conduct was 'impossible' – 'He is a megalomaniac who imagines that he is managing the Universe.' (Baines, 350.)

Transition: 1911–19

This was in two senses a period of transition. Firstly, some of the novels and tales of this period are very good, while others show signs of a decline in Conrad's powers; and secondly, there was to be a rapid improvement in his income.

In order, the publications of this phase are: *'Twixt Land and Sea* (three tales); *A Personal Record*, by far the more enjoyable of his two books of autobiographical reminiscence; *Chance*, serialised in the *New York Herald* in 1912 and published as a book in 1913; *Victory*; *Within the Tides* (a collection of four of his more trival tales); and *The Shadow-Line*. Of the novels, most critics concur in regarding *The Shadow-Line* as the best: a vivid study of the stresses on a young captain whose first command is a disease-haunted and becalmed sailing-ship. *Victory* is much more problematic for the critics, some seeing it as one of the Conradian masterpieces, others seeing it as a flawed and tainted work. The publication which most deeply affected Conrad's fortunes was, of course, *Chance*. Until then, Conrad had needed to have his earnings augmented by loans from friends and agents and by grants from the British taxpayer (£500 from a special fund in 1904, £100 as a Civil List pension in 1911). However, *Chance* became a best-seller in both Britain and the United States. Why this should have been so is not easy to understand. The book is certainly not one of Conrad's better novels; nor is it obviously 'popular', for the narrative is unfolded with elaborate deviousness. However, its discussion of feminism had some topicality; serialisation in the *New York Times* may have helped; the American publishers, Doubleday, made zealous promotional efforts; Garnett claimed that 'it is probable that the figure of the lady on the "jacket" of *Chance* did more to bring the novel into favour than a long review by Sir Sidney Colvin in *The Observer*'; and the main narrative had what, by Conradian standards, was a happy ending, with its inhibited hero and heroine eventually experiencing the long-delayed sexual embrace. Jocelyn Baines has suggested that Conrad's reputation may simply have been ripe and ready at last – ripe for general celebrity, ready for popular interest to burgeon. Even when in debt, Conrad had never stinted himself: he had dressed like a dandy, owned a succession of expensive early motor-cars, and moved into gradually larger and more impressive houses; but now, at last, he had an income more than adequate to his life-style.

His agent, J. B. Pinker, was able to sell the serial rights of *Victory* for £1,000, and the money helped Conrad to take his family on a visit to Poland in 1914; but the sentimental journey to Cracow and Zakopane was ruthlessly interrupted by the outbreak of the First World War, and it was with extreme difficulty that the family eluded internment and returned to England via Italy. Ironically, it was a war that Conrad had long prophesied; and his own son Borys served as a soldier at the front, and was gassed and shell-shocked. After the armistice, Conrad was pessimistic about the establishment of the League of Nations, but at least could take consolation from the re-establishment of the Polish State – a new republic.

Decline

In the closing years of his life he produced *The Arrow of Gold*, *The Rescue*, *Notes on Life and Letters* (a collection of essays and occasional pieces) and *The Rover*. Posthumously-published volumes were *Suspense* (never completed), *Tales of Hearsay* (four minor stories) and *Last Eassys*. All four of the novels of this late phase are disappointing: the narrative too often meanders, as though Conrad has lost his creative energy; and the further back in the past they are set (*The Rover* and *Suspense* are novels of the Napoleonic period), the more Conrad seems to be turning his back on the problems of the present and the perennial to which he had given such ferociously intense attention in *Heart of Darkness* and *Nostromo*.

However, as his writing lost its bite, public adulation increased. Film rights brought him thousands of pounds; collectors sought his manuscripts; and in 1919 he moved into Oswalds, a large Georgian house at Bishopsbourne, near Canterbury. On a visit to the USA, where he gave a talk, he was lionised: 'To be aimed at by forty cameras held by forty men that look as if they came in droves is a nerve-shattering experience', he wrote to his wife. He evidently enthralled his American audience by a reading of the death of Lena, the heroine of *Victory*. His Polish accent was still thick, rendering good as 'goot', blood as 'bloot'; but the hearers were moved – Conrad noticed 'audible snuffling'. In England, a further accolade was the offer of a knighthood from the Labour Prime Minister, Ramsay Macdonald: an offer that Conrad courteously and diplomatically declined:

above *Oswalds, Bishopsbourne, near Canterbury.*
This Georgian house with its bowling green and walled gardens was Conrad's home from 1919 until his death.

left *Conrad in old age, near the time of his visit to the USA.*

As a man whose early years were closely associated in hard toil and unforgotten friendships with British working men, I am especially touched on this offer being made to me during your Premiership.
(*CP*, 47)

When the sculptor Epstein visited Oswalds in 1924 to make a bust of the author, he found Conrad 'crippled with rheumatism, crotchety, nervous, and ill. He said to me, "I am played out".' In July Conrad suffered a heart attack: 'I begin to feel like a cornered rat', he remarked. Another attack followed, on 2 August; and at 8.30 the next morning he fell dead to the floor.

His funeral took place in Canterbury during the week of the annual cricket festival: the streets and shopfronts were decorated with gay bunting. After the service at the Roman Catholic church of St Thomas's, the body was buried beneath a stone which bore the words he had chosen as epigraph for *The Rover*:

Sleep after toyle, port after stormie seas,
Ease after warre, death after life, does greatly please.

By a further irony, these are the words uttered in Spenser's *Faerie Queene* by 'a man of hell, that calls himself Despair'. Though Conrad

Conrad's grave at Canterbury. The stone bears the pessimistic quotation from Spenser which had served as the epigraph to The Rover.

was buried with Catholic obsequies, the paradoxical inscription is a reminder of the radical scepticism which gave so much power to his writings; and by reminding us, furthermore, of old Peyrol, the hero of *The Rover*, who lives and dies by his work as a seaman, they appropriately recall the dual career of Conrad, the seaman turned writer, who was still toiling at his literary work at the time of his death.

Subsequent reputation

Around the end of Conrad's life there were some significantly discordant notes amid the general crescendo of praise. E. M. Forster, reviewing *Notes on Life and Letters* (1921), made the complaint – which subsequently became famous – that 'the secret casket of his genius contains a vapour rather than a jewel'. Leonard Woolf made much the same point when he remarked of *Suspense*: 'I had the feeling which one gets on cracking a fine, shining, new walnut . . . . . only to find that it has nothing inside. Most of the later Conrads give one this feeling'. And *The Spectator* said in 1925: 'We begin to see that he was an impressive rather than a likeable writer . . . . . He had stories to tell. And oddly enough he had nothing to say'. However, though such sceptical notes were sounded, Conrad's prestige remained generally high with critics and commentators during the 1920s; and by means of the cinema, with its films of *Victory* (1920), *Lord Jim* (1925), *Nostromo* (1926), *Romance* (1927) and *The Rescue* (1929), his fame was reaching a larger audience than he could have imagined possible when he had embarked on his literary career. In the 1930s, as later generations of writers (Lawrence, Joyce, Huxley and Auden among them) moved into the foreground of discussion, there was a slackening of interest in him; the novelist Elizabeth Bowen remarked: 'Conrad is in abeyance. We are not clear yet how to rank him; there is an uncertain pause'.

If any single publication signalled the end of that 'uncertain pause', it was F. R. Leavis's *The Great Tradition*, 1948, which ranked Conrad 'among the very greatest novelists in the language – or any language'; and thereafter the great and still-continuing surge of critical interest swelled, with many of the subsequent commentators taking as their starting-point the bold discriminations made in Leavis's account. Of course, the vast post-war expansion of higher education in many lands meant that the majority of interesting literary figures soon became, inevitably, the centres of expanding industries of research and commentary. But in the case of Conrad, the scale of the renewed attention has been particularly impressive. In addition to numerous critical and biographical studies, there have been several lengthy bibliographies; computers have produced concordances to *Heart of Darkness*, *Lord Jim* and *Almayer's Folly*; work is proceeding on a scholarly edition of the entire canon; and Conrad is now served by the international Joseph Conrad Society (which has branches in the USA, Great Britain, France, Italy and Poland) and the quarterly periodical *Conradiana*, published in Texas. There have been post-war adaptations for the cinema of *An Outcast of the Islands*, 'The Secret Sharer', *Lord Jim* and 'The Duel' (filmed as *The Duellists*); and films of *The Shadow-Line* and 'Amy Foster' have been made for television, the latter being incorporated in a biographical programme. Of these films, *An Outcast of the Islands* (directed by Carol Reed), *The Shadow-Line* (Andrzej Wajda) and *The Duellists* (Ridley Scott) have been the more successful as adaptations, though all three took quite gross liberties with the text, and (since cameras are dumb and seduced by surfaces) it is difficult to conceive of a close cinematic equivalent to a Conradian masterpiece. One critic, John Simon, has offered the following rule for the dramatisation of fiction: 'If it is worth doing, it can't be done; if it can be done, it isn't worth doing.' Coppola's *Apocalypse Now* (1979) almost solved the problem by being a film *on* rather than *of* a Conradian text: a spectacular transposition of much of *Heart of Darkness* from the Congo of circa 1890 to the Vietnam War circa 1970: a selective magnification of the more ruthlessly prophetic aspects of the original. In recent decades, even operas have sprung from Conrad's pages: the novel *Victory* and the tale 'Tomorrow' have been transformed into operas by Richard Rodney Bennett and Tadeusz Baird respectively.

Conrad has been admired by, and has influenced in various ways, an important sequence of writers ranging from T. S. Eliot to the Kenyan novelist James Ngugi; and that influence will be the subject of a later section.

2 Cultural background

The tensions

There is no morality, no knowledge and no hope.

Conrad: letter to Cunninghame Graham

It must not be supposed that I claim for the artist in fiction the freedom of moral Nihilism. I would require from him many acts of faith of which the first would be the cherishing of an undying hope. . . . .

Conrad: 'Books' in *Notes on Life and Letters*

Those who read me know my conviction that the world, the temporal world, rests on a few very simple ideas; so simple that they must be as old as the hills. It rests notably, among others, on the idea of Fidelity.

Conrad: 'A Familiar Preface' to *A Personal Record*

We live, as we dream – alone.

Marlow in Conrad's *Heart of Darkness*

A list of the salient features of Conrad's work would include pessimism, a pessimism capable of modulating deeply towards cynicism or even nihilism, yet coupled with some very ancient and traditional moral affirmations; and it would include pyrrhonism, a scepticism so thorough as to entail scepticism even about the value of scepticism. As the four epigraphs remind us again, Conrad is a janiform writer: morally he may seem radically paradoxical or self-contradictory. In Conrad's writing we see a combination of nineteenth-century and twentieth-century preoccupations; he stands at the intersection of the late Victorian and the early modernist cultural phases; he is both romantic and anti-romantic, both conservative and subversive. Morally and politically, psychologically and philosophically, he can be a probing and challenging writer; yet he can also be, on occasion, embarrassingly conventional. Albert Guerard, in *Conrad the Novelist*, has offered a useful list of some of the main paradoxes or duplicities that we encounter in Conrad's works:

A declared fear of the corrosive and faith-destroying intellect – doubled by [i.e. coupled with] a profound and ironic skepticism;
A declared belief that ethical matters are simple – doubled by an extraordinary sense of ethical complexities; . . . . .

A declared distrust of generous idealism — doubled by a strong idealism . . . . . ;

A declared commitment to authoritarian sea-tradition — doubled by a pronounced individualism . . . . . ;

A declared and extreme political conservatism, at once aristocratic and pragmatist — doubled by great sympathy for the poor and disinherited of the earth . . . . . ;

A declared fidelity to law as above the individual — doubled by a strong sense of fidelity to the individual . . . . . ;

Briefly: a deep commitment to order in society and in the self — doubled by incorrigible sympathy for the outlaw, whether existing in society or the self.

And these tensions are implicit in exciting stories, full of graphic incident, with characters who engage our sympathies and anti-pathies, in locations which extend richly before the imaginative eye. Conrad's ability to endure as a writer may be strongly related to his janiformity, for contrasting cultural periods will each find that Conrad can reflect yet salutarily criticise their preoccupations. Like all men, Conrad was influenced by the climate of ideas of his day; yet like all great writers, he responded more intelligently and imaginatively to those ideas than the mass of men would have done. A consideration of that background, under various headings, may help to explain him; it will not explain him away.

My method in the ensuing sections is the obvious one of saying 'What and why?' 'What are the salient features of Conrad's work, and why are they there? What are the circumstances that permitted or encouraged their development?' The discussion of Conrad's pessimism permits an appropriate transition from the biographical to the broader cultural factors; similarly, discussion of his political views entails consideration not only of his Polish background but also of the imperialistic fervour of the late nineteenth century. Scientific ideas had a multitude of philosophical and literary consequences: we will see how the sense of determinism induced by the prestige of the empirical method helped to engender a literary race of 'superfluous men' and encouraged Conrad and other writers to reflect that perhaps the central choice in life lay between passive rationality (the Hamlet-like) and irrational activity (the Quixotic). Other sections discuss some effects of evolutionary ideas on religion, politics and psychology, and their consequences for Conrad. Finally, we narrow the discussion to a survey of literary texts which certainly or probably influenced Conrad's writings; and that section appropriately prepares us for the final main part of this book, the account of 'The Art of Conrad' itself.

Conrad's pessimism

Conrad's works place heavy emphasis on death and isolation, on inadequate understanding between people and on the bitterness of experience. In his first novel, the protagonist dies a drug-addict's suicidal death; in the second, the protagonist is shot; in *The Nigger of the 'Narcissus'*, the 'nigger' dies, while patriarchal Singleton comes to recognise his own impending death; in *Heart of Darkness*, Kurtz dies, while Marlow gains bitter knowledge; in *Lord Jim*, Jim is killed by the natives he had tried to help; in *Nostromo*, Nostromo is shot, Decoud commits suicide, and Mrs Gould comes to disillusionment; in *The Secret Agent*, Winnie stabs her husband and subsequently drowns herself. Even in his later works, which are less bleak and uncompromising, death enjoys wide privileges: in *Victory*, Lena is shot dead and Heyst throws himself into a burning building to perish; in *The Rover*, old Peyrol sacrifices his life in a fatal voyage. In the shorter works, murder and (more frequently) suicide are just as common. Frequently the deaths come as a *coup de grâce* to those who have been misunderstood, frustrated or disillusioned. The isolation Conrad depicts is not merely the physical isolation of individuals or groups on ships surrounded by sea or in outposts surrounded by jungle: more tellingly it is the covert loneliness that occurs within crowds or within marriages when seeming mutuality has been rotted inwardly by egotism. There are very few happy marriages in Conrad's pages (I can recall only the comfortable domesticity of Herman and his wife in 'Falk', and that is mocked for its petit-bourgeois cosy conventionality by the narrator); and on the joys of parenthood, on happy family reunions, on sociable celebrations, he has conspicuously little to say: loss, separation and the conflict of desires are his preferences.

When we look forward to Conrad from Dickens, we see that the warmths, genialities and festivities to which Dickens attunes us are absent from Conrad; he excludes, too, those tender moments of mutuality which for George Eliot are local triumphs of humanity. Again, if we look back from D. H. Lawrence (who said 'I can't forgive Conrad for being so sad and for giving in'), we see that Conrad lacks Lawrence's sense of nature's miraculously potent vitality and of man's rich emotional and instinctual depths. Conrad has his own specialisations, his own eloquences, his own kinds of measured affirmation; but it is clear that his outlook is generally bleaker and more defensive than that of most other novelists. Memorable moments in his pages suggest the vulnerable littleness of man set against some great and threatening environment – the captain in *The Shadow-Line*, beset by an all-obliterating night; Decoud in *Nostromo*, marooned on a tiny island amid the empty immensity of sea and sky; or Marlow in *Heart of Darkness*, surrounded by vast tangles of a

Somewhere in the Pacific. *This cartoon of Conrad by Max Beerbohm is the frontispiece to Beerbohm's* A Survey *(1921).*

Conrad, observing the emblems of death and evil, remarks: 'Quelle charmante plage! On se fait l'illusion qu'ici on pourrait être toujours presque gai.' ('What a charming beach! One has the illusion that here one could for ever be almost cheerful.')

jungle which seems poised to annihilate intruding men.

Such symbolically-charged contrasts between the lonely individual in the foreground and the neutral or threatening vastness of the background may remind us of Thomas Hardy's work. Conrad is more cosmopolitan than Hardy, not only in location and characterisation, but also in thematic range: Conrad has a larger and more systematic network of political, philosophical and psychological observations. Their pessimisms have different emphases: Hardy has a bitter sense of the ways in which destiny tortures the innocent and sensitive; Conrad has a more Augustan sense of the general vanity of human wishes. Yet there are clearly some common features in their pessimism which point to causes extending beyond private experience to the general background. In both writers, there is a strong sense that the heavens, once thought to be benevolent to man, are empty or even hostile. In both, there is a keen post-Darwinian sense that man and his struggles are but part of a 'Nature, red in tooth and claw'. In both, there is a strong element of anti-rational primitivism: the sense that 'Where ignorance is bliss /'Tis folly to be wise'. And in both, we often hear the plangent tones of the disillusioned romantic.

Any consideration of the sources of Conrad's pessimism should be prefaced by a reminder that Conrad is an artist with free will, with freedom of choice: a causal sequence is not a determining sequence. There are times when a pessimistic emphasis can be seen as tactical, as an attempt to offer a dissenting voice to a discussion in which, in the world at large, optimistic tones have sounded too frequently. Nevertheless, our biographical survey of Conrad's career up to the time when he started to produce his novels gives many reasons why he should have found the tones of pessimism readily available to himself. There was the upbringing in a beleaguered Poland; the early deaths of his mother and father; long years at sea when he was first a Pole among Frenchmen and next a Pole among Englishmen. Even with marriage, his haunting sense of isolation was slow to fade, as is suggested by the tale 'Amy Foster'. In that tale, a Polish emigrant who has been shipwrecked off the English coast comes ashore and after cruel tribulations marries a simple country girl, but he is deserted by her when he is suffering a feverish illness: he calls for water, but in his native language, and she, frightened by the strange sounds, runs away. He dies, having been 'cast out mysteriously by the sea to perish in the supreme disaster of loneliness and despair'. In this tale Conrad may partly be recalling the time on his honeymoon when he was ill with fever. In her memoirs, his widow Jessie was to write:

For a whole long week the fever ran high and for most of the time J. C. was delirious. To see him lying in the white canopied bed, dark-faced, with gleaming teeth and shining eyes, was sufficiently impressive, but to hear him muttering to himself in a strange tongue (he thinks he must have been speaking Polish), to be unable to penetrate the clouded mind or catch one intelligible word, was for a young inexperienced girl truly awful. . . . . The sense of there being nobody at hand to help overpowered and silenced me.

(*Personal Recollections*, 1924, pp. 25–7)

However, although the circumstances of his early life and subsequent voyages may well have predisposed Conrad towards a pessimistic sense of isolation, there were general cultural factors which operated to reinforce this sense. We have noted some connections with Hardy's writing, and we may recall, too, the pessimism of so much major poetry between the mid-nineteenth century and the early twentieth, from Tennyson's 'In Memoriam' and Matthew Arnold's 'Dover Beach' to T. S. Eliot's 'The Waste Land'. One obvious reason for this pessimism was the decline of religious belief (partly as a consequence of the rising prestige of science) and the resultant growth of the sense of loss.

Religious matters

In the nineteenth century, if there was still religion for the masses there was, increasingly, scepticism for the intelligentsia. The decline of religious belief can generate a keen and pervasive sense of loss. If one is brought up to believe that the existence of God makes moral sense of the universe and gives a happy ending (regeneration in Paradise) to all virtuous lives on earth, then the loss or absence of faith may entail a grim awareness that the universe is no longer man's homeland but a ruthlessly amoral territory on which man, with his ideals, sensitivities and aspirations, is an intruder. Conrad had a keen sense of this – of man decoyed into an alien and perhaps senseless creation. 'C'est comme une forêt où personne ne connaît la route' – 'It's like a forest in which nobody knows the way', he told Cunninghame Graham. 'Faith is a myth and beliefs shift like mists on the shore'; and even Spring could seem a cruel fraud:

> There is twilight and soft clouds and daffodils – and a great weariness. . . . . Spring? We are an[n]ually lured by false hopes. Spring! Che coglioneria! [What balls! What nonsense!] Another illusion for the undoing of mankind.
>
> (*LCG*, 82–3)

Not surprisingly, then, the novels and tales sound that recurrent theme of the seeming sanctuary which proves to be a baited trap.

Conrad maintained some connections with the Catholic Church – his son Borys was baptised a Roman Catholic and was sent to a

51

Catholic preparatory school, for example; but there is no doubt of the thoroughness of Conrad's personal scepticism. His attitude to Christianity resembles not an agnostic's nostalgia for certitude (a common Victorian attitude) but rather an Augustan's distaste for fanaticism. He read with pleasure the work of the Augustan satirist, Swift, and compared himself with Swift's Gulliver. At Christmas 1920, Conrad told a fellow-sceptic, Edward Garnett:

> It's strange how I always, from the age of fourteen, disliked the Christian religion, its doctrines, ceremonies and festivals..... Nobody – not a single Bishop of them – believes in it. The business in the stable isn't convincing; whereas my atmosphere (vide reviews) can be positively breathed.
>
> (*EG*, 188–9)

And later:

> Christianity.....is distasteful to me. I am not blind to its services but the absurd oriental fable from which it starts irritates me.
>
> (*EG*, 265)

Conrad could also complain that Christianity's moral standards were (*a*) too high and (*b*) too low.

> (*a*) Great, improving, softening, compassionate it may be but it has lent itself with amazing facility to cruel distortion and is the only religion which, with its impossible standards, has brought an infinity of anguish to innumerable souls – on this earth.
>
> (*EG*, 265)

> (*b*) The doctrine (or theory) of expiation through suffering .....is quite simply an infamous abomination when preached by civilized people. It is a doctrine which, on the one hand, leads straight to the Inquisition and, on the other, discloses the possibility of bargaining with the Eternal.....Each act of life is final .....I am strong enough to judge my conscience rather than be its slave.
>
> (*LMP*, 36)

It was to his friend Cunninghame Graham, who himself asserted on the public platform that 'God was a man of the very best intentions who died young', that Conrad wrote 'There is no morality, no knowledge and no hope'. Dostoyevsky had claimed: 'If God is dead, everything is permitted'; and for those who lose the sense of God's reality, ethical relativism – the sense that morality is merely a matter of convention which varies from place to place, without there being any objective enduring test of right and wrong – presses particularly strongly. In 'Dover Beach', Matthew Arnold spoke of the present as a time of doubt and confusion,

> Swept with confused alarms of struggle and flight
> Where ignorant armies clash by night;

Tennyson reflected in 'In Memoriam' that if there were no after-life, the Creation, however beautiful, would seem the work of

> some wild Poet, when he works
> Without a conscience or an aim;

and Conrad, with the dry irony of a matured and poised scepticism, remarks in *A Personal Record*:

> I have come to suspect that the aim of creation cannot be ethical at all. I would fondly believe that its object is purely spectacular
> . . . . .

(92)

For the growth of scepticism in the nineteenth century there are various familiar causes. One was the prestige of science in general, which seemed to be producing impressive results by following procedures that ignored, or even seemed to defy, religious tradition. The prestige of physics and technology encouraged men to think of the universe as a vast mechanism and of man himself not as the image of God with an immortal soul but as a mechanism endowed with consciousness. T. H. Huxley, the evolutionist, said 'We are conscious automata'; the youthful Bertrand Russell confided to his journal in 1888: 'I do wish I believed in the life eternal, for it makes me quite miserable to think man is merely a kind of machine endowed, unhappily for himself, with consciousness.' Furthermore the spread of evolutionary ideas made the Book of Genesis seem manifestly a fable and by hinting at man's continuity with the animal kingdom offered a humiliating threat to his dignity. Even before the publication of Darwin's *Origin of Species*, the implications of the evolutionary theories in such works as Lyell's *Principles of Geology* had shocked Tennyson into sombre reflection:

> Are God and Nature then at strife,
>   That Nature lends such evil dreams?
>   So careful of the type she seems,
> So careless of the single life. . . . .

> 'So careful of the type?' but no.
>   From scarped cliff and quarried stone
>   She cries, 'A thousand types are gone;
> I care for nothing, all shall go.

> 'Thou makest thine appeal to me.
>   I bring to life, I bring to death;
>   The spirit does but mean the breath:
> I know no more.' And he, shall he,

Man, her last work, who seem'd so fair,
　　Such splendid purpose in his eyes,
　　Who roll'd the psalm to wintry skies,
Who built him fanes of fruitless prayer,

Who trusted God was love indeed
　　And love Creation's final law –
　　Tho' Nature, red in tooth and claw
With ravine, shriek'd against his creed –

Who lov'd, who suffer'd countless ills,
　　Who battled for the True, the Just,
　　Be blown about the desert dust,
Or seal'd within the iron hills?

(*LV–LVI*)

And a further blow to man's dignity came with the popularisation of Lord Kelvin's second law of thermodynamics – the law of entropy, which emphasised that in course of time there would be a levelling of all the temperature-differences in the universe; so that the sun, instead of pouring out its energy indefinitely, would eventually cool and die in the heavens, and man would die a chilly death on earth.

'What makes mankind tragic', said Conrad, 'is not that they are the victims of nature, it is that they are conscious of it.' (*LCG*, 70). Given the bleakness of the vistas opened by scientific discovery, it is not surprising that many writers entertained the idea (paradoxically, since they *were* writers) that ignorance might after all be bliss. As we shall see later, the anti-rational primitivism which burgeoned in the late nineteenth century and which has its finest efflorescence in the twentieth, with D. H. Lawrence, is of great importance in Conrad. In the meantime, we must turn to some political matters.

Poland and Conrad's political outlook

We would expect Conrad, the son of a renowned patriot, to have inherited his father's defiant love of Poland; and indeed this patriotism can be found explicitly and implicitly in many of his works. Most obviously, there are political essays bearing directly on the subject: 'Autocracy and War' and 'The Crime of Partition' (*NLL*). Then there is the late tale 'Prince Roman' (*TH*), in which Conrad recalls how, as a child, he was privileged to meet the deaf, aged prince who had once been sentenced for life to the Siberian mines as his punishment for fighting the Russians in the uprising of 1831 – fighting for

> that country which demands to be loved as no other country has ever been loved, with the mournful affection one bears to the unforgotten dead and with the unextinguishable fire of a hopeless

passion which only a living, breathing, warm ideal can kindle......
(TH, 51)

Then there are the poignant reminiscences of *A Personal Record* and the accounts of later visits: 'First News' and 'Poland Revisited' (*NLL*). And in 1916 Conrad actually visited the Foreign Office in London with a memorandum, later adapted as 'A Note on the Polish Problem' (*NLL*), arguing the importance of establishing, after the war, a protectorate of allied powers to nurse Poland to independence. (In fact she regained complete independence in 1918, and promptly was at war with her old enemy, Russia, whose invading armies were routed in 1920; but her democratic system crumbled: Marshal Piłsudski held power from 1926 to 1935, and after his death a military junta ruled the nation.)

One of the most interesting tensions in Conrad's nature is that between patriotic loyalty to his homeland and the need to gain and maintain his independence. He may well have felt some guilt at having left his native land as a youth, at having taken British nationality, and at working in English and under the anglicised name of Joseph Conrad – the surname Korzeniowski having been so often garbled by linguistically-slothful Englishmen. And Poles themselves debated the ethics of his action. In the Polish weekly *Kraj*, in March 1899, Wincenty Lutosławski said that men of talent had the right to emigrate from an oppressed Poland; and he cited Conrad's novels when explaining that their works, even if in a foreign language, could still 'preserve the national spirit'. This view was bitterly contested by Eliza Orzeszkowa, herself a well-known novelist, who wrote in a subsequent article:

> Creative ability is the very crown of the plant, the very top of the tower, the very heart of the heart of the nation. And to take away from one's nation this flower, this top, this heart and to give it to the Anglo-Saxons who are not even lacking in bird's milk, for the only reason that they pay better for it – one cannot even think of it without shame.....Over the novels of Mr Conrad Korzeniowski no Polish girl will shed an altruistic tear.....

(KRZ, 114)

Conrad may well have heard of this debate; and certainly there is a passage in *A Personal Record* which seems intended as a defence against such accusations. He is referring to his decision to leave Poland to go to sea:

> Alas! I have the conviction that there are men of unstained rectitude who are ready to murmur scornfully the word desertion. Thus the taste of innocent adventure may be made bitter to the palate. The part of the inexplicable should be allowed for in appraising the conduct of men in a world where no explanation

is final. No charge of faithlessness ought to be lightly uttered.

(35)

So it is clear that Conrad was sensitive to the idea that he could be regarded as having deserted his country; yet had he stayed at home he could, as we have noted, have been conscripted into the Russian army – no honour for a Pole. It is not surprising, then, that his later work should have had such a strong thematic preoccupation with loyalty and betrayal, and particularly with ambiguous situations in which loyalty to one code or group entails betrayal of another. Some Poles have claimed to see a strong autobiographical, political element in *Lord Jim*. Jim leaps from what he believes to be a sinking ship, the *Patna*, later experiences shame and disgrace because of this act, and strives to redeem himself by his toils in a far-off land. Gustav Morf, in *The Polish Heritage of Joseph Conrad*, once suggested that Conrad was thus sublimating his feelings of guilt at leaving Poland, the name *Patna* standing for *Polska* (another suggestion is *Patria*).

Allegorical interpretations of Conrad's works, and particularly interpretations which treat them as autobiographical confessionals or psychological self-therapies, can be crudely reductive: as Conrad the guilty is pushed to the fore, Conrad the truth-teller, the astute observer of many lives, the artist capable of generalising objectively from a private basis, tends to be pushed to the rear. However, a preoccupation with the ambiguities of loyalty and betrayal is certainly one of *Lord Jim*'s most important features: as when the villainous Gentleman Brown plays on a sense of complicity with Jim, who finds that his loyalties are divided between his native followers and his race, and between a practical but ruthless ethic and a chivalrous but risky one.

There are other ways in which Conrad's Polish background attuned him to such ethical ambiguities. His father, Apollo, had been loyal to Poland – yet, for that very reason, 'an enemy of the state', a subversive, law-breaking figure in the eyes of the Russian authorities. Loyalty to a nation could entail disloyalty to its rulers. And furthermore, Apollo's nationalism, which resulted in trial and exile, led to sufferings not only for himself but for his wife and young son, who was so soon orphaned. So Conrad was capable of seeing ways in which loyalty to nation might entail disloyalty to family – or at least a sacrifice of family happiness on the altar of a patriotic ideal. We may recall that in *Nostromo*, Gould sacrifices his wife's happiness for the sake of his increasingly inflexible devotion to his ideal of developing the mine; in *Under Western Eyes*, Haldin's devotion to the revolutionary cause results in his death and also thereby in the death of his heartbroken mother; and in *Lord Jim*, Jim's determination to offer himself as sacrifice to the natives who feel he has betrayed them entails his desertion of his closest friends, the girl Jewel and the servant Tamb'Itam. (Conrad once wrote of himself: 'His life .....presented itself to his conscience as a series of betrayals.' [*NLL*, 149])

His multiple perspectives, his readiness to see both the under-dog's and the top dog's viewpoints, help to make Conrad the most incisive, mature and subtle political commentator of all the novelists. Born into the Polish gentry, with nobles and wealthy land-owners (whose serfs spoke Russian) among his relatives and contacts, Conrad would know what it felt like to be socially the top dog of a given society. Yet since the Poles were politically subjugated by Prussia, Russia and Austria, he also knew what it was like to be the under-dog in an imperialist situation. During his sea-life, his voyages took him to some of the outposts of empire – Bombay, the Dutch East Indies, Singapore; and when domiciled in England, he could exper-ience at first hand the jingoistic enthusiasms within a nation which was very much the top dog of imperialism – for in the late nineteenth century Britain was proud mistress of the greatest empire the world had ever known, an empire stretching round the globe, the empire 'on which the sun never sets'. Thus Conrad, who like so many Poles was an anglophile, respecting British traditions of regard for individual liberties, could share some imperialist enthusiasms: and in the closing pages of *The Nigger of the 'Narcissus'*, he writes of Great Britain, the 'ship mother of fleets and nations', with a patriotic fervour which would have delighted a Kipling or a W. E. Henley or an Edmund Bentley. (*The Nigger* was first published in Henley's jingoistic *New Review*, which may partly account for that fervour.) Nevertheless, since he had known at first hand the ruthlessness of Russian imperialism (and later the iniquities of Belgian imperialism) he was capable of asking searching questions about the justification of the imperial ethos, questions which too few in the late nineteenth century were prepared to ask; and his *Heart of Darkness* is the most brilliant fictional account of the rapacity and brutality which some-times flourished in the name of imperial progress.

Given the sufferings of his nation and his family at the hands of the Russian overlords, one would expect a bitterness against Russia to be prominent in Conrad's writings, and in certain works this is indeed the case. In 'Autocracy and War' he expresses a contempt which might be a little more persuasive were it a little less sweeping:

She [Russia] is not an empty void, she is a yawning open chasm between East and West; a bottomless abyss that has swallowed up every hope of mercy, every aspiration towards personal dignity, towards freedom, towards knowledge, every ennobling desire of the heart, every redeeming whisper of conscience.

(*NLL*, 100)

And in this essay of 1905 he also makes the astute prophecy – a prophecy that was, of course, fulfilled in 1917 and the subsequent years – that though a Russian revolution will come, her people are so immured to slavery that the overthrow of Tsarism will simply inaugurate a further tyranny:

> In whatever form of upheaval Autocratic Russia is to find her end, it can never be a revolution fruitful of moral consequences to mankind. It cannot be anything else but a rising of slaves..... It is safe to say tyranny, assuming a thousand protean shapes, will remain clinging to her struggles for a long time before her blind multitudes succeed at last in trampling her out of existence under their millions of bare feet.
>
> (102–3)

(The rhetoric may remind us of the indignation of a much more recent exile from Russian rule, Alexander Solzhenitsyn.) Three years after the Russian Revolution had taken place, Conrad recorded in the 'Author's Note' to *Under Western Eyes*:

> These people [the revolutionaries] are unable to see that all they can effect is merely a change of names. The oppressors and the oppressed are all Russians together; and the world is brought once more face to face with the truth of the saying that the tiger cannot change his stripes nor the leopard his spots.

Conrad's inherited bitterness against Russia makes the more notable his ability in the novels and tales to register the complexity of Russian experience and outlooks. It is true that in *The Secret Agent* the arch-villain is the sinister Russian diplomat, Mr Vladimir; but in *Heart of Darkness* the altruistic (if gullible) admirer of Kurtz is also a Russian, while 'The Warrior's Soul' (*TH*) notes the pity which Tsarist officers felt for the exhausted troops of Napoleon's retreating Grand Army. Most notably: in *Under Western Eyes* Conrad discriminates finely among both the defenders of Tsarist autocracy and the revolutionary groups: on each side he notes both relative turpitude and relative nobility; he observes that the ordinary people may be downtrodden by the régime – or casually killed by a revolutionary's bomb; and he even observes that the extremities of Russian experience may give to life there an intensity compared with which the life of a Swiss citizen may be tame, and the life of a British citizen may be emotionally muted and inhibited. This rendering of complexities shows that Conrad's nature is most fully present in his best works of fiction: there we come closer to the true Conrad than in letters or non-fictional writing – closer even than we would come if we were to interview him in person. The disciplines of good fiction are truth-seeking disciplines; and at its best Conrad's preoccupation with ambiguity and paradox is a sign neither of uncertainty nor of a fence-sitting attitude, but, on the contrary, of an uncompromising commitment to the true complexities of human experience.

Imperialism

Politically, Conrad is janiform. He is in some respects very conservative; yet he has also a keen radicalism of temperament which can lead him to observations which seem socialistic or even anarchistic.

In one early letter (commenting on the 1885 General Election in England) he says:

> The International Socialist Association are triumphant, and every disreputable ragamuffin in Europe feels that the day of universal brotherhood, despoliation and disorder is coming apace, and nurses daydreams of well-plenished pockets amongst the ruin of all that is respectable, venerable and holy. The great British Empire went over the edge, and yet on to the inclined plane of social progress and radical reform . . . . .
>
> England was the only barrier to the pressure of infernal doctrines born in continental back-slums. Now, there is nothing! . . . . .
>
> Socialism must inevitably end in Caesarism . . . . .
>
> The whole herd of idiotic humanity are moving in that direction at the bidding of unscrupulous rascals and a few sincere, but dangerous, lunatics.
>
> *(LL* I, 84)

Considering that this election, with the newly-extended franchise, had brought to power Mr Gladstone's Liberals, Conrad's response seems a little hysterical; but it is meet to recall that during the nineteenth century numerous British writers had the sense that democracy could lead to mobocracy and violent chaos. Dickens conveys the fear vividly; so too did Ruskin, Carlyle, Arnold, George Eliot and Elizabeth Gaskell. The reason is obvious: the memory of the French Revolution was a recurrent nightmare: the Revolution with its idealistic slogans, its frenzies of bigotry, its waves of carnage, its bloody futility. When Conrad said 'Socialism must inevitably end in Caesarism', he might have been recalling various lessons of history: that the republicanism of ancient Rome gave way to the rule of the Caesars; that at the English Civil War, victory for the parliamentarians led to the tyranny of Cromwell; and that the French revolutionaries' talk of 'liberty, equality and fraternity' yielded to the autocracy of Napoleon.

Nevertheless, as we have noted, Conrad's closest literary friendship was to be with the brilliant pioneer socialist, R. B. Cunninghame Graham, a man who worked on the extreme left wing of British politics. To him Conrad wrote:

You with your ideals of sincerity, courage and truth are strangely out of place in this epoch of material preoccupations. What does it bring? What's the profit? What do we get by it? These questions are at the root of every moral, intellectual or political movement. Into the noblest cause men manage to put something of their baseness; and sometimes when I think of You here, quietly[,] You seem to me tragic with your courage, with your beliefs and your hopes. Every cause is tainted: and you reject this one, espouse that other one as if one were evil and the other good while the same evil you hate is in both, but disguised in different words. I am more in sympathy with you than words can express yet if I had a grain of belief left in me I would believe you misguided. You are misguided by the desire of the impossible – and I envy you. Alas! What you want to reform are not institutions – it is human nature. Your faith will never move that mountain. Not that I think mankind intrinsically bad. It is only silly and cowardly.

(*LCG*, 68)

And in a further letter to Cunninghame Graham he was even more cynical:

Fraternity means nothing unless the Cain-Abel business. . . . . Man is a wicked animal. His wickedness has to be organised. . . . . . Society is essentially criminal – otherwise it would not exist. It's egoism which preserves everything – absolutely everything – everything that we hate, everything that we love. And everything holds together. This is why I respect extreme anarchists. – 'I wish for general extermination' – Very well. It is just; and what's more, it's clear.

(*LCG*, 117. I have translated Conrad's French.)

What is obvious in these varied and not entirely consistent pronouncements is the distrust of human nature: the sense that society, at best, holds in check the ever-present tendencies to disruption. If the temperamental conservative is one who takes a very pessimistic view of human nature, then for much of the time Conrad is such a conservative. However, we should remember that his father was not only a scion of the gentry, but also a leader of the 'Reds' amongst the Polish patriots: he hoped that the Russians might be cast out as a result of a popular uprising which would unite high and low. So although Conrad's distrust of human nature is in a very ancient sceptical tradition, which can be traced back via such philosophers as Schopenhauer and Voltaire to Mandeville and Hobbes and eventually to Lucretius, there is a complication caused by that sympathy with the under-dog which can sometimes be found among aristocrats – particularly when, as Polish aristocrats, they are in some sense under-dogs themselves. *Noblesse oblige.*

It is often the case that scions of the land-owning gentry feel themselves threatened by the business-minded middle class, and this for the very good reason that history is on the side of the middle classes: as a feudal-agrarian economy gives way to a mercantile-industrial economy, so economic and political power gradually passes from the land-owning interests to business interests. So it is not entirely unusual for noblemen to espouse popular causes, seeking alliance with the poor against the common bourgeois enemy (Cunninghame Graham, as a land-owning aristocrat with a heavily-mortgaged estate, is a perfect example), or to offer criticisms of the middle-class outlook which sound much like those offered by socialists. Like Cunninghame Graham, Conrad had a keen eye for the way in which high-sounding phrases and slogans might mask the ruthless acquisitiveness of individuals or of nations. 'Holy Russia' he had experienced in childhood as unholy tyranny. In *Heart of Darkness* he was to write, with laconic audacity:

> The conquest of the earth, which mostly means the taking it away from those who have a different complexion or slightly flatter noses than ourselves, is not a pretty thing when you look into it too much.
>
> > (*Y*, 50–1)

And he has a keen eye for the way in which democracy under capitalism may approach pseudo-democracy, since the man who pays the piper calls the tune:

> Industrialism and commercialism – wearing high-sounding names in many languages (*Welt-politik* may serve for one instance).....
> – stand ready, almost eager, to appeal to the sword as soon as the globe of the earth has shrunk beneath our growing numbers by another ell or so. And democracy, which has elected to pin its faith to the supremacy of material interests, will have to fight their battles to the bitter end.....
>
> > ('Autocracy and War', *NLL*, 107)

(This is virtually a prophecy of the First World War.) And in Africa, Conrad notes in that essay, 'territorial spheres of influence' have been marked out 'to keep the competitors for the privilege of improving the nigger (as a buying machine) from flying prematurely at each other's throats.'

'Competitors for the privilege of improving the nigger (as a buying machine)': a definition to savour and relish: an astonishingly cynical – and penetratingly accurate – remark for the time (1905). It sounds like the sort of observation that a Marxist might make; but it is a mistake to assume that Marxists have the monopoly of political scepticism. On the contrary: Conrad had little to learn from Marxists, and he could have taught them a good deal. He had seen exploitation in the Congo; in the tropics he had often been in 'frontier situations' where white confronts black or brown, and where one is obliged to ask what, if anything, really distinguishes the civilised from the barbaric; and he had developed a keen eye for disparities between word and fact, slogan and deed.

From a survey of Conrad's works we can infer how he would probably have ranked various imperial nations in order of demerit. Beginning with the least corrupt and descending to the most corrupt, the order would be: Great Britain; France; Spain; Japan; Austria; Holland; USA; Belgium; Prussia; Russia. Prussia and Russia are at the bottom of the list, mainly because of their treatment of the subjugated Poles. The Belgians are close to the bottom, largely because of their predatory activities in the Congo. The Americans occupy a low position because Conrad was inclined to see North American society as the arch-capitalist society, dominated by the quest for the silver dollar. Furthermore, in the 1890s the United States had emerged as a newly aggressive imperial power by going to war with Spain over possession of Cuba and the Philippines; and though the Americans were the victors, Conrad (like many British and European observers) was inclined to have a pitying sympathy for Spain, on the grounds that though this old nation was now shorn of her former grandeur, at least she could boast cultural riches far exceeding those of the USA. 'But, perhaps, the race is doomed?' asked Conrad. 'It would be a pity. It would narrow life, it would destroy a whole side of it which had its morality and was always picturesque and at times inspiring. The others may well shout Fiat lux! [Let there be light!] It will be only the reflected light of a silver dollar and no sanctimonious pretence will make it resemble the real sunshine.' (*LCG*, 84.) Of Dutch imperialism Conrad took a mixed but generally rather hostile view, to judge from *Almayer's Folly* and 'Freya of the Seven Isles'. Austria's place in the list is fairly high, because although she was one of the partitioning powers in Poland, her rule had often been relatively easy-going and tolerant. Conrad's respect for the Japanese stemmed mainly from the fact that they had defeated the Russians in 1905 and were allies of Britain in the early years of the century. France has a high position partly because Poland was culturally a francophile nation and partly because Poles had fought under Napoleon against Russia: indeed, Conrad's great-uncle Nicholas had himself been one of the survivors of the retreat from Moscow (starving, he had eaten dog). And Britain has her position at the top of the table largely because of her liberal traditions of concern for the liberty of the individual (the traditions of free speech, of the jury system in courts of law, of the parliamentary electoral system, and the principle of sanctuary for foreign refugees), and because – notwithstanding many barbarities inflicted by her in Ireland and elsewhere – her imperialism had been relatively paternalist and less ruthlessly exploitative than that of other nations.

In his letters, Conrad can speak proudly of that 'liberty, which can only be found under the English flag'. But although he could speak like a proud British patriot on many occasions, he still held the view that imperialism in itself was always suspect and that the world would be a better place if there were no imperialism at all. In his very first novel, *Almayer's Folly*, he had dared to imply that what the imperial nations do on a big scale, with their gunboat diplomacy and their international rivalry for 'spheres of influence', is essentially no different from what the 'uncivilised' natives do on a small scale in their jungle settlements. In that novel, the Dutch are in rivalry with the British for control of Borneo; the Arabs are in competition with the Malays for control of Almayer's trading district; and Almayer himself competes with the Balinese, Dain, for possession of his half-caste daughter. And she, Nina, who has lived among both natives and Europeans, reflects bitterly that whatever the race, nationality, colour or creed, all men seem alike in their egoistic questing for material profit. In *Heart of Darkness*, Conrad makes the point that Kurtz, who becomes corrupt in the African wilderness, is the product of all Europe – including England. 'All Europe contributed to the making of Kurtz'; he was 'educated partly in England'; 'his mother was half-English, his father was half-French'.

The boldness and originality of Conrad's criticisms of imperialism are enhanced when we recall that the 1890s, when *Almayer's Folly* and *Heart of Darkness* appeared, were the great heyday of imperialism, as trade rivalry grew between the various industrialised nations; and it was certainly a time when the majority of British people – whatever their social class – were enthusiastic jingoists: indeed a popular music-hall song of the day (by G. W. Hunt) was the origin of that term jingoist:

> We don't want to fight; but, by Jingo, if we do,
> We've got the ships, we've got the men, and we've got the money too.

'An Outpost of Progress', that scathing attack on colonialism in Africa, was published in the magazine *Cosmopolis* for June and July 1897 – Victoria's Jubilee Year. In the June issue of the magazine, Sir Richard Temple's article 'The Reign of Queen Victoria' is a eulogy of the growth of British economic power, military strength, and territory; while in 'The Globe and the Island', the regular political commentator, Henry Norman, praises British gunboat diplomacy in Africa. The July number of the magazine, in which

Conrad's Kayerts shoots the unarmed Carlier and hangs himself from a cross, contains a commentary on the Jubilee celebrations in which Norman remarks:

> Britain is Imperialistic now. The 'Little Englander' has wisely decided to efface himself. The political party which should talk of reducing the navy or snubbing the Colonies would have a short shrift. We are Imperialists first, and Liberals or Tories afterwards. I said this, for my own part, years ago, when the sentiment was not quite so popular. Now it has happily become a commonplace. The Jubilee is its culminating expression.....

The issue of *Blackwood's Magazine* for March 1899 contained an article called 'An Unwritten Chapter of History: the Struggle for Borgu', of which the following remarks are typical:

> The little bush-fighting that was done against Lapai and elsewhere proved the superiority of the hard bullet over that used in the Sniders. The soft bullet is apt to break up when volleys are fired into bush where natives are hiding; but the Lee-Metford projectiles went through the cover so completely that the hidden party always ran before our men could get close.....;

and this article accompanies the episode of *Heart of Darkness* in which the 'pilgrims' empty their futile rifles into the bush, and in which Kurtz scrawls 'Exterminate all the brutes!'

Conrad's pessimistic sense that human nature is largely corruptible and fallible leads him to the humanitarian insight that since we 'civilised' men are not likely to be much better than the so-called 'inferior races', if at all, we might as well leave them alone. His anti-rational primitivism sometimes leads him to imply that the 'savage' man may in fact be healthier, more vital and better attuned to his environment than is the restless European – this is implied, for example, in the famed description in *Heart of Darkness* of the natives paddling their canoe powerfully through the surf:

> 'They shouted, sang; their bodies streamed with perspiration; they had faces like grotesque masks – these chaps; but they had bone, muscle, a wild vitality, an intense energy of movement, that was as natural and true as the surf along their coast. They wanted no excuse for being there.'

> (*Y*, 61)

In ironic contrast to such vitality is the absurd automatism of the French warship shelling a continent (*Y*, 61–2) and the moribund apathy of the natives who have been used as slave-labour and abandoned to the grove of death by the Europeans (*Y*, 66–7).

Conrad is particularly acute in his sense that aggression on the part of individuals *and* of nations may stem not from strength but from weakness, insecurity, fear and immaturity. In 'Autocracy and War' he eloquently says:

> The intellectual stage of mankind being as yet in its infancy, and States, like most individuals, having but a feeble and imperfect consciousness of the worth and force of the inner life, the need of making their existence manifest to themselves is determined in the direction of physical activity. The idea of ceasing to grow in territory, in strength, in wealth, in influence – in anything but wisdom and self-knowledge [–] is odious to them as the omen of the end. Action, in which is to be found the illusion of a mastered destiny, can alone satisfy our uneasy vanity and lay to rest the haunting fear of the future.....It will be long before we have learned that in the great darkness before us there is nothing that we need fear. Let us act lest we perish – is the cry. And the only form of action open to a State can be of no other than aggressive nature.
>
> (*NLL*, 108–9)

The claims are bold, simple, polemical and profound. The linkage of the immaturity of a State to the immaturity of an individual is striking – and suggests that one source of the power of Conrad's novels is that they offer simultaneously public and private histories: they are simultaneously political, psychological and moral analyses of life. Here Conrad argues that just as the mature individual does not go punching and elbowing his way about the world but leads a more quiet, contemplative and cultured life, so the mature nation does not concern itself with imperialisic aggression and expansion but cultivates its own human, cultural riches. (Conrad may partly be thinking of the way the national life of subjugated Poland found expression in a flourishing artistic heritage.) Naturally Conrad's ideal invites some criticism: e.g. that historically it is an era of imperial expansion that generally provides the economic pre-conditions of flourishing culture (the Athenian empire produced the Athenian civilisation of the fifth century BC; and exploited subject-territories paid for the later Roman splendours); but nevertheless his ideal is nobly pacific and is even more relevant to today's conditions than it was to yesterday's.

There is a further aspect of imperialism which is of particular importance in Conrad's work. Conrad was greatly interested in 'one-man imperialism' – in the small, personal empires established by adventurous Europeans in far-off places: for example, by Clunies-Ross in the Cocos Island chain, by the real Lingard in Borneo, and by James (later Sir James) Brooke on Sarawak. Almost single-handedly, Brooke established himself as revered ruler of the natives on Sarawak: he became 'the first White Rajah'; the land became his property, and on his retirement was passed from one Brooke to another until eventually, in 1946, it was taken over by the British Government. Conrad wrote to the Lady Margaret Brooke, Dowager Ranee of Sarawak, in 1920:

> The first Rajah Brooke has been one of my boyish admirations, a feeling I have kept to this day strengthened by the better understanding of the greatness of his character and the unstained rectitude of his purpose.

> (*LCG*, 210)

Conrad drew heavily on the life of James Brooke (particularly as recorded in Rodney Mundy's *Narrative of Events in Borneo and Celebes*, 1848) when writing *Lord Jim* and *The Rescue*; and there is no doubt that Conrad could feel the romantic appeal of such daring, personal achievements. Yet it is noticeable that even when dealing with these one-man empires, Conrad still, in the novels, makes consistently the point that fools rush in where angels fear to tread: that in the long run even the benevolent paternalist does more harm than good. Though Jim helps his tribe of natives to conquest and prosperity, his presence provokes the massacre in which the old chief's son is slain; and in *The Rescue*, though Lingard for a while is saviour, counsellor and ally to his native friends Hassim and Immada, his infatuation with a white woman leads him to ignore their plight, and they, betrayed, perish. Even Kurtz of *Heart of Darkness* had left his savage followers mourning and distraught by his decision to return with the whites.

In *Lord Jim*, the philosophical Stein muses regretfully: 'This magnificent butterfly finds a little heap of dirt and sits still on it; but man will never on his heap of mud keep still. He want to be so, and again he want to be so . . .' His words, a comment on Jim and human nature, may serve also as a wry comment on imperialism.

Finally, we should notice the relationship between Conrad's attitude to imperialism and his attitudes to racial and sexual prejudice – for these are interlinked matters. With the surface of his imagination he can reflect and in some measure endorse imperialistic enthusiasms, but the depths of his imagination question and subvert such enthusiasms. Similarly, at a superficial level his works reflect and in some measure endorse the prejudices (of white against black, of Gentile against Jew, of male against female) which were taken for granted by the majority of people of all classes in the Europe of his day; but the more fully his imagination is engaged, the more thoroughly those prejudices are challenged.

Science and determinism

In the nineteenth century, science enjoyed greater prestige than ever before, and probably more than it has enjoyed since. In this century, two world wars, in which scientific knowledge was so ingeniously employed to multiply slaughter and destruction, have shown that advances in science are far from synonymous with advances in civilisation, and that a decent quality of life is far more dependent on human kindness than on scientific qualifications. Nevertheless, in the last century the prestige of science was so great that even areas of thought that had little to do with empirical experimentation (for example, the psychological speculations of Freud, or the political rhetoric of Marx and Engels) claimed to be 'scientific' and – a word supposedly entailed by 'scientific' – 'objective'.

Today, we are much more aware that scientific laws change from age to age, and that scientific fact in one period is fantasy in another. In the middle ages, it was 'scientific fact' that the sun went round the earth; but the cosmology of Ptolemy has been superseded by that of Copernicus, and Newton has been superseded by Einstein. Although there has, on the whole, been an accumulation of new knowledge about the universe, it is also the case that what often seemed to be a great advance in science was merely a re-orientation of the known facts so as to suit the changing values of society. We are also far more aware that a scientist's conclusions are implicit in his premises; that he often sees only what he wants to see; and that his researches may help to support an oppressive political system.

But when Conrad was a young man, science seemed to be making vast progress in many areas. Astronomy, biology, physics, engineering: the burgeoning of European industrial technology was transforming Europe and changing the world. New weapons, new machines, new means of transport: and, dominating a submissive globe, a thriving and expanding 'workshop of the world'. Here, in the spectacular advances of the capitalist economies, lay some of the reasons for science's prestige and the notion that it was unfailingly 'objective'.

Some scientific 'laws' are analytic propositions or deductions; they are tautologies: the rules of a game rather than facts about the world. (An example is the law that in normal conditions water freezes at $0°$ Centigrade and boils at $100°$ Centigrade.) Many other scientific 'laws' are synthetic propositions, or inductions: they are often generalisations inferred from a number of experimental observations. These are not rigid, binding, permanent laws: they are potentially refutable and may be revised, corrected or scrapped in the light of further observations; they are generalisations by men, not things built into the physical world. Again, though event is linked to event by a sequence of cause and effect, that sequence is not a binding, compelling sequence. I am here now because a bus has brought me from the station: but the sequence has not been a determined or determining one: events could have happened otherwise. The train was not magically compelled to bring me – it might have been cancelled; and the bus was not compelled to bring me – the driver might have been ill, or I might have chosen to walk.

Now these limitations may seem obvious today; but they were not so obvious in the mid-nineteenth century. Many people then thought that the laws of science were objective laws, immanent in nature; and those people often confused causality with determinism, thinking that causal laws had power to determine or predestine. And these erroneous beliefs had profound consequences (as we shall see in the subsequent sections) in the thought and the literature of the period. We may note at once that an intermittent but powerful sense of the universe as a soulless mechanism determining human lives is one of the obvious sources of Conrad's pessimism, as the following words to Cunninghame Graham indicate:

> There is a – let us say – a machine. It evolved itself (I am severely scientific) out of a chaos of scraps of iron and behold! – it knits. I am horrified at the horrible work and stand appalled. I feel it ought to embroider – but it goes on knitting.....And the most withering thought is that the infamous thing has made itself; made itself without thought, without conscience, without fore-sight, without eyes, without heart. It is a tragic accident – and it has happened. You can't interfere with it. The last drop of bitter-ness is in the suspicion that you can't even smash it.....
>
> It knits us in and it knits us out. It has knitted time space, pain, death, corruption, despair and all the illusions – and nothing matters. I'll admit however that to look at the remorseless process is sometimes amusing.

> (*LCG*, 56–7)

If 'nothing matters', then man, as a moral being, is superfluous. And as we shall now see, 'Superfluous Men' soon manifest themselves.

The Superfluous Man

The Superfluous Man is a distinctive type of man who is commonly to be found in Russian literature of the nineteenth century. He is the offspring of certain rather lonely, self-pitying and unlucky heroes of the Romantic period: notably Goethe's sorrowful young Werther and Byron's moody Childe Harold. In turn, he is the progenitor of certain neurotically self-conscious and rather impotent figures of twentieth-century literature: Rilke's Malte Laurids Brigge, Sartre's Roquentin (for yesterday's Existentialist is last week's Superfluous Man), Camus's Clamence, and even Nabokov's Humbert Humbert, and the numerous futile protagonists of Samuel Beckett's works.

The name of the type, established by Lermontov, was used by Conrad's favourite Russian novelist, Turgenev, in his tale 'The Diary of a Superfluous Man' (1850). Tchulkaturin, the central figure of that tale, is the son of fairly well-to-do landowners in Russia. The estate has been sold; he has enough money to live in idleness, but not enough to have power. He lives in the countryside, which is relatively inexpensive compared with Moscow, but excruciatingly boring. He is extremely egoistic; his 'sensibility' makes him self-conscious to the point of paralysis or derangement. He is a romantic without a cause; socially superfluous. His style combines sentimental self-absorption, emotional exhibitionism, and ironic, even comic, self-deflation:

> Farewell, life!..... Farewell, Liza! I wrote these two words, and almost laughed aloud. This exclamation strikes me as taken out of a book. It's as though I were writing a sentimental novel and ending up a despairing letter.....
>
> Tomorrow is the first of April. Can I be going to die tomorrow? That would be really too unseemly. It's just right for me, though .....
>
> How the doctor did chatter today!

Even Tchulkaturin's last words combine pathos with irony:

> Sinking into nothing, I cease to be superfluous.

Characteristics of this type, then, are an egoistic, albeit intelligent, sensibility, rather decadent or neurotic in its oscillations of mood; a cynical or ironic quality; and above all that sense of being super-fluous, without role or function; isolated from society. Other examples of the type are: Pechorin, central figure of Lermontov's *A Hero of Our Time* (1840), the eponymous protagonist of Turgenev's *Rudin*, the protagonist of Chekhov's 'A Moscow Hamlet', and a variety of prominent figures in Chekhov's plays – the hero of *Ivanov*, Vanya in *Uncle Vanya*, Cherbutykin in *The Three Sisters*. Others can be found in the pages of Goncharov, Dostoyevsky and Tolstoy; and the Super-fluous Man also exists as a state of being through which pass various characters who may not eventually belong to this type. If we ask why Superfluous Men are so common in *Russian* literature of the nineteenth century, the men themselves provide numerous answers. One is that for various economic reasons (inflation, increase of labour costs after the emancipation of the serfs, the high cost of living in the fashionable cities of Moscow and St Petersburg) there then existed a large class of educated, idle, discontented, bored gentlemen. Sufficiently well-to-do not to be obliged to work, yet too poor to enjoy the pleasures of power; often forced to live in the countryside, which was inexpensive but, to their civilised natures, oppressively boring. Another reason is that the Russian state, autocratically ruled and with a rigid hierarchy, already virtually a police state with ruthless powers of censorship, offered few outlets for romantic idealism and radicalism. In the chilly vastness of Tsarist Russia, it was easier for a man to feel 'superfluous' than in other parts of Europe. And the sense of fatalism that this engendered could make him particularly receptive to deterministic arguments.

In his powers of philosophical self-vindication, the narrator of Dostoyevsky's *Notes from Underground* is by far the most fully developed of the Superfluous Men. However he looks at his situation, this morbid Hamlet feels himself threatened by 'the stone wall' of laws, whether they be those of the utilitarian economists or of evolutionary scientists; men can appear to him 'the keys of a piano, which the laws of nature threaten to control so completely'. He considers various responses to this sense of determinism. One is to be Hamlet-like: to shrug one's shoulders and do nothing, submitting to inertia. (If action is compelled, perhaps inaction manifests, perversely, a sense of independence.) The second way is to assert one's independence by acting in apparent defiance of rational laws: to be quixotic, using one's will wilfully; acting capriciously, even anarchically. If 'the direct, legitimate fruit of consciousness is inertia', nevertheless 'reason is nothing but reason . . . . . while will is a manifestation of the whole life'; 'caprice . . . . . preserves for us what is most precious and most important – that is, our personality, our individuality'; 'it is just his fantastic dreams, his vulgar folly, that he will desire to retain, simply in order to prove to himself . . . . . that men still are men and not the keys of a piano'; 'he will contrive destruction and chaos . . . . . only to gain his point'. The narrator actually adds, as though prophesying the coming of Conrad's Mr Kurtz, 'It may be at the cost of his skin, it may be by cannibalism!'

We can see that in his neurotic self-consciousness, his impotence and his habitation of a waste-land of boredom, the Superfluous Man anticipates many twentieth-century figures, from Eliot's Prufrock to the static Jeremiahs of Samuel Beckett. On the other hand, in his sense of absurdity and alienation, and in his idea that one could prove one's selfhood by some defiant, anarchic, seemingly irrational action, he anticipates existentialist or absurdist protagonists: Sartre's Roquentin or Camus's Meursault and Clamence. We could perhaps say that the existentialist is a Hamlet who chooses to become a Don Quixote.

The Hamlet/Don Quixote dichotomy

From the mid-nineteenth century onwards, the increasing erosion of religious belief reduced the sense that moral standards had absolute, objective warrant. One of the numerous cultural consequences of this was that Cervantes's Don Quixote came to be regarded not just as a lovable literary eccentric but increasingly as a symbol of modern idealism: for his idealism had patently lacked objective sanction. So in the later half of the nineteenth century, a cult of Don Quixote

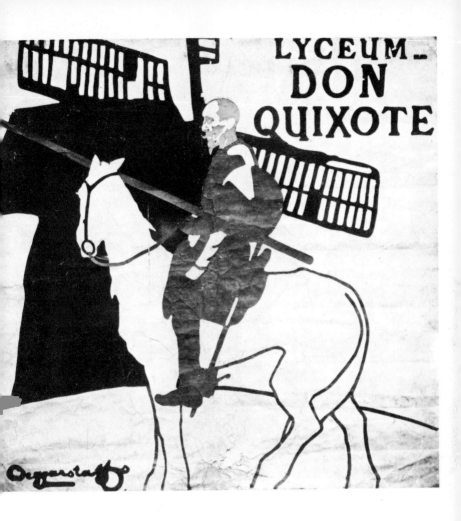

William Nicholson ('W. Beggarstaff') : a poster for a dramatisation by Henry Irving of Don Quixote.

In 1898 Nicholson sent this poster to Conrad (who was gratified), possibly because the head of Quixote bore some resemblance to Conrad's.

The Quixote cult reached its zenith around 1900; it finds a reflection in Conrad's characterisations.

developed in Europe. The number of translations of Cervantes's classic multiplied rapidly; and characters in literature or in life who manifested questing idealism were likely to be compared to Quixote. The cult's extreme was probably reached in 1906, when Miguel de Unamuno published *Our Lord Don Quixote*, a philosophical and religious commentary which proposed that we adopt Cervantes's deluded knight as the Christ for our times. 'I believe', said Unamuno, 'we might undertake a holy crusade to redeem the Sepulchre of the Knight of Madness from the power of the champions of Reason.'

This cult was anticipated by some of the Russian writers. We have noted that Dostoyevsky's Superfluous Man considered two contrasting responses to his plight: one that of passivity, a Hamlet-like response; the other that of irrational, rather Quixotic action. In another Russian writer of the time, this Hamlet/Don Quixote dichotomy became quite explicit as a means of analysis of contemporary states of mind. The writer was, again, Conrad's favourite Russian writer, Turgenev; and the item in question is his influential lecture, 'Hamlet and Don Quixote' (1860), which was first published in England in 1894.

In the lecture, Turgenev claims that Hamlet and Don Quixote represent 'the twin antitypes of human nature, the two poles of the axle-tree on which that nature turns'. Shakespeare's Hamlet was a sceptical procrastinator: in him 'the native hue of resolution/Is sicklied o'er with the pale cast of thought'; and the Hamlet type is similarly a sceptical egoist, his will paralysed by reflection. Don Quixote, on the other hand, is an active campaigner, a credulous idealist: he can act, though, alas, he is often misguided or deluded: his giants are only windmills.

> So on the one side we see the Hamlets of this world – that is to say, types that are thoughtful and discriminating, persons of wide and profound understanding, but persons who are useless in the practical sense, inasmuch as their very gifts immobilize them – and on the other, crack-brained Don Quixotes, who are only useful to humanity and can set its feet marching because they see but one sole point on the horizon, a point the nature of which is often not at all what it seems to their eyes.

A pessimistic disjunction, then: rationality that leads to inaction, versus activity that may be deluded.

Chekhov read and admired this piece, and it influenced the characterisation in his plays, most explicitly in *Ivanov*. Conrad, who warmly admired Turgenev's 'unerring instinct for the significant, for the essential in human life and in the visible world' (*EG*, 269), would have known the dichotomy through its use in Turgenev's novels and tales even if he had not known the lecture itself. What is certain is that the Hamlet/Don Quixote dichotomy has obvious

The Second Sally *by William Strang.*
   Conrad's friend, Cunninghame Graham, was the model for the Don in this picture from Strang's Series of Thirty Etchings . . . . . illustrating
. . . . . 'Don Quixote' *(1902).*

application both to Conrad's janiform personality and to the loom of characterisation in his works.

We have seen that Conrad's tutor called him 'an incorrigible, hopeless Don Quixote' for his decision to go to sea, and that the Don figures almost as a patron saint in the autobiographical *Personal Record*; we have also seen that Conrad was reproached for being a brooding Hamlet by his cousin, Marguerite Poradowska, and that jeremiads about the native hue of resolution's being sicklied o'er with the pale cast of thought are a recurrent feature of his letters. Again, we have seen that Conrad's closest literary friendship was with Cunninghame Graham, a man who was celebrated in his lifetime as 'a modern Don Quixote' (and who was referred to as 'the Don Quixote' by Conrad); who often paid tribute to both Cervantes and Shakespeare, and who even posed as the Don for a series of etchings by Strang to illustrate Cervantes's masterpiece; and yet whose tales and letters (like this one to Edward Garnett in 1899) reveal a profound and often Hamlet-like scepticism about the value of action:

> Significance in things, Ha, Ha, why even atoms themselves are all in a jumble.
>
> Fornication, my masters, murder, adultery, cheating, lies, & the offertory, those are the leading motives of life, & ever will be . . . . . A dingy farce played by fools & harlots, on a poor stage, with an incompetent stage manager, & the only laugh in it, being at one's own antics & folly for continuing to act.
>
> (*LCG*, 27)

If we turn to Conrad's works, we find that the Hamlet/Don Quixote dichotomy is almost alarmingly applicable to a wide range of characters. I say 'almost alarmingly' because this fact suggests a certain schematic ruthlessness about Conrad's characterisation on occasion and because we are thus reminded of Conrad's pessimistic emphasis on impotence and futility. Many of the patently honourable characters can be seen as quixotic either because their values are anachronistic or incongruous, given the nature of the environment in which those values operate, or because their idealism has the quality of a delusion or monomania. Both factors operate in the case of Tom Lingard, the brave adventurer with a fatal capacity for wishing to foster protégés. In *Almayer's Folly*, *An Outcast* and *The Rescue*, his well-intentioned schemes bring bitterness and death to others. (And he is explicitly likened to Don Quixote, of course: D'Alcacer in *The Rescue* calls him 'a descendant of the immortal hidalgo errant upon the sea'.) More subtly, several of the major works, and *Nostromo* in particular, suggest that all conduct governed by pursuit of some ideal is quixotic both in the sense that it will be betrayed by the facts of harsh actuality – 'There was something inherent in the necessities of successful action which carried with it the moral degradation of the idea' (*N*, 521) – and in the sense that the quester will appear deranged in proportion to his degree of devotion to that ideal – 'Every conviction, as soon as it became effective, turned into that form of dementia the gods send upon those they wish to destroy' (200). When trying to sum up the political confusions of South America, Decoud in that novel says: 'There is a curse of futility upon our character: Don Quixote and Sancho Panza, chivalry and materialism, high-sounding sentiments and a supine morality.....' (171). A central thematic statement of *Under Western Eyes* is: 'Hopes grotesquely betrayed, ideals caricatured – that is the definition of revolutionary success' (135).

Conrad has ambivalent feelings, of course, about quixotic individuals. The Romantic tradition, which places a high value on lonely, intense idealism, encourages Conrad to look with some sympathy on such characters; but various Augustan and Enlightenment traditions (commending balance, restraint and sociability) encourage him to look sceptically on conduct tending to the fanatical and extreme. An excellent resolution of the ambivalence is found in the characterisation of Charles Gould in *Nostromo*, whose courage, rectitude and sense of honour win measured respect even though his progress towards what is virtually a cold monomania is systematically delineated. As the narrator observes of Gould:

A man haunted by a fixed idea is insane. He is dangerous even if that idea is an idea of justice; for may he not bring the heaven down pitilessly upon a loved head?

(379)

Looking beyond particular characters, we can see that in his more sceptical moods, Conrad could regard any and every apparently purposeful action as quixotic. If men were pre-determined beings, the puppets of causality, in a universe devoid of God, of responsiveness, of ultimate purpose, they were all, in a sense, quixotic: futile and deranged, the sense of effective action being only an illusion. The point is uncompromisingly made in the most famous epigram in *Nostromo*, an epigram which deploys dauntingly the words 'illusion' and 'helpless':

In our activity alone do we find the sustaining illusion of an independent existence as against the whole scheme of things of which we form a helpless part.

(497)

The idea is repeated with variations in *Nostromo* and in other writings of Conrad:

Action is consolatory. It is the enemy of thought and the friend of flattering illusions.

(*N*, 66)

He [Anatole France] wishes us to believe and to hope, preserving in our activity the consoling illusion of power and intelligent purpose.

(*NLL*, 34)

Action, in which is to be found the illusion of a mastered destiny, can alone satisfy our uneasy vanity and lay to rest the haunting fear of the future.....

(*NLL*, 108)

One implication of these words was to be developed extensively later by absurdist and existentialist authors: the implication that man, as a moral and meaning-seeking creature, is an absurdity in the creation. And Conrad fully recognised this implication, as the following passages show:

Humanity presses from all sides upon the narrow waters desecrating with the whisper of its hopes and fears, with the cry of its strife, with the sigh of its longings, the august unconcern of a limitless space.

(MS of *The Rescue*)

Man on this earth is an unforeseen accident which does not stand close investigation.

(*V*, 196)

If we now consider the other half of the Hamlet/Don Quixote dichotomy, we see that Turgenev's Hamlet has sired many offspring in Conrad's pages. The most familiar example is probably *Nostromo*'s Decoud, the sophisticated sceptic who sees the follies of activities that others take seriously (though it must be said that his scepticism is surpassed by the narrator's), and who, when isolated on an island, experiences 'the crushing, paralysing sense of human littleness', comes to doubt even his own individuality, and eventually shoots himself. A more extreme example is Axel Heyst, the hero of *Victory*. Heyst has been indoctrinated into scepticism by his father, a cynical philosopher (probably based by Conrad on Schopenhauer) who with 'strange serenity, mingled with terrors', had contemplated 'the universal nothingness' and had taught his son that life was a cruel joke, a snare and a cheat. Consequently:

The young man learned to reflect, which is a destructive process, a reckoning of the cost. It is not the clear-sighted who lead the world. Great achievements are usually accomplished in a blessed, warm mental fog, which the pitiless cold blasts of the father's analysis had blown away from the son.

'I'll drift,' Heyst had said to himself deliberately.

(91–2)

Nevertheless, though he strives to be detached and uncommitted, he is twice drawn into involvement with his fellow men, once through pity and once through a mixture of pity and sexual desire; and both acts conspire to bring about the disastrous dénouement in which the girl who loves him, Lena, is killed. Heyst appears to disavow his father's sceptical philosophy with the words, 'Woe to the man whose heart has not learned while young to hope, to love – and to put its trust in life!' – but having said this, he commits suicide; and if the elder Heyst could be invited to comment on the novel, he would doubtless observe that the plot vindicates his cynicism, since his son's altruistic acts have actually provoked the final disasters; and as if echoing his pronouncements on nothingness, the novel's last word is 'Nothing!'

Just as the more quixotic characters were only the extreme examples in an extensive discussion, within Conrad's fiction, of an essential quixotry about all human action, so the more Hamlet-like characters (intelligent, sceptical, distrustful of action) are only the extreme instances in an extensive preoccupation with the idea that reflection may paralyse will. In *The Shadow-Line*, when the narrator is afflicted with acedia, a sense of the pointlessness of action, his phrasing echoes the play *Hamlet* as he speaks of 'this stale, unprofitable world of my discontent'; and his imagination proves to be a subversive power which leads him almost to the point of mental breakdown on his ship. Generally in Conrad's fiction it seems to be the rule that the more reflective the man, the more likely he is to prove fallible or unreliable in action, and the more stolidly imperceptive the man, the more likely he is to prove resiliently dependable in action. If you wish to ally yourself to one who is consistent and seems designed for survival, you should ally yourself with Sancho Panza or Horatio rather than with their masters. And in Conrad's pages such dependables are represented by Singleton (*Nigger of the 'Narcissus'*), MacWhirr ('Typhoon'), the boiler-maker (*Heart of Darkness*), Don Pepe (*Nostromo*), Wang (*Victory*) and many others.

Anti-rational primitivism

A writer is a primitivist in so far as he says or implies that a relatively primitive state of being (in individuals or societies) is better than a relatively sophisticated state of being. A writer is an anti-rational primitivist in so far as he says or implies that a relatively primitive state of consciousness is better than a relatively sophisticated one: he may, for example, commend instinctive awareness or 'blood consciousness' and condemn rational calculation or 'mental con-

77

sciousness'. Such a writer is often a nostalgic chronological primitivist, too: one who postulates some kind of golden age in the past,
before the Fall into our present unhappy state. The story of Adam
and Eve in the Garden of Eden is, among other things, a myth of
chronological anti-rational primitivism. (I phrase matters so as to
evoke a wince at the jargon, which hails from A. O. Lovejoy and
G. Boas; but even jargon may have its uses, as here.)

Consciousness imposes its gifts and its burdens on all of us; civilisation bestows on us amenities and problems. In all ages, men have
intermittently yearned for a release from the burdens of consciousness; in all civilisations, there has been some degree of nostalgia for
the bygone simplicity of the imagined Golden Age. However, a
particularly remarkable burgeoning of anti-rational primitivism
took place among numerous writers in the mid to late nineteenth
century. The reasons for this burgeoning are clear: this was a time
when the vistas of thought were particularly depressing, since so
many of the advances of science and technology seemed to blight
man's faith in God and a benevolent universe. Of the philosophers,
Schopenhauer, Nietzsche, Kierkegaard, Sorel and later Bergson
were among those who in various ways sought to disparage conventional rational awareness and to emphasise the potency of instinctual or anti-rational being. We have seen that in 1888 the young
Bertrand Russell, who was later to have a brief but intense friendship
with Conrad, could think of man as just 'a kind of machine endowed,
unhappily for himself, with consciousness'; and seventy-three years
later the same Bertrand Russell, after a long lifetime dedicated to
rational enquiry, told me:

> I think I have always felt that there were two levels, one that of
> science and common sense, and another, terrifying, subterranean
> and chaotic, which in some sense held more truth than the everyday
> view. You might describe this as a Satanic mysticism.

For Russell, this subterranean level appears to hold not only 'more
truth' but also more potency.

Amongst literary figures of the mid to late nineteenth century,
anti-rational primitivism took a diversity of forms. Walter Pater,
for example, looked back nostalgically to the instinctive awareness
of the child and of the 'childhood' of man in Homeric Greece:

> A world.....under Homeric conditions, such as we picture to
> ourselves with regret, for which experience was intuition, and life
> a continuous surprise, and every object unique, where all knowl-
> edge was still of the concrete and particular, face to face
> delightfully.

> *(Plato and Platonism,* 1893)

Samuel Butler, throughout his works, championed instinct and intuition as against conscious reflection and calculation. The following wry reflections, in *Life and Habit* (1877), are characteristic:

> Dog-fanciers tell us that performing dogs never carry their tails; such dogs have eaten of the tree of knowledge, and are convinced of sin accordingly – they know that they know things, in respect of which, therefore, they are no longer under grace, but under the law, and they have yet so much grace left as to be ashamed. So with the human clever dog; he may speak with the tongues of men and angels, but so long as he knows that he knows, his tail will droop.....In that I write at all, I am among the damned.

Anti-rational primitivism has its fullest, richest and most complex expression in the novels, tales and essays of D. H. Lawrence, above all in *The Rainbow* and *Women in Love*. In his letters, particularly in those of 1915–16 to Bertrand Russell, Lawrence could reduce it to crude, stark terms:

> There is the blood-consciousness, with the sexual connection holding the same relation as the eye, in seeing, holds to the mental consciousness. One lives, knows, and has one's being in the blood, without any reference to nerves and brain. This is one half of life, belonging to the darkness. And the tragedy of this our life, and of your life, is that the mental and nerve consciousness exerts a tyranny over the blood-consciousness.....
>
> Do for your very pride's sake become a mere nothing, a mole, a creature that feels its way and doesn't think.....
>
> When you make your will, do leave me enough to live on.

Russell, who was to outlive Lawrence by forty years, tartly observed later: 'The only difficulty with this programme was that if I adopted it I should have nothing to leave.' He also claimed that Lawrence's doctrine of blood-consciousness 'led straight to Auschwitz'. This, however, does Lawrence some injustice. Anti-rational primitivism has contributed to every part of the spectrum of political beliefs, though it has been far more conspicuous as a contributor to politics of the extreme left (libertarian anarchism) and extreme right (fascism) than as a contributor to democratic liberalism. This diversity is not surprising when we recall that anti-rational primitivism is an important element in both the Augustan and the Romantic movements. The Augustan writer (Swift in *Gulliver's Travels*, Pope in *The Dunciad*, for example), condemns abstruse, fanatical, and seemingly impractical reasoning – in fact the so-called Age of Reason was one which feared intense reasoning and commended instead common sense, a reasoning strictly controlled by criteria of practicality and social utility. The Romantic, on the other hand, condemns 'the mind-forg'd manacles', the meddling intellect which murders to dissect, and strives to defend the life of the emotions or instincts.

There is *hard* primitivism and *soft* primitivism. Soft primitivism occurs when the Golden Age postulated is a slothful one, a place of idleness and ease, like the legendary Land of Cockayne or the Isle of the Lotos Eaters. Hard primitivism occurs when the Golden Age is a time of toil and austerity. In so far as he is an anti-rational primitivist, Conrad upholds hard primitivism: his simple, dependable, constructive types are workers: Singleton, the patriarchal helmsman of *The Nigger of the 'Narcissus'*; the boiler-maker of *Heart of Darkness*; Jörgenson in *The Rescue*. Once Cunninghame Graham sent Conrad a letter which apparently complained that Singleton was too much the ignorant Uncle Tom, the inarticulate loyal workman, and should have been granted an education. Conrad's response has become one of the most famous anti-rationalist statements in the history of modern literature:

> You say: 'Singleton with an education'.....But first of all – what education? If it is the knowledge how to live my man essentially possessed it. He was in perfect accord with his life. If by education you mean scientific knowledge then the question arises – what knowledge, how much of it – in what direction? Is it to stop at plane trigonometry or at conic sections? Or is he to study Platonism or Pyrrhonism or the philosophy of the gentle Emerson? Or do you mean the kind of knowledge which would enable him to scheme, and lie, and intrigue his way to the forefront of a crowd no better than himself? Would you seriously, of malice prepense cultivate in that unconscious man the power to think. Then he would become conscious – and much smaller – and very unhappy. Now he is simple and great like an elemental force. Nothing can touch him but the curse of decay – the eternal decree that will extinguish the sun, the stars one by one, and in another instant shall spread a frozen darkness over the whole universe. Nothing else can touch him – he does not think.
>
> Would you seriously wish to tell such a man: 'Know thyself'. Understand that thou art nothing, less than a shadow, more insignificant than a drop of water in the ocean, more fleeting than the illusion of a dream. Would you?

$(LCG, 53-4)$

It's a letter of characteristic rhetorical eloquence – characteristic in the way the argument gathers a rhythmic roll and surge of momentum. It demonstrates that Conrad's primitivism is strongly defensive and pessimistic, and therefore closer in spirit to the Augustan varieties than to the Romantic. The reference to the frozen darkness is further evidence that in the late nineteenth century anti-rationalism was in large measure an imaginative refuge from the bleak vistas offered by science.

In *The Nigger of the 'Narcissus'*, there is a claim that the Golden

Age of simplicity was the age of the uneducated seaman, a breed of whom Singleton is the last representative:

> Yet he was only a child of time, a lonely relic of a devoured and forgotten generation. He stood, still strong, as ever unthinking . . . . . The men who could understand his silence were gone . . . . . They were the everlasting children of the mysterious sea. Their successors are the grown-up children of a discontented earth. They are less naughty, but less innocent; less profane, but perhaps also less believing; and if they had learned how to speak they have also learned how to whine. But the others were strong and mute . . . . .
>
> (*NN*, 24–5)

In *Victory*, Heyst suggests that the Fall of Man occurred far earlier – and not when Eve ate the forbidden fruit but rather at the very moment when Adam gained conscious awareness of his surroundings:

> That first ancestor . . . . ., as soon as he could uplift his muddy frame from the celestial mould, started inspecting and naming the animals of that paradise which he was so soon to lose.
>
> Action – the first thought, or perhaps the first impulse, on earth! The barbed hook, baited with the illusion of progress, to bring out of the lightless void the shoals of unnumbered generations!
>
> (*V*, 173–4)

Conrad is not being wholly ironic when, in the 'Author's Note' to that novel, he remarks: 'The habit of profound reflection . . . . . is the most pernicious of all the habits formed by the civilised man.' And in another of the letters to Cunninghame Graham, he again shows how anti-rational primitivism is largely a defensive reaction against the bleak findings of nineteenth-century science – though this time it is Darwinian evolutionism rather than Kelvinian thermodynamics which is cited:

> Systems could be built, and rules could be made – if we could only get rid of consciousness. What makes mankind tragic is not that they are the victims of nature, it is that they are conscious of it. To be part of the animal kingdom under the conditions of this earth is very well – but as soon as you know of your slavery the pain, the anger, the strife – the tragedy begins.
>
> (*LCG*, 70)

Such preoccupations help to give the rich charge and swelling glow of symbolic suggestion to memorable Conradian passages like this one in *Nostromo*:

> Nostromo woke up from a fourteen hours' sleep, and arose full length from his lair in the long grass. He stood knee deep amongst

the whispering undulations of the green blades with the lost air of a man just born into the world. Handsome, robust, and supple, he threw back his head, flung his arms open, and stretched himself with a slow twist of the waist and a leisurely growling yawn of white teeth, as natural and free from evil in the moment of waking as a magnificent and unconscious wild beast. Then, in the suddenly steadied glance fixed upon nothing from under a thoughtful frown, appeared the man.

$$(\mathcal{N}, 411-12)$$

This is, of course, an admirably written passage. It tells us much about the character of Nostromo and his fictional environment; but at the same time it reminds us of our own lives and tells us things about ourselves which we have often sensed but never quite been able to get into apt words. Shimmering within this film of Nostromo awakening is another vision, of a savage tigerish Adam stirring (with 'a leisurely growling yawn of white teeth'). It tells us that man is an eternally divided creature – part of the animal kingdom yet alienated from it by the burden of consciousness. And the passage also tells us about our everyday transition from the pleasure of awakening to the pain of realisation of the day's tasks and problems. As in all great writing, we are at the intersection of the particular and the general, of the strange and the familiar.

Determinism and solipsism

Determinism is the belief that all things are determined, so that free will is an illusion. Solipsism is the belief that the individual self constitutes the sole reality. On the one hand, man is the puppet of the universe and its causal laws; on the other, man is a flame of awareness glowing in the midst of a dark flux of the unknown. They are contrasting, mutually contradictory notions; yet both flourished in the late nineteenth century; and both derive from the prestige of empiricism.

As we have seen previously, scientific empiricism, by postulating and verifying innumerable causal laws, could create in those who failed to distinguish between causality and compulsion the sense that man is the passive subject of those laws. But solipsism, too, develops with the prestige of empiricism. Since the empirical outlook of science has the basic assumption that the foundation of all worthwhile knowledge is the evidence of the senses, recognition that the senses can deceive us can appear to reveal a threat to the basis of all certainty. We are all familiar with optical illusions – with the apparent bending of a straight stick in water, for example; and we all confuse illusion with reality when we dream. Since our senses deceive us some of the time, it is theoretically possible that they may deceive us all the time; in which case we can be certain only of our own existence, it seems, and of nothing beyond.

Common sense revolts against such a notion (and Dr Johnson expressed his revolt by kicking a stone), but philosophers have encountered remarkable difficulty when they have attempted to vindicate common sense. We could argue, perhaps, that our faith that the world is substantially as common sense assumes it to be rests not on any naïve belief in the infallibility of the senses but rather on the value-judgement that it is good for our assumptions about the status of the world to be fulfilled. We know that predictions based on the assumption that the world is as stable as common sense assumes it to be are, on the whole, sufficiently fulfilled; while predictions based on the assumption that the world is essentially 'private' or phantasmagoric tend not to be fulfilled. Such arguments are still open to challenge, though it is notable that the solipsist's case often seems to thrive on a confusion of terminology, as A. J. Ayer shows in *The Foundations of Empirical Knowledge*; and it is cheering that the most brilliant early expounder of the solipsist case, David Hume, recorded in his *Treatise of Human Nature* (1739–40) that when logic would not rescue him from solipsism,

> I dine, I play a game of backgammon, I converse, and am merry with my friends; and when after three or four hours' amusement, I wou'd return to these speculations, they appear so cold, and strain'd, and ridiculous, that I cannot find it in my heart to enter into them any farther.

As scientific empiricism gained prestige in the nineteenth century, so the undercurrent of solipsistic fear grew. A diversity of philosophers gave varied expression to it. Nietzsche's works, for example, generate solipsistic epigrams which, like this one in *The Dawn*, sometimes anticipate Conrad's: 'Beliefs are illusions of which we have forgotten that they are illusions'. Schopenhauer, too, a philosopher studied by Conrad, modulates towards solipsism when he emphasises 'the frailty, vanity and dream-like quality of all things'; and in Walter Pater's *Marius the Epicurean* (which Conrad read in 1897), Marius reflects

> that the ideas we are somehow impelled to form of an outer world, and of other minds akin to our own, are, it may be, but a day-dream, and the thought of any world beyond, a day-dream perhaps idler still. . . . .

Conrad's letters frequently express the contradictory paradigms. Sometimes, as we have noted, he talks of the universe as a hard, remorseless machine – the deterministic paradigm. Yet he can also talk of the individual as a solitary consciousness amid mirage-like flux – the solipsistic paradigm.

The machine is thinner than air and as evanescent as a flash of lightning ..... The ardour for reform, improvement[,] for virtue, for knowledge, and even for beauty is only a vain sticking up for appearances as though one were anxious about the cut of one's clothes in a community of blind men. Life knows us not and we do not know life – we don't even know our own thoughts..... Faith is a myth and beliefs shift like mists on the shore.

(*LCG*, 65)

There is a quality of emotive rhetoric about this passage: it develops a certain lyrical-descriptive momentum, even approaching the tone of an incantation – particularly when, in the last sentence, alliteration and assonance set the prose singing; it is writing to convey a mood as much as to define an argument. Nevertheless, the fears were genuine: when Conrad told Graham, 'Sometimes I lose all sense of reality in a kind of nightmare effect produced by existence', he was telling the cold truth.

Now this sense of extreme subjectivity has numerous consequences in the works of Conrad. There are direct expressions: Marlow in *Heart of Darkness* says 'We live, as we dream – alone'; and one of the phrases that Conrad was most fond of quoting was Calderón's 'La vida es sueño' ('Life is a dream'), which is recalled by Decoud's thought: 'All this is life, must be life, since it is so much like a dream.' (*N*, 249.) Conradian narrators (particularly those of *Nostromo* and *Lord Jim*) have the cynical habit of applying the term 'illusions' to ideals, thoughts, observations and feelings – even love is termed merely 'the strongest of illusions' in *Nostromo*. Max Beerbohm acutely parodied this tendency in his tale 'The Feast' with the splendidly mock-Conradian lines:

In his upturned eyes.....the stars were reflected, creating an illusion of themselves who are illusions.....

Within the hut the form of the white man, corpulent and pale, was covered with a mosquito-net that was itself illusory like everything else, only more so.

(*A Christmas Garland*, 1912, pp. 125, 126)

(Beerbohm thus solicits the paradox that if all is illusory, so is the belief that all is illusory.) Conrad's solipsistic intuitions magnify his awareness of the gulfs in comprehension between people who ostensibly are in accord; and this awareness generates many of the ubiquitous Conradian ironies which reach their extreme in *The Secret Agent* when the recumbent Verloc summons, in tones of sexual desire, the wife who is about to stab him to the heart. Their different worlds, instead of coinciding, collide lethally.

There is another, related, consequence. In the works of Walter

Pater, whom Conrad admired, we find both an eloquent presentation of the solipsist case and a nostalgia for a time when all knowledge was 'of the concrete and the particular'. Pater's phrase, and the criteria it commends, subsequently became clichés of modern literary criticism. A recent writer, Professor A. D. Nuttall, has argued that the modern taste for vivid concreteness in literature may be compensatory: it may be caused by a widespread (and not always fully recognised) fear that the solipsist case may be valid, generating a demand for reassurance that the world has tangibly solid objectivity. In *A Common Sky* (1974), p. 262, Nuttall remarks: 'If a man feels the real world slipping from him, he tightens his grip upon it.' Although Nuttall did not discuss Conrad, Conrad's work appears to provide an excellent illustration of this thesis. On the one hand, the explicit solipsistic comments are supported by descriptive passages which strongly emphasise a dreamlike, phantasmagoric quality of experience; yet, on the other hand, there are innumerable passages which emphasise the tangible solidity of our environment. Thus, the remarkably varied textural richnesses of Conrad's writing stem in part from his paradoxical imaginative grasp of both determinism and solipsism.

I conclude this section, and anticipate the next, by quoting from *The Shadow-Line* two passages which illustrate what Nuttall would term 'ontological security and insecurity' respectively. In the first, the narrator seems to have a confident grasp of the world; in the second, the world seems treacherously to be vanishing from him.

I went aft, ascended the poop, where, under the awning, gleamed the brasses of the yacht-like fittings, the polished surfaces of the rails, the glass of the skylights. Right aft two seamen, busy cleaning the steering gear, with the reflected ripples of light running playfully up their bent backs, went on with their work, unaware of me and of the almost affectionate glance I threw at them in passing towards the companion-way of the cabin.

(pp. 50–1)

Ransome stepped back two paces and vanished from my sight.
At once an uneasiness possessed me, as if some support had been withdrawn. I moved forward too, outside the circle of light, into the darkness that stood in front of me like a wall. In one stride I penetrated it. Such must have been the darkness before creation. It had closed behind me. I knew I was invisible to the man at the helm. Neither could I see anything. He was alone, I was alone, every man was alone where he stood. And every form was gone too, spar, sail, fittings, rails; everything was blotted out in the dreadful smoothness of that absolute night.

(pp. 112–3)

That the latter passage implies a grimly ironic comment on the former is characteristic of the art of Conrad.

Darkness and the dying sun

In the 1850s William Thomson (later to be Lord Kelvin) had defined the Second Law of Thermodynamics: the law of entropy, which says that the amount of 'available' energy in the universe must gradually dwindle to nothing as heat flows from warmer into cooler masses until equalisation of temperatures prevails. The aspect of this law which most captured the popular imagination was the notion that the sun, instead of burning seemingly inexhaustibly, must inevitably burn itself out, like a great Victorian coal-fire in the sky, and that as it does so, the human race must perish as icy darkness palls the earth. (Today, scientists have alternative notions: one being that the sun, like a perfect atomic reactor, may be able perpetually to replenish its energies, and another being that it may grow vaster, consuming the earth before collapsing.) Nowadays our vision of the ultimate doomsday is probably one of the nuclear holocaust, brighter than a thousand suns; but for men of the late nineteenth century – and particularly in the 1890s, when thoughts of *fin de siècle* led to thoughts of *fin du globe* – the foreseen doomsday was a very dark and cold one.

It stirred the imagination. Even a scientist, Professor Alexander Winchell, was moved to sombre eloquence in his article 'The Sun Dying Out', published in *Scientific American* in 1891:

> The treasury of life and motion from age to age is running lower and lower. The great sun which, stricken with the pangs of dissolution, has bravely looked down with steady and undimmed eye upon our earth ever since organization first bloomed upon it, is nevertheless a dying existence.

In *The Golden Bough*, a massive study of myth, ritual, legend and intellectual evolution, Sir James Frazer wrote:

> In the ages to come man may be able to predict, perhaps even to control, the wayward courses of the winds and clouds, but hardly will his puny hands have strength to speed afresh our slackening planet in its orbit or rekindle the dying fire of the sun.

One of the most memorable descriptions of the dark doomsday comes in H. G. Wells's *The Time Machine* (1895; a tale which Conrad read, admired and remembered), when the Time Traveller voyages almost to the end of time:

> So I travelled, stopping ever and again, in great strides of a thousand years or more, drawn on by the mystery of the earth's

fate, watching with a strange fascination the sun grow larger and duller in the westward sky, and the life of the old earth ebb away . . . . .

. . . . . In another moment the pale stars alone were visible. All else was rayless obscurity. The sky was absolutely black.

A horror of this great darkness came on me.

The idea of the dying sun obviously augmented Conrad's pessimism by suggesting the ultimate futility of all action in this alien universe; and it added importantly to the symbolic vistas of his imagination. In 1898 he told Cunninghame Graham:

The mysteries of a universe made of drops of fire and clods of mud do not concern us in the least. The fate of a humanity condemned ultimately to perish from cold is not worth troubling about. If you take it to heart it becomes an unendurable tragedy. If you believe in improvement you must weep, for the attained perfection must end in cold, darkness and silence.

(*LCG*, 65)

Yet when, seven years later, Conrad wrote his essay 'Henry James', the tone had modulated from the sardonically magisterial to the stoically affirmative:

When the last aqueduct shall have crumbled to pieces, the last airship fallen to the ground, the last blade of grass have died upon a dying earth, man, indomitable by his training in resistance to misery and pain, shall set this undiminished light of his eyes against the feeble glow of the sun. The artistic faculty, of which each of us has a minute grain, may find its voice in some individual of that last group. . . . . The artist in his calling of interpreter creates (the clearest form of demonstration) because he must. He is so much of a voice that, for him, silence is like death; and the postulate was, that there is a group alive, clustered on his threshold to watch the last flicker of light on a black sky, to hear the last word uttered in the stilled workshop of the earth.

(*NLL*, 13–4)

This passage from the essay has obvious connections with Marlow's tale in *Heart of Darkness*, which also has the theme that in course of time all man's technology may be annulled by the non-human environment; and in both cases we have an artist-narrator speaking to a small group which is beset by an apparently all-encompassing darkness. Conrad is celebrated for his 'nightscapes'; for descriptions like that of the black night in the Placid Gulf through which Decoud sails in *Nostromo*, the perilous approach to the looming darkness of Koh-Ring in 'The Secret Sharer', or the oppressive blackness of the night which engulfs the becalmed ship in *The Shadow-Line*. And such descriptions, which attribute an annihilating dynamism to the darkness, have a peculiarly haunting power. By these scenes Conrad conveys to us, directly or subliminally, a wide array of his fears: the fear that decency may be fighting a doomed rearguard-action against barbarism, the fear that human rationality is opposed by a cruel irrationality in the universe, and the fear that an infinity of blank extinction awaits mankind as a race, just as surely as it awaits man as a mortal individual. Nevertheless, as Conrad remarked in 'Henry James': 'The creative art of a writer of fiction may be compared to rescue work carried out in darkness.'

Darwinism

We have previously noted that evolutionary ideas were already current before Charles Darwin's *The Origin of Species* appeared in 1859; but Darwin's book was the summation of the evolutionary ideas of the period. He held that complex creatures such as men had not been specially created (as the Bible said) but had gradually, over aeons of time, evolved into their present form in accordance with natural laws. The laws he listed as follows: growth with reproduction; inheritance; variability; 'a Ratio of Increase so high as to lead to a Struggle for Life, and as a consequence to Natural Selection' – whereby those who are fittest for survival in the given environment do survive while the others perish.

In its stress on ruthless competition this theory of evolution is largely a product of its economic times. It appeared in the heyday of Victorian *laissez-faire* capitalism; and Darwin himself mentions that he had been strongly influenced by the economic theories of the Reverend Thomas Malthus. Malthus had been sternly utilitarian in outlook: he believed that the poor tended to breed and over-breed improvidently until they starved, so that charity (if intelligently applied) should be punitive, rewarding the poor who had few children and being withheld from the poor who had many. In short, Darwin's theory reflects the ethos of its day by over-emphasising competition and under-emphasising co-operation. Partly because of this reflection, *The Origin of Species* became rapidly and bleakly influential as a work of scientific fact. There is no doubt that its influence was, on the whole, a bleak one. George Bernard Shaw wrote: 'When its whole significance dawns on you, your heart sinks into a heap of sand within you. There is a hideous fatalism about it.' This was in spite of the fact that in the concluding pages of *Origin of Species* Darwin had striven to give his theory a consolatory form by postulating a Creator who works (albeit deviously and somewhat wastefully) to raise ever higher forms of life:

And as natural selection works solely by and for the good of each being, all corporeal and mental endowments will tend to progress towards perfection . . . . . Thus, from the war of nature, from famine and death, the most exalted object which we are capable of conceiving, namely, the production of the higher animals, directly follows. There is grandeur in this view of life, with its several powers, having been originally breathed into a few forms or into one; and that, whilst this planet has been cycling on according to the fixed law of gravity, from so simple a beginning endless forms most beautiful and most wonderful have been, and are being, evolved.

During this determinedly consolatory peroration, Darwin had urged the reader to take heart from the contemplation of 'an entangled bank':

It is interesting to contemplate an entangled bank, clothed with many plants of many kinds, with birds singing on the bushes, with various insects flitting about . . . . . and to reflect that these elaborately constructed forms, so different from each other . . . . . have all been produced by laws acting around us.

Conrad responded deeply to Darwinism. His texts are full of 'entangled banks'. In his early novels and tales, in *Almayer's Folly*, *An Outcast*, 'An Outpost of Progress', *Heart of Darkness* and *Lord Jim*, he is very fond – some critics would say too fond – of describing fecund jungly settings. And Conrad is Darwinian and anti-Darwinian. He emphasises the struggle for survival which is constantly taking place in these jungles – and on the whole, though he sees the exotic beauty, he emphasises the savage violence and wastefulness of the struggle, rather than the achievement of 'forms most beautiful and most wonderful'. Thus in *Almayer's Folly*:

The intense work of tropical nature went on: plants shooting upward, entwined, interlaced in inextricable confusion, climbing madly and brutally over each other in the terrible silence of a desperate struggle towards the life-giving sunshine above – as if struck with sudden horror at the seething mass of corruption below, at the death and decay from which they sprang.

(p. 71)

Such descriptions can rapidly become tedious and skippable: they have too much melodrama, too predictably emotive and insistent an application of adjectives and amplifications; yet they are characteristic of Conrad's early work in their presentation of a Darwinian struggle so ruthless as to appal even the plants that are involved in it.

In the late nineteenth century, many apologists for aggressive imperialism propped their arguments with illicit inferences from

Darwinian principles – illicit, because Darwin was dealing with competition between species and species, or between species and environment, but not between nations or races. The illicit argument went like this: It is a law of nature that creatures should compete, and that the 'fittest' should survive and prevail over the 'unfit'. Therefore, if Europeans seize Africa and subjugate the Africans, they are simply doing what they are naturally obliged to do – the fit cannot help but prove their fitness. This argument was implicit in, for example, Lord Salisbury's distinction (which Conrad noted and mocked) between 'living' and 'dying' nations:

> The living nations will gradually encroach on the territory of the dying. . . . . It is not to be supposed that any one nation of the living nations will be allowed to have the profitable monopoly of curing or cutting up these unfortunate patients. . . . . We shall not allow England to be at a disadvantage in any re-arrangement.
>
> (*LCG*, 129)

In *Heart of Darkness*, Conrad retorts by turning Darwinism against the political Darwinians. If a goal of the evolutionary process is an equilibrium between the creature and its environment (as *The Origin of Species* had suggested), then that goal has in Africa been reached by the natives whom Marlow observes on the coast, who 'wanted no excuse for being there' and who blend with their setting, rather than by the Europeans, who appear absurdly anomalous and perish rapidly there or survive as grotesques or brutal automata. Conrad is particularly good at showing that in a struggle for survival the victors may simply be the more ruthless or cunning (or physically tough), like the manager in *Heart of Darkness*, rather than those who in any moral sense are 'higher'. Similarly, Conrad is skilled at deflating the pride of those who think that civilised Europeans offer a complete contrast to savage Africans. From time to time (as here in 'An Outpost') he asserts that 'civilised' values are matters of social convention, without real roots:

> The courage, the composure, the confidence; the emotions and principles; every great and every insignificant thought belongs not to the individual but to the crowd: to the crowd that believes blindly in the irresistible force of its institutions and its morals.
>
> (*TU*, 89)

More paradoxically, he can undercut Darwinian teleology by suggesting that the rifle is merely a more powerful version of the bow, fashionable dress an elaborated loin-cloth, romantic love a sophistication of carnal lust, and the appetite for roast meat a modern vestige of cannibalism. *Nostromo*'s Decoud reflects that whereas in the past, 'barbarism. . . . . went about yelling, half-naked, with bows and arrows', today it wears 'the black coats of politicians' (*N*, 231).

In both *Heart of Darkness* and the tale 'Falk', Conrad describes civilised men who have become cannibals; in the former case, with Kurtz, the attitude taken by the narrator is largely one of horror; in the latter case, the attitude is one of cool acceptance – 'Don't be shocked', he says. Conrad even likes to hint that Christianity may differ little from the rites of savages: Marlow describes the sound of distant drums as 'weird, appealing, suggestive, and wild – and perhaps with as profound a meaning as the sound of bells in a Christian country.' (*Y*, 71.) In some respects, indeed, the primitive may be morally preferable to the civilised:

> Not perhaps that primitive men were more faithless than their descendants of to-day, but that they went straighter to their aim, and were more artless in their recognition of success as the only standard of morality.
>
> (*N*, 386)

We have stressed that Conrad relishes paradox, and though at times he suggests that civilisation is just a hypocritical sophistication of savagery, at other times he will suggest that it is a precious achievement to be guarded. Such paradoxes often hinge on ambiguous key terms; and as we elucidate the meanings of the ambiguous term (like those of 'civilisation' here) the apparent self-contradiction dwindles into sound sense. If civilisation is represented by a humane fellow like Marlow, then Conrad can see it as indeed a worthy achievement. If it is represented by jingoistic statesmen and the commercial exploitation of Africa, Conrad can see it as a hypocritical fraud.

Darwinism and psychology

In the last chapter of *The Origin of Species*, Darwin claimed that with the arrival of his theory of evolution, 'Psychology will be based on a new foundation'; and he was quite right. An eager devotee of Darwinian evolutionism was Sigmund Freud, who, as a young medical student, conducted zoological research which supported Darwinism by demonstrating continuity between the cell-structures of lower and higher animals. And in later years, when Freud became the great pioneer of psycho-analysis, he was fond of equating himself with Darwin, claiming that just as Darwin had inflicted one great blow on man's pride by having 'robbed man of his peculiar privilege of having been specially created, and relegated him to a descent from the animal world, implying an ineradicable animal nature in him', so Freud had inflicted a further great blow by proving that every person's 'ego' 'is not even master in his own house', but must constantly battle with unruly sexual drives. Obviously, Freudian theory is, in its origins, largely an inference from Darwin: for if

Darwin suggests that each of us has 'an ineradicable animal nature', it is likely that beneath the conscious surface of our minds there may be numerous primitive urges and impulses linking us with more barbaric or bestial forebears. Hence Freud's bold 'conflict model' of the human mind, with its constant tussle between the anarchic drives from the id and the controlling endeavours of the more prudent and civilised ego; or, in his later and quite inconsistent scheme, the tussle between life-affirming libido and life-denying death-wish. Hence, too, Freud's sceptical readiness to see ostensibly civilised phenomena as mere 'sublimations' – i.e., as respectable transformations of relatively base source-material.

It will already be clear that there are some interesting similarities between the thought of Conrad and that of Freud. The presentation of Mr Kurtz in *Heart of Darkness* may suggest the Freudian conflict-model of the self by indicating that his civilised qualities were 'sub-limated' versions of repressed barbaric powers which, in the wilderness, can display their original lustful and murderous nature. Again, Marlow makes it clear there that a conflict-model is appropriate to his own nature: for in spite of his civilised outlook, something within him responds sympathetically both to the charisma of the fallen Kurtz and even to the throbbing of drums on the bank. (One commentator, Albert Guerard, has carried this idea to absurd extremes by suggesting that Kurtz is really meant to be the 'id' of Marlow.) There are also ways in which the dramatisation of human psychology in *Heart of Darkness* differs from the Freudian scheme, and here Conrad may be wiser than Freud. Many of the Europeans are depicted as conscienceless automata who carry death and exploitation abroad almost as a matter of mechanical habit: indeed, the tale emphasises that such men as the accountant at the central station, the manager and the brickmaker are 'hollow men', not men with striving ids. This is a debatable matter, but I think that the psychology here is both un-Freudian and sound. The Nazi extermination camps of the 1940s (in which so many millions of Jews and Poles died) were, in many cases, run by individuals who, like Conrad's accountant, were prepared to do their duty without qualms, as a matter of routine, even when such duty entailed the administration of mass murder. Adolf Eichmann, for example, when captured by the Israelis after the war, betrayed no remorse at his trial and was inclined to shrug off the indictments. Incidentally, it is worth noting that one of Freud's precursors, William James, had in his *Principles of Psychology* (1890) commended the value of habit as a force which maintains social harmony. Conrad looks now with sympathy and now with deep suspicion on predictably habitual activity.

Even where there are similarities between Conrad's work and Freud's, these are not the result of any direct indebtedness of Conrad to the elder man. When *Heart of Darkness* was first published, Freud was virtually unknown in England, and by the time that Freud had established an international reputation (1909–10) most of Conrad's best work had been completed. Quite likely Conrad's first direct encounter with Freud's writings was the very late one, during a holiday on Corsica in 1921. There he met a French disciple of Freud's, H.-R. Lenormand, who persistently (and irritatingly) urged him to psycho-analyse such characters as Lord Jim and Almayer. Conrad was predictably resistant: 'I'm nothing but a story-teller', he would say; 'I don't want to get to the bottom.....I want to look on reality as something rough and coarse over which I pass my fingers. Nothing more.' Lenormand lent Conrad two of Freud's books, but Conrad, 'who spoke of Freud with scornful irony', returned them apparently unread, and urged the Frenchman to write a novel on 'the decline of men who had arrived at certitude'.

Atavism and doubles

The Freudian conflict-model of the human psyche emerged from that great mass of writing which explored with varying degrees of plausibility the possible implications of evolutionary theory. Atavism (the reversion to an ancestral or primitive type) and the fear of atavism became important subjects for fiction-writers, who seized rapidly on the dramatic notion that in individuals civilisation and even humanity might be only skin-deep.

A richly symbolic forerunner of the later fictional treatments is Herman Melville's *Benito Cereno* (1855), in which a crew of supposedly docile and deferential blacks prove to be cunning, vengeful killers who, rising from slavery, have murdered the white crewmen and taken the Spanish captain hostage. In England, H. G. Wells, in *The Island of Doctor Moreau* (1896), offered one of the most subversive and starkly antitheistic discussions of the atavistic theme. Moreau acts on the assumption that since men have evolved from beasts, he should be able by means of skilled surgery to convert various animals – pumas, apes, etc. – into the likeness of men. He has some success: victims of his experiments can pass for men at a distance and shamble around docilely enough,. Moreau having indoctrinated them with the notion that he is their God and can punish disobedience with inflictions of pain like those the creatures have already suffered beneath his scalpel. But, of course, these humanoids gradually regress; every experiment seems doomed; and eventually Moreau himself is killed in a rebellion by the very creatures he had thought to dominate as God. It is in the epilogue that the narrative modulates most steeply into the subversive. The narrator, a traveller who by chance had witnessed the crisis on the island, returns to Europe – and finds that ordinary men have frightening resemblances to the humanoids of Dr Moreau:

I could not persuade myself that the men and women I met were not also another, passably human, Beast People, animals half-wrought into the outward image of human souls, and that they would presently begin to revert, to show first this bestial mark and then that.....

I would go out into the streets to fight with my delusion, and prowling women would mew after me, furtive craving men glance jealously at me, weary pale workers go coughing by me, with tired eyes and eager paces like wounded deer dripping blood.....Then I would turn aside into some chapel, and even there, such was my disturbance, it seemed that the preacher gibbered Big Thinks even as the Ape Man had done; or into some library, and there the intent faces over the books seemed but patient creatures waiting for prey. Particularly nauseous were the blank expressionless faces of people in trains and omnibuses; they seemed no more my fellow-creatures than dead bodies would be, so that I did not dare to travel unless I was assured of being alone. And even it seemed that I, too, was not a reasonable creature, but only an animal tormented with some strange disorder in its brain, that sent it to wander alone, like a sheep stricken with the gid.

(Heinemann, 1896, pp. 216, 217–8)

This ending has some similarities to part of the ending of *Heart of Darkness*: the part where Marlow, on his return to Europe, has a partly-deranged hostility to the masses of people in the streets around, who seem ludicrous, arrogant and stupid in their folly – in their failure to comprehend the abyss which is so near, the abyss of corruption or atavism into which Kurtz has fallen. Again, Moreau's humanoid animals may remind us that in Conrad's *Victory* the hero's island sanctuary is invaded by three beings who seem to represent three stages in evolution: Gentleman Jones, an intelligent but decadent, enfeebled, and sterile villain; his henchman Ricardo, who seems more tiger than man in movements, outlook and appearance; and their servant Pedro, who is so ape-like that his knuckles almost brush the ground. 'Here they are before you', says Heyst; 'Evil intelligence, instinctive savagery, arm in arm. The brute force is at the back.' Atavism of a kind – some reversion of 'civilised' men to the savage or bestial when they are taken from the familiar supports offered by urban Europe – is a theme in *Almayer's Folly*, when the isolated Almayer descends to the stupor of opium addiction; in *An Outcast*, with Willems's descent into demoralisation; in 'An Outpost of Progress', as Kayerts and Carlier cast aside tolerance and restraint, becoming slave-traders and finally fighting each other to the death; and in 'Falk', in which two seamen fight so that the victor may eat the flesh of the vanquished.

Atavism found its way into the pseudo-science of Conrad's day.

In Italy, Cesare Lombroso claimed that criminals and madmen were in fact instances of atavism, throwbacks in the evolutionary sequence. The various types of degeneration, he claimed in *L'uomo delinquente* (1876), were physically identifiable: for example, they often had crinkly hair, thick lips and a Mongoloid slant to the eyes. Conrad knew of Lombroso's theories, and in *The Secret Agent* he plays an elaborate game of ironic endorsement and mocking reversal of them. Ossipon, the parasitic anarchist, is a disciple of Lombroso, and accordingly detects in young Stevie all the physiological characteristics of the 'mongoloid degenerate' defined by the Italian. The first irony is that Stevie, in his innocent benevolence, is a living contradiction of the doctrine; the second is that Ossipon totally fails to see that he himself, with his crinkly hair, flattened nose, and mouth 'of the Negroid type' is a perfect example of the 'negroid degenerate' described by his master. And the third is that though Mr Vladimir had justified the attack on Greenwich Observatory by claiming that science was the 'sacrosanct fetish' of the middle classes, the blindest worshipper of 'science' is in fact Ossipon himself in his devotion to Lombroso.

In England, the chief disciple of Lombroso was Max Nordau, who corresponded with Conrad in 1898. (He wrote to praise *The Nigger of the 'Narcissus'*; Conrad, a little embarrassed, remarked 'Praise is sweet, no matter whence it comes'.) Nordau was author of *Degeneration*, a best-selling pseudo-scientific work of 1895. In this, there is a type-description of the 'ego-maniac', which appears to have influenced Conrad's presentation of the Professor in *The Secret Agent*; and Nordau also discusses the 'highly-gifted degenerate', a type in whom some mental gift is exceptionally developed at the cost of the remaining faculties, and who may be exceptionally tall. Nordau says:

> Highly-gifted degenerates . . . . . corrupt and delude; they do, alas! frequently exercise a deep influence, but this is always a baneful one . . . . . They are guides to swamps like will-o'-the-wisps, or to ruin like the ratcatcher of Hammelin.

This account may have provided elements of the character of Kurtz in *Heart of Darkness*, for Kurtz has the gift of exceptional eloquence, he signally has a Pied Piper quality, and he even has the characteristic of exceptional height, for to Marlow 'he looked at least seven feet long'.

Evolution, aestheticism and sex

Aestheticism was a movement amongst English and French writers and artists which flourished (if that is not too robust a term) in the period 1850–1905 and particularly in the 1890s. It can be traced back to the Romantic Movement's emphasis on the importance of private, intense experience and on the role of the artist as a seer who is not to be judged by mundane laws. Amongst the English Romantics the forerunner of Aestheticism is Keats, whose work is quiveringly self-conscious, treating the vocation of the poet as a high mystery to be entered only by the Elect, and is rich in sensuous descriptions yet poor in social, political and moral debate. (Indeed this isolation of the sensuous makes Keats seem more sensuous than he really is: Ben Jonson is equally sensuous in descriptions but is doing many other things at the same time.) One of the most famous slogans of the Aesthetes, 'Art for Art's sake', derives from Gautier's 'L'Art pour l'Art', which in turn derives from Victor Cousin's 'Il faut de la religion pour la religion, de la morale pour la morale, de l'art pour l'art' ('We need religion for religion's sake, morality for morality's sake and art for art's sake').

Now if an Aesthete is one who believes that the artist should dedicate himself to the creation of beautiful works of art, it would at first appear that there is nothing at all objectionable in his belief, since artists down the ages have striven to create things of beauty. What matters, though, is what the Aesthete thinks should be sacrificed, ignored or rejected in that pursuit of the beautiful. An art which achieves an identity largely by means of massive exclusions can be a very trivial art. Perhaps the most useful 'Aesthete's Creed' is that offered by Oscar Wilde in the Preface to *The Picture of Dorian Gray*:

> The artist is the creator of beautiful things.
> To reveal art and conceal the artist is art's aim.....
> There is no such thing as a moral or an immoral book. Books are well written, or badly written. That is all.....
> The moral life of man forms part of the subject-matter of the artist, but the morality of art consists in the perfect use of an imperfect medium. No artist desires to prove anything. Even things that are true can be proved.
> No artist has ethical sympathies. An ethical sympathy in an artist is an unpardonable mannerism of style.....
> All art is quite useless.

It's a splendidly insolent, provocative preface, and it makes very good sense when we consider which enemies Wilde had in mind. He is opposing the puritanical moralistic critics of the day, who would fetter art by imposing conventional moral values upon it; and he is defying critics of a utilitarian disposition, who would value art only in proportion to its evident social utility. In the opposition to censorship and social control, there is much to respect here. It is also the case that such a creed can encourage a trivial, narcissistic art which turns its back on much of life and thus debases itself. The most characteristic work of the Aesthetic Movement is slight and ephemeral: poetry variously languorous or precious, hinting at decadent vice or murmuring of lethargic raptures amid veiled somnolent vistas of melancholy twilight. In the largely-forgotten poems of Lionel Johnson, Ernest Dowson, Arthur Symons or Theodore Wratislaw, for example, and in the prose essays of Pater, Wilde or Crackanthorpe, the predictably narcissistic connoisseurship of a limited range of experience continues. However, though most of the work of the Aesthetes was ephemeral, the movement helped to generate a number of Preter-Aesthetes: artists who in various ways grew through and beyond Aestheticism, having some sympathies with it yet also a keen sense of its limitations. The great Preter-Aesthetes include W. B. Yeats, whose early poetry so often sounds the melancholy, languorous and lethargic tones of Aestheticism, yet who came to quarrel with the movement and to exploit the tension between Aesthetic concerns and public political concerns. Another Preter-Aesthete is James Joyce, whose *Portrait of the Artist as a Young Man* is very much a portrait of the student as a would-be Aesthete, but whose *Ulysses* looks in criticism as well as sympathy on Stephen Dedalus, who after all has not produced any significant work of art and who could not conceivably produce a work with the vitality of *Ulysses* itself. A third is Ezra Pound, whose 'Hugh Selwyn Mauberley' looks with pity and scorn on the narcissistic poet: significantly, commentators experience great difficulty in distinguishing between parts of the poem which represent Mauberley's work and parts which represent Pound's comments on Mauberley. And Conrad too belongs to this august company.

Conrad has defined very precisely for us the point at which the element of Aestheticism in his outlook gives way to the larger concerns of Preter-Aestheticism. The definition comes in Conrad's famous Preface to *The Nigger of the 'Narcissus'*. There Conrad says of the true artist:

He . . . . . cannot be faithful to any one of the temporary formulas of his craft. The enduring part of them – the truth which each only imperfectly veils – should abide with him as the most precious of his possessions, but they all: Realism, Romanticism, Naturalism, even the unofficial sentimentalism (which like the poor, is exceedingly difficult to get rid of), all these gods must, after a short period of fellowship, abandon him – even on the very threshold of the temple – to the stammerings of his conscience and to the outspoken consciousness of the difficulties of his work. In that uneasy solitude the supreme cry of Art for Art, itself, loses the exciting ring of its apparent immorality. It sounds far off. It has ceased to be a cry, and is heard only as a whisper, often incomprehensible, but at times faintly encouraging.

So even 'the supreme cry of Art for Art, itself' eventually sounds merely as a 'faintly encouraging' whisper behind the dedicated artist as he proceeds on his lonely and agonisingly difficult quest – seeking 'by the power of the written word to make you hear, to make you feel . . . . ., to make you *see*', and to 'awaken in the hearts of the beholders that feeling of unavoidable solidarity . . . . . which binds men to each other and all mankind to the visible world'. Thus, although Conrad shows respect for the spirit of priestly dedication to one's art which Aestheticism may evoke, his emphasis on social solidarity indicates clearly enough his Preter-Aestheticism. And it is quite typical of Conrad's janiformity that the very preface which upholds the duty of establishing solidarity between men should also be a preface which makes the plight of the creative artist seems an arduously solitary one. 'Art is long and life is short, and success is very far off.'

The extent to which Aestheticism is a defensive reaction against evolutionary ideas has been under-estimated. Yet the implication seems quite clear. In Baudelaire and Huysmans, in Pater and Wilde, there is heavy emphasis on the value not only of art but also of the artificial and the sterile: and one reason for this initially novel and puzzling emphasis is that Darwin and the evolutionists had made the natural and the fecund seem, to some sensitive observers in some moods, a bloody battleground – nature, red in tooth and claw. Such observers might reflect that if nature was a battleground, man proved his superiority by detaching himself from it as far as possible. Hence not only the decadents' connoisseurship of the artificial in literature and life-style but also their preoccupation, in literature and in life, with sterile forms of sexuality: for example, heterosexuality whose object is a courtesan, or homosexuality. ('Woman is natural – which means abominable', claimed Baudelaire.)

This post-Darwinian imaginative recoil from the implications of fecund procreative sexuality is strongly evident in Conrad's work: sometimes he even seems to anticipate Jean-Paul Sartre's bizarre assertion that 'the sexual act is the castration of the man'. Again and again in Conrad's pages, a passionate sexual encounter seems, paradoxically, to emasculate the man, to be subversive, making him bewildered and self-doubting, and it sometimes results in his

Drawing by Conrad: Woman with Serpent.
'*Both his writings and his drawings are liberally sprinkled with references to birds and snakes . . . . . When Lena [in* Victory] *finally succeeds in inducing [Ricardo] to surrender his knife, the writer observes: "The very sting of death was in her hands; the venom of the viper in her paradise, extracted, safe in her possession . . . . ." In short, Ricardo has been "de-snaked".'*
(Bernard C. Meyer: Joseph Conrad: A Psychoanalytic Biography, *1967, p. 331.*)

This sketch must have been done
between the years of 1892 - 1894
They came into my possession
at my marriage in 1896.

Jessie Conrad

Drawing by Conrad: The Diffident Suitor.
'*A remarkable pictorial re-affirmation of the bizarre and distorted relationships encountered in his love stories..... As if retreating from both beast and lady, the man sits retracting his pigeon-toed feet, his knees pressed firmly together like a well-behaved girl, with his left forearm guarding the vicinity of his genitals.*' (*Meyer*, op. cit., *p. 329.*)

destruction. This pessimistic pattern extends from the earliest novel, *Almayer's Folly*, to much later ones like *Victory* and *The Rescue*. In *Almayer's Folly*, the young warrior, Dain, feels that because of his passion for Nina, 'he had lost faith in himself, and there was nothing else in him of what makes a man'; and when he copulates with her, 'the heavens were suddenly hushed up in the mournful contemplation of human love and human blindness'. In *Victory* we are told that Heyst 'used to come out of her [Lena's] very arms with the feeling of a baffled man', and he too finds that attachment to Lena has sapped his power to defy the invaders of his island.

Now in this preoccupation of Conrad's there is some obvious common sense: a man with marital responsibilities is less likely to rush into a duel than an unattached bachelor. There is also the ex-seaman's notion that if a man brings his wife or mistress on board, he can't be giving his energies to his work. ('I was never married myself. A sailor should exercise self-denial,' says Captain Mitchell in *Nostromo*.) A more exalted influence is Schopenhauer's *The World as Will and Idea*, which emphasised that the woman, whose prime loyalty is to the life-force and its procreative drive, is basically in opposition to the man, who at his highest should be a stoical spectator of nature's battles. And the influence of the post-Darwinian recoil from fecund nature is made clear when Conrad describes his passionate native seductresses as though they were emanations from the torrid jungle, as in this passage of second-rate waffling Conradese in *Heart of Darkness*:

> The immense wilderness, the colossal body of the fecund and mysterious life seemed to look at her, pensive, as though it had been looking at the image of its own tenebrous and passionate soul.
>
> (*Y*, 136)

(As has been noted, Conrad's inhibitions in dealing with the sexual often result in second-rate writing like this.)

If the passionate mistresses are emanations from the jungle, the idealised heroines are emanations from the world of art. In Shakespeare's *The Winter's Tale*, the statue of Hermione comes, apparently miraculously, to life; but we soon realise that Hermione has been flesh and blood all the time and has only been *imitating* a statue. In Conrad's fiction, I am tempted to say, the reverse is apparent: several of his beautiful heroines purport to be flesh and blood but really belong to the condition of statuary. They linger in the imagination as a series of statuesque poses and gestures, inviting classical or allegorical titles. Examples include the Intended in *Heart of Darkness*, light shining on her white brow; Antonia, 'lovely like an allegorical statue', in *Nostromo*; Felicia Moorsom in 'The Planter of Malata', who resembles 'a being made of ivory and precious metal';

Alice Jacobus, 'a seated statue' in 'A Smile of Fortune'; and Hermann's niece in 'Falk', who 'appeared to look at the world with the empty white candour of a statue' and who 'could have stood for an allegoric statue of the earth'. On at least one occasion, however, Conrad suggests that even when feminine beauty has the apparent dignity of a marble artefact, marble was once primeval mud: and that is when, in *Heart of Darkness*, the Intended stretches out her arms towards the Kurtz of memory, in a gesture which exactly duplicates that of Kurtz's savage mistress.

Literary influences

We have noted that Conrad's father was a poet and an accomplished linguist: a translator into Polish of works by Shakespeare, Victor Hugo and others. Thus Conrad was from early years familiar with a wide range of French and English literary texts as well as with Polish works, and in later years he retained a habit of wide, indeed voracious, reading, of texts ancient and modern, popular and specialised. Whether among poetry or prose, drama or essay, his range was impressively wide. He recalled being 'fed on French and English literature', and claimed to have bought, with his first earnings in England, a thick, green-covered volume of Shakespeare. The epigraphs to his works give some idea of his diversity of interests as a reader: they are taken from Amiel, Shakespeare, Spenser, Boethius, a nursery rhyme, Chaucer, Milton, Sir Thomas Browne, Novalis, Baudelaire.....So a full discussion of possible literary influences would be a book in itself – and that book would probably not have room for all the memoirs, biographies, autobiographies, travel accounts and ephemera consulted by Joseph Conrad during the writing of his own works. Here, however, we may note selectively some aspects of Conrad's literary heritage.

Polish writing

We have seen that Conrad's very name – Conrad or Konrad – is a mnemonic of the long tradition of Polish patriotic writing, often romantically lyrical or religiose, which has its culmination in Mickiewicz's *Konrad Wallenrod* and *Dziady*. However, when we look back to these Polish classics of the nineteenth century, they tend to throw into relief, by contrast, some very distinctive features of Conrad's work. Against the lyrical and religiose patriotism of Mickiewicz, what comes to the fore in Conrad is the circumspect emphasis on the ambiguity of political situations, on the murky entanglements of politics, on the fear that 'there was something inherent in the necessities of successful action which carried with it the moral degradation of the idea' (*N*), and on the way in which political rhetoric can delude both speaker and hearer. But in 'Prince Roman' and the political essays, there can still be found that note of intense, unqualified patriotism which might have gladdened a Mickiewicz. A small but significant link between the two writers is that Yankel, the patriotic Polish-Jewish innkeeper of 'Prince Roman', is clearly a literary reincarnation of Yankiel, the patriotic Polish-Jewish innkeeper of Mickiewicz's *Pan Tadeusz*.

In other areas, various debts to Polish literature have been cited. Dr Najder, the leading Polish expert on Conrad, claims that the plot of 'Karain' is based on Mickiewicz's ballad *Czaty*; that there are verbal echoes of *Konrad Wallenrod* in *Almayer's Folly* and *An Outcast*, borrowings from *Dziady* in *Under Western Eyes*, an influence of *Pan Tadeusz* on *Lord Jim* (the theme of heroic atonement for past disgrace) and of Bobrowski's *Memoirs* on *A Personal Record*. Again, Dr Irmina Pulc notes that Conrad's syntax often seems reminiscent of Polish usages. His fondness for asyndeton (the omission of conjunctions), as in 'An empty stream, a great silence, an impenetrable forest. The air was thick, warm, heavy, sluggish.' (*HD*), may have been encouraged by the relative looseness of Polish syntax compared with English in this respect; and in the work of Prus, Żeromski and Iwaszkiewicz, for example, one frequently encounters the device of anaphoric parallelism (repetition of the same word at the beginning of two or more parallel phrases) which is one of Conrad's stylistic thumb-prints – as in 'the sea, blue and profound, remained still, without a stir, without a ripple, without a wrinkle – viscous, stagnant, dead.' (*Lord Jim*, 15–6.) In such stylistic matters it is difficult to be conclusive, however, since English and French precedents for them can also be found.

French influences

That last quotation could equally well, in fact, be cited as an instance of Gallic influence, for, as is common in French writing, its adjectives are arranged in pairs and triplets after the noun ('the sea, blue and profound . . . . . viscous, stagnant, dead'): one of the parody-inviting signs of 'Conradese'. Jocelyn Baines suggests that Conrad's over-fondness for polysyllabic privative adjectives ('inconceivable', 'inscrutable', 'impenetrable') may have been encouraged by the inflated phraseology of Pierre Loti.

Though not accurate in French, Conrad was so fluent in that language that he sometimes unthinkingly used French words in his English texts, as in this sentence of *The Nigger*: 'They lay in a solid mass more inabordable than a hedgehog'. (*Inabordable* means un-approachable.) In correspondence with English acquaintances, Conrad readily turns to French (*a*) when offering courteous gal-lantries, (*b*) when expressing highly sceptical or cynical ideas ('la société est essentielment [*sic*] criminelle' – society is essentially criminal), or (*c*) when expressing some of his own positive moral convictions – as in a letter to Sir Sidney Colvin in 1917:

> The humorous, the pathetic, the passionate, the sentimental *aspects* come in of themselves – mais en vérité c'est les valeurs idéales des faits et gestes humains qui se sont imposés à mon activité artistique. [But truly my artistic activity has been governed by the ideal values of human facts and deeds.]
>
> (*LL* II, 185)

Conrad's shifts to French indicate sometimes a shift to a more confidential, intimate mode, and sometimes a need for the language which lends courtliness to politeness and which invests abstract terms with greater sonority than does English.

Of the French authors, it was probably Gustave Flaubert (1821–80) who had the greatest influence on Conrad. Flaubert set the standard of extreme literary dedication: for him, literature was the central concern of life, and the great writer was one who was prepared to sacrifice all other concerns in order to build laboriously, phrase by phrase, with intense concentration and concern for *le mot juste*, his fictional worlds. Conrad's attitudes to his art form a protean cluster, but part of that cluster is certainly a note of Flaubertian dedication, an obsessive concern with literary truth and beauty, and a related contempt for those who would prostitute letters on the altars of commerce. Significantly, Flaubert's strengths as a writer were much in his mind at the very beginning of his literary career, for in a letter of 1892, while he was slowly building *Almayer's Folly*, Conrad wrote in French to Marguerite Poradowska:

> I have just re-read *Madame Bovary* in respectful admiration. . . . .
>
> Now here is a man who had enough imagination for two realists. There are few authors who are as creative as he. One never for a moment questions the characters or the events in his pages; one would rather doubt one's own existence.
>
> (*MPL*, 101. My translation)

Flaubert had striven for cool lucidity in seeing life as it is, warts and all, and not as convention, polite society or romantic notions see it. He brought a new scrupulous diligence of attention to ostensibly mediocre lives in mediocre settings; and though he scandalised some of his earlier readers (he was prosecuted for offending public morals), and gave an impression of life-denying aestheticism to many subsequent readers, not only a new honesty but also a new kind of human poignancy emerges from his apparently ruthless observations. The world of *Madame Bovary* is finally a chill, depressing one in which incomprehension, frustration and waste seem the norm; but Flaubert does note the aspirations which are frustrated, the love wasted too; quietly he points to the child, Berthe, who must suffer because of the follies of the parents. Certainly Flaubert could have strengthened Conrad's preoccupation, so evident in his first novel, with incommunication and egoistic delusion.

Another feature in which Flaubert was of the literary vanguard was the use of starkly ironic counterpoint or juxtaposition. For example, when Rodolphe is using his eloquence to seduce Emma Bovary, his words are counterpointed by cries from the Agricultural Show beyond the window:

> 'A hundred times I've wanted to abandon you, and yet I've always followed and stayed by you!'
> 'Manure!'

Again: at the book's climax, Emma has poisoned herself and is lying in her death-pangs:

> As the death-rattle grew louder, the priest hurried his prayers; they blended with Charles Bovary's stifled sobs . . .
> Suddenly, on the pavement outside, there was a clacking of big clogs and the scraping of a stick, and a harsh voice rose, singing:
> 'When the hot sun shines above,
> A young girl often dreams of love . . . . .
> The wind blew very hard that day –
> Her petticoat flew far away!'

(My translation)

Against the pious words of the priest, a bawdy song from a hideous blind beggar. This technique of extremely discordant juxtaposition is an incisively ironic technique, often jarring and cruelly aggressive in effect, like a callous practical joke. Among English writers, it is Conrad's contemporary Thomas Hardy who, particularly in *Jude the Obscure*, and particularly in the sequence depicting Jude's death, comes closest to this Flaubertian example; but in Conrad's work there are many kindred effects. In *Almayer's Folly*, Lakamba's decision to have Almayer poisoned is counterpointed by Verdi's *Il Trovatore* played on a barrel-organ amid the jungles of Sambir: 'The Trovatore fitfully wept, wailed, and bade good-bye to his Leonore again and again in a mournful round of tearful and endless iteration'. In *Nostromo*, the pious rhetoric of politicians is interrupted by the squawk of 'Viva Costaguana!' from a parrot. In *The Secret Agent*, the Professor's sinister discussion with Ossipon is concluded by a selection of 'national airs' on the automatic pianola, among them 'The Blue Bells of Scotland'.

Another French writer admired by Conrad was Guy de Maupassant (1850–93), the prolific writer of drily ironic tales. Conrad claimed to be 'saturé de Maupassant' – saturated by him; when established as a writer, he provided an introduction to a selection of Maupassant's tales; and various debts can be postulated. The Preface to *The Nigger of the 'Narcissus'* owes some debts of phrasing to Maupassant's Preface to *Pierre et Jean*, and *The Nigger* may owe occasional descriptive touches (particularly at the death of Wait, which has a few similarities to that of Forestier) to *Bel-Ami*. It must be said, however, that the tale of Conrad's which, in subject and treatment, most resembles one of Maupassant's is not particularly successful. This tale is 'The Idiots' (*TU*), a drably pessimistic account of a blighted marriage amid the harsh environment of the Breton coast. (Conrad wrote it during his honeymoon ...)

In two book-reviews (in *The Speaker* for 16 July 1904 and in *The English Review* for December 1908) Conrad paid tribute to the 'princely' genius, the sceptical humanity, of Anatole France (1844–1924). From the pages of France, Conrad derived not only reinforcement for his own bleak view of history and human nature but also (as Owen Knowles has shown) instances of lucidly epigrammatic phrasing. To take one of several possible examples: in the essay 'Mérimée', France sums up as follows the character of the novelist Prosper Mérimée:

> What should he regret? He had never recognised anything but energy as virtue or anything but passions as duties. Was not his sadness rather that of a sceptic for whom the universe is only a succession of incomprehensible images.....?
>
> (*Œuvres complètes*, VI, 1926, 383. My translation)

And years later, in *Nostromo*, Conrad sums up as follows the character of Decoud:

> What should he regret? He had recognised no other virtue than intelligence, and had erected passions into duties.....His sadness was the sadness of a sceptical mind. He beheld the universe as a succession of incomprehensible images.

(498)

As Shakespeare took ideas and phrases from Plutarch and Holinshed, seizing and re-animating, so Conrad used his French mentors.

English influences

One of the many possible English examples is Coleridge's visionary, nightmarish poem of the sea, 'The Rime of the Ancyent Marinere' (1798), which influenced *The Shadow-Line*. In both, an accursed ship is a place of torment for the central figure. In the poem, the mariner bears a burden of guilt and feels that he is subject to reproachful gazes from the crew; so does the young captain of the novel. Above all, Conrad's work rivals Coleridge's in its attempt to render the horror of a becalmed ship. The captain reflects:

> No confessed criminal had ever been so oppressed by his sense of guilt.....The sun climbs and descends, the night swings over our heads as if somebody below the horizon were turning a crank..... This death-haunted command ..... I had had visions of a ship drifting in calms and swinging in light airs, with all her crew dying slowly about her decks.

At the climax of the poem, there comes a sudden rain and wind, and the dead crew begin to haul on the ropes. At the climax of the novel, there comes a sudden rain and wind, and the crew – virtually all of whom have been very ill – man the ropes like ghosts:

> Those men were the ghosts of themselves, and their weight on a rope could be no more than the weight of a bunch of ghosts.

In the 'Author's Note' to *The Shadow-Line*, Conrad repudiates the supernatural in fiction:

> This story.....was not intended to touch on the supernatural ....., which (take it any way you like) is but a manufactured article, the fabrication of minds insensitive to the intimate delicacies of our relation to the dead and to the living.....

Yet it is typical of Conrad's janiformity that in spite of this repudiation, just as supernatural motifs are strongly evident in *The Nigger*, *Heart of Darkness* and 'The Secret Sharer', so in *The Shadow-Line* there are counterparts to the supernatural elements of Coleridge's poem. Though Conrad almost certainly did not consciously intend this to happen, his novel can in part, like the poem, be read as a religious allegory of guilt and redemption through suffering and divine grace. In both cases the descriptive strength lies mainly in the vivid evocation of the nightmarish journey of an apparently accursed ship. In *The Shadow-Line* the captain's most loyal helper is a fellow who is mysteriously immune to fever, who is uncannily attentive and calm, and whose 'grace' (a term connoting both physical and metaphysical beauty, both ease of movement and spiritual virtue) is repeatedly and explicitly stressed; and this fellow is called Ransome. In the particular context that Conrad provides, the name Ransome evokes memories of the Christ who suffered to redeem man from sin, the Christ whom the Bible describes as man's ransom: in Matthew 20, v.28, and Mark 10, v.45 ('the Son of man came.....to give his life a ransom for many'), and in 1 Timothy 2, v.5–6 ('Christ Jesus .....gave himself a ransom for all'). Of course, at the end of the novel, the supernatural suggestions fade like ghosts at cock-crow, and we learn that Ransome's grace of movement is largely a consequence of his weak heart, which makes him move cautiously; but those ghosts were deliberately conjured up, to enrich the texture and meaning of the fiction, by Conrad's creative imagination.

There is no doubt that Conrad had a detailed familiarity with 'The Ancyent Marinere': I notice that among his unpublished papers is a letter to John Livingstone Lowes, the Coleridge scholar, complaining that an albatross was unlikely to be encountered in such southerly latitudes as the poem describes. Nevertheless, both Conrad and Coleridge could draw on a traditional fund of legends of the sea, legends about becalmed, haunted or crewless ships (like the *Marie Celeste*) or of interminable purgatorial voyages inflicted on a sinful mariner: a tradition as old as Jonah and which culminates in the legend of the Flying Dutchman. Conrad, who admired Wagner's music, must have known his opera, *Der fliegende Holländer*; and there are explicit references to the Flying Dutchman in 'Falk' as well as in *The Shadow-Line*.

Among novelists, it is probable that the Englishman whose work Conrad most enjoyed was Charles Dickens. As a boy, he had read Dickens in Polish: 'My first introduction to English imaginative literature was *Nicholas Nickleby*. It is extraordinary how well Mrs Nickleby could chatter disconnectedly in Polish' (*PR*, 71); and Conrad's letters and fictional works are peppered with Dickensian references. Thus in *Chance* (p. 162), the narrator notes that once de Barral had clung to his child beside his wife's grave and later walked hand in hand with his daughter at the seaside, and comments: 'Figures from Dickens – pregnant with pathos'. In *The Mirror of the Sea*, Conrad remarks that a forbidding acquaintance of his Marseilles days, Madame Delestang, reminded him of Lady Dedlock in *Bleak House*. And in 'Poland Revisited' (*NLL*, 152) he says that his first visit to London was in order to call at a shipping office which turned out to be in

> A Dickensian nook of London, that wonder city, the growth of which bears no sign of intelligent design, but many traces of freakishly sombre phantasy the Great Master knew so well how to bring out by the magic of his understanding love. And the office I entered was Dickensian too. The dust of the Waterloo year lay on the panes and frames of its windows.....

'Freakishly sombre phantasy': the similarity between the two writers lies mainly in their powers of creation of grotesquerie. In *The Secret Agent* particularly, Conrad makes London a place of savage farce by using the Dickensian technique of investing the inanimate with an unexpected degree of life (a pianola plays spontaneously, houses have apparently strayed from their correct locations) while investing the animate – the men and women – with an alarming degree of automatism. Again, there is a rather Dickensian quality about Conrad's atmospheric rendering of London in that novel: to live there is like living at the bottom of a filthy, muddy and

stagnant aquarium (the slimy London of *Bleak House* comes to mind);
and the scene in which Winnie Verloc's bewigged mother crosses
the city in a rattling cab drawn by an emaciated horse approaches
a Dickensian vividness.

It is still not a *very* close approach: there are important differences
between the two men. Dickens has a rich creative exuberance, an
eruptive fecundity of comic and absurd invention, which the more
austere and laborious Conrad lacks; and Conrad has a more mature
control of the elements of his works than the relatively manic and
immature Dickens possesses. (One un-Dickensian subtlety of *The
Secret Agent* is that the virtue which prevails is distinctly sullied:
the right thing is done, but for wrong reasons: the Assistant Commissioner expels Mr Vladimir, but he does so partly in order to
protect Michaelis, because Michaelis is the protégé of a wealthy
and influential hostess who, in turn, is a friend of the Assistant
Commissioner's wife.)

Both Dickens and Dickens's admirer, Thomas Carlyle (whose
Sartor Resartus Conrad knew), provide British precedent for some
aspects of Conrad's political radicalism. Dickens and Carlyle are
majestically eloquent when exposing and denouncing the injustice
and brutality of industrialism in the nineteenth-century, yet their
attack proceeds not from socialist premises but from 'organicist
conservative' premises: they seek a hierarchic society in which the
concept of *noblesse oblige* guides the high, while grateful deference
guides the low – an attempt to convert industrial society into an
idealised harmonious feudal state. And certainly, in *The Nigger of
the 'Narcissus'* Conrad came close to recommending that 'feudal'
pattern of society: a corporate, hierarchic and authoritarian community. By the time of *Nostromo*, however, Conrad's increasing
awareness of the inevitability of class conflict had led him to outgrow
that model.

Part Two
The Art of Conrad

3 Conrad on his art

From the Preface to *The Nigger of the 'Narcissus'*, 1897:

> A work that aspires, however humbly, to the condition of art should carry its justification in every line. And art itself may be defined as a single-minded attempt to render the highest kind of justice to the visible universe..... My task which I am trying to achieve is, by the power of the written word to make you hear, to make you feel – it is, before all, to make you *see*.

From a letter to William Blackwood, editor of *Blackwood's Magazine*, 12 February 1899 (*BB*, 50–1):

> The cheque for £60 now received and the previous one of £40 on account of the same tale [*Heart of Darkness*] will probably overpay it as I do not think it will run to 40,000 words. I did write that number or even more but I've been revising and compressing the end not a little.

From a letter to Edward Sanderson, 12 October 1899 (*LL* I, 283):

> I am at it day after day, and I want all day, every minute of it, to produce a beggarly tale [i.e. tally] of words or perhaps to produce nothing at all.....
>
> And oh! dear Ted, it is a fool's business to write fiction for a living. It is indeed.
>
> It is strange. The unreality of it seems to enter one's real life, penetrate into the bones, make the very heartbeats pulsate illusions through the arteries. One's will becomes the slave of hallucinations.....

From a letter to John Galsworthy, 20 July 1900 (*LL* I, 295):

> The end of *L.J.* [*Lord Jim*] has been pulled off with a steady drag of 21 hours.....A great hush. Cigarette ends growing into a mound similar to a cairn over a dead hero. Moon rose over the barn, looked in at the window and climbed out of sight. Dawn broke, brightened. I put the lamp out and went on, with the morning breeze blowing the sheets of MS. all over the room. Sun rose. I wrote the last word and went into the dining-room. Six o'clock I shared a piece of cold chicken with Escamillo [his dog].....

From a letter to the *New York Times*, 2 August 1901:

> Fiction, at the point of development at which it has arrived,

demands from the writer a spirit of scrupulous abnegation. The only legitimate basis of creative work lies in the courageous recognition of all the irreconcilable antagonisms that make our life so enigmatic, so burdensome, so fascinating, so dangerous – so full of hope. They exist! And this is the only fundamental truth of fiction.

From a letter to William Blackwood, 31 May 1902 (*BB*, 155):

I am *modern*, and I would rather recall Wagner the musician and Rodin the Sculptor who both had to starve a little in their day – and Whistler the painter who made Ruskin the critic foam at the mouth with scorn and indignation. They too have arrived. They had to suffer for being 'new'. And I too hope to find my place in the rear of my betters. But still – my place.

From a letter to H. G. Wells, 7 February 1904 (*LL* I, 326–7):

I've started a series of sea sketches [*The Mirror of the Sea*] and have sent out P. [Pinker, his literary agent] on the hunt to place them. This must save me. I've discovered that I can dictate that sort of bosh without effort at the rate of 3,000 words in four hours. Fact. The only thing now is to sell it to a paper and then make a book of the rubbish.

From 'Henry James', January 1905 (*NLL*, 13):

Action in its essence, the creative art of a writer of fiction may be compared to rescue work carried out in darkness against cross gusts of wind swaying the action of a great multitude.

From 'Books', July 1905 (*NLL*, 7–8, 9):

Liberty of imagination should be the most precious possession of a novelist. To try voluntarily to discover the fettering dogmas of some romantic, realistic, or naturalistic creed in the free work of its own inspiration, is a trick worthy of human perverseness which, after inventing an absurdity, endeavours to find for it a pedigree of distinguished ancestors.....

To be hopeful in an artistic sense it is not necessary to think that the world is good. It is enough to believe that there is no impossibility of its being made so.....I would wish him [the artist] to look with a large forgiveness at men's ideas and pre-judices.....

From 'A Familiar Preface', 1912 (*PR*, xix–xx):

At a time when nothing which is not revolutionary in some way or other can expect to attract much attention I have not been revolutionary in my writings. The revolutionary spirit is mighty convenient in this, that it frees one from all scruples as regards ideas. Its hard, absolute optimism is repulsive to my mind by the menace of fanaticism and intolerance it contains. No doubt one should smile at these things; but, imperfect Aesthete, I am no better philosopher.

From a letter to Sir Sidney Colvin, 18 March 1917 (*LL* II, 185):

I have been called a writer of the sea, of the tropics, a descriptive writer, a romantic writer – and also a realist. But as a matter of fact all my concern has been with the 'ideal' value of things, events and people. That and nothing else.

From a letter to Barrett H. Clark, 4 May 1918 (*LL* II, 204–5):

My attitude to subjects and expressions, the angles of vision, my methods of composition will, within limits, be always changing – not because I am unstable or unprincipled but because I am free. Or perhaps it may be more exact to say, because I am always trying for freedom – within my limits. . . . . A work of art is very seldom limited to one exclusive meaning and not necessarily tending to a definite conclusion. And this for the reason that the nearer it approaches art, the more it acquires a symbolic character.

4   The pressure towards paradox

Conrad's janiformity entails an impulsion towards paradox in matters large, small and intermediate; an impulsion so great as to lead at times even to self-contradiction.

To begin with small matters: even in his habits of phrasing, that preoccupation with the paradoxical emerges. Conrad likes an oxymoronic construction which can be rendered by the formula: $A = B + (-B)$. Examples in *Heart of Darkness*: the cry of the Intended is 'an exulting and terrible cry, ... the cry of inconceivable triumph and of unspeakable pain'; and the words of Kurtz are 'the bewildering, the illuminating, the most exalted and the most contemptible, the pulsating stream of light, or the deceitful flow from the heart of an impenetrable darkness.' (As the examples suggest, this device can become facile and automatic.)

In his descriptive paragraphs, Conrad has a predilection for a variety of techniques which lend an air of absurdity, futility or nightmare to what, presented by more orthodox techniques, would appear quite rational and natural. Such techniques are sometimes termed 'impressionistic', but 'absurdist' is more appropriate, particularly when we recall that Conrad generally regarded literary impressionism as vivid but shallow – he said that Stephen Crane was '*the only* impressionist and *only* an impressionist'. One of these absurdist techniques is use of the *dwarfing perspective* – a viewpoint that offers a reductive view of human activities. It may be a bird's-eye view or, so to speak, a star's, jungle's or mountain's view of man. Here is an example from *Nostromo*, describing a battle:

> Horsemen galloped towards each other, wheeled round together, separated at speed . . . . . The movements of the animated scene were like the passages of a violent game played upon the plain by dwarfs mounted and on foot, yelling with tiny throats, under the mountain that seemed a colossal embodiment of silence.
>
> (*N*, 26–7)

Another absurdist technique is the use of the *frustrating context*: the given context appears to render unattainable the goal of an activity: the actions appear blind or impotent. A good example is the account of the railway-building in *Heart of Darkness*:

> A heavy and dull detonation shook the ground, a puff of smoke came out of the cliff, and that was all. No change appeared on the face of the rock.
>
> (*Y*, 64)

Both this and the previous technique combine when, in the same tale, Marlow describes a French warship shelling the coast:

> In the empty immensity of earth, sky, and water, there she was, incomprehensible, firing into a continent. Pop, would go one of the six-inch guns; a small flame would dart and vanish, a little white smoke would disappear, a tiny projectile would give a feeble screech – and nothing happened. Nothing could happen. There was a touch of insanity in the proceeding, a sense of lugubrious drollery in the sight. . . . .
>
> (Υ, 61–2)

A third absurdist technique – and one which is of immense importance, as it applies to large-scale matters as well as to local descriptive passages – is that of *delayed decoding*. (The term is Ian Watt's, though I extend its application.) Here the writer confronts us with an effect while withholding or delaying knowledge of the cause; and the eventual explanation may not entirely erase the strong initial impression of the event's strangeness. In *Heart of Darkness* (which is extremely full of such examples):

> Something big appeared in the air before the shutter, the rifle went overboard, and the man stepped back swiftly, looked at me over his shoulder in an extraordinary, profound, familiar manner, and fell upon my feet. The side of his head hit the wheel twice, and the end of what appeared a long cane clattered round and knocked over a little camp-stool. It looked as though after wrenching that thing from somebody ashore he had lost his balance in the effort.
>
> (Υ, 111)

Not until several lines later is the decoding supplied: the man has been slain by a spear hurled by a native on the river-bank. To be aware of the technique of delayed decoding is to discover the secret of much vivid, immediate writing by Conrad and by others. The impressions are often appropriate to those of a mind under stress or illness, when the awareness of events outstrips the ability to understand or interpret those events. A narrative which, like *Heart of Darkness*, frequently uses this technique will, almost inevitably, be asking one of the defining questions of Modernism: Is it the case that all life, truly perceived, is absurd and senseless? (Later novels by Jean-Paul Sartre and Albert Camus carried to extremes this 'de-familiarisation device'.)

Where characterisation is concerned, the impulsion to paradox has various consequences. One is the presence of characters who themselves are walking paradoxes. There is Mr X, for example, the aristocratic revolutionary, the elegant firebrand, of the tale 'The Informer'. (Evidently he was prompted by Cunninghame Graham, an aristocratic revolutionary in real life.) Then there is Mr

Kurtz, the crusading idealist who has become a savage god. And in *The Nigger of the 'Narcissus'*, James Wait is a negro from St Kitts who speaks with the accents of an English gentleman ('Won't some of you chaps lend a hand with my dunnage?') and claims to be ill when he is relatively well, and well when he is mortally ill. As we have noted earlier, Conrad is fond of the *Doppelgänger* motif, in which complicity is established between ostensibly contrasting characters: e.g., between the apparently law-abiding captain and the murderous fugitive in 'The Secret Sharer', between Heyst and Gentleman Jones in *Victory*, and even between Gould and the bandit Hernández in *Nostromo*: indeed, *Nostromo* is bound by a network of such connections. It should be noted, though, that Conrad's conventions of characterisation may vary from work to work as the imaginative environment of the characters changes: thus, in *Nostromo* the narrator is able to sum up the characters with laconic aphorisms, whereas in the earlier *Heart of Darkness* the emphasis fell rather on the unknowability of personality: there we encountered numerous characters who had a vivid question-raising extern and an answer-frustrating inner opacity. Conrad's interest in this *opacity factor* is another of his anticipations of Modernism.

A further anticipation is provided by his interest in the *covert or elided plot-sequence*. Conrad likes to conceal or withhold narrative elements that a more orthodox novelist would have made evident and prominent. Examples are the covert murder-plot of *Heart of Darkness*, the wiles of Jacobus in 'A Smile of Fortune', and the attempt to defraud the hero of his first command in *The Shadow-Line*. On other occasions, as in *Nostromo* and *The Secret Agent*, the omniscient narrator, by juggling with the sequence of events or leaving large elisions in his representation of them, obliges us to do a great deal of reconstitution. Delayed decoding takes place on a large scale. A student once told me that this is what happens in a detective novel, but I think he was wrong. In a detective novel, we soon know what the crime is, and our interest lies in fitting together the clues to identify the villain. In Conrad's work, we may initially be unaware of any 'crime' and we may not be consciously engaged in 'detection'. Characteristically, we share the experiences of a protagonist who is at first unaware that he is the object of machinations or manipulations by others; events strike him as odd rather than sinister; and only tardily does realisation come to him and us of the scheme being woven about him. So this method of 'the covert plot' may initially give a strong sense of absurdity and later a strong sense that the world is a place of ambushes in which virtue needs to be vigilant.

5   The covert plot: two examples

1   *The conspiracy against Kurtz in*
Heart of Darkness

When Marlow approaches the Central Station, he expects to take command of a paddle-steamer which will voyage upstream to aid Kurtz. But on arrival he finds that the steamer has been wrecked. Looking back on that time, he reflects: 'I did not see the real significance of that wreck at once. I fancy I see it now, but I am not sure – not at all. Certainly the affair was too stupid – when I think of it – to be altogether natural.' The circumstances of the wrecking are peculiar: two days before his arrival, 'They had started.....in a sudden hurry up the river with the manager on board, in charge of some volunteer skipper, and before they had been out three hours they tore the bottom out of her on stones.' At Marlow's first interview with the manager, the latter suggests that the repair will take three months. 'Afterwards . . . . . it was borne in upon me startlingly with what extreme nicety he had estimated the time requisite. . . . .'

The repair is delayed because there are no rivets at the Central Station. There are many rivets at the Outer Station, but though Marlow requests them they do not arrive. Later we learn that the manager has been in a position to block the requests.

We gradually infer what Marlow has come to suspect. Before Marlow had arrived at the Central Station, the manager had persuaded 'some volunteer skipper' to steer the vessel on to rocks, and had then impeded the repairs for three months by withholding materials. A further two months are taken by the steamer's eventual journey – and by the time relief arrives, Kurtz, who has thus been isolated for well over a year, is dying. The manager's motive is that Kurtz, a successful and influential ivory-gatherer, is his main rival for promotion in that area.

Conrad succeeds in eating his cake and having it. The elliptical presentation of this plot enables him to maintain the general atmosphere of futile, purposeless activity, while the plot when we eventually perceive it makes a bitter comment on the evolutionary doctrine of the 'survival of the fittest' and on the political doctrine that the white man has a moral right to rule over Africa.

2   *The attempt to defraud the hero in*
The Shadow-Line

He couldn't see me anywhere this morning. He couldn't be expected to run all over the town after me.

'Who wants you to?' I cried. And then my eyes became opened to the inwardness of things and speeches the triviality of which had been so baffling and tiresome.

(p. 26)

At this point the hero at last begins to realise that the 'inwardness' of things at the Officers' Sailors' Home at Singapore has included a trick to defraud him of his first command. The master of a British ship has died at Bangkok; the Consul has cabled to the Harbour-Master at Singapore for a new captain; and the Harbour-Master, knowing that the hero, a first mate with excellent references, has no ship at present, sends word to the Sailors' Home that the job is available. The shifty steward at the Home decides to pass the message not to our hero but to Hamilton, his motive being that Hamilton has not been paying his bills and this may be a way to get rid of him. Luckily the quietly observant Captain Giles sees the trick and warns the hero, who eventually secures the command of the beautiful sailing-ship at Bangkok. Heavy irony stems from the fact that our man originally fails to see the point of Giles's hints and is slow to realise that Giles, far from being irritatingly inane, is in fact astutely safe-guarding his interests. There is also a subtle suggestion that Giles, by securing the command for the hero, saves him from degenerating into the states of surly dishonesty, torpor or dissipation manifested by other people at the Home.

One of Conrad's great strengths as a narrator lies in engaging our interest in a protagonist who has much to learn and who is aware of facts which he is only gradually coming to comprehend. One implication is that the meaning of life is what we make of it.

6   Textual commentaries

The opening of Almayer's Folly, *1895*

'Kaspar! Makan!'

The well-known shrill voice startled Almayer from his dream of splendid future into the unpleasant realities of the present hour. An unpleasant voice too. He had heard it for many years, and with every year he liked it less. No matter; there would be an end to all this soon.

He shuffled uneasily, but took no further notice of the call. Leaning with both his elbows on the balustrade of the verandah, he went on looking fixedly at the great river that flowed – indifferent and hurried – before his eyes. He liked to look at it about the time of sunset; perhaps because at that time the sinking sun would spread a glowing gold tinge on the waters of the Pantai, and Almayer's thoughts were often busy with gold; gold he had failed to secure; gold the others had secured – dishonestly, of course – or gold he meant to secure yet, through his own honest exertions, for himself and Nina. He absorbed himself in his dream of wealth and power away from this coast where he had dwelt for so many years, forgetting the bitterness of toil and strife in the vision of a great and splendid reward. They would live in Europe, he and his daughter. They would be rich and respected. Nobody would think of her mixed blood in the presence of her great beauty and of his immense wealth.....

Such were Almayer's thoughts as, standing on the verandah of his new but already decaying house – that last failure of his life – he looked on the broad river. There was no tinge of gold on it this evening, for it had been swollen by the rains, and rolled an angry and muddy flood under his inattentive eyes, carrying small drift-wood and big dead logs, and whole uprooted trees with branches and foliage, amongst which the water swirled and roared angrily.

The novel's title will prove to be characteristically ambiguous. 'Almayer's Folly' is both name and fact. It is the name jocularly given to the shell of a large building erected to accommodate the traders and workmen of the British Borneo Company – but the company had to leave to the Dutch this area of Borneo, so the building remains empty. And 'Almayer's Folly' also refers to Almayer's habit, throughout his life, of making foolish misjudgements: his loveless marriage for gain, his belief that his half-caste daughter could be bred to European ways, his faith in the trading station and the coming of the British; and now, as the tale opens, his faith that with the help of Dain Maroola, a trader and native prince from Bali, he can equip an expedition to find gold in the interior of Borneo and thus return proudly to Europe with the daughter.

The quoted passage bears some signs of being the opening of a 'first novel': the author is cramming in rather too much expository information; but the scene is well set: we see the European against an oppressive exotic background which is ominously turbulent. And the passage is very rich in latent ironies. 'Kaspar! Makan!' means 'Kaspar Almayer! Come to dinner!', and the tones are those of Almayer's wife, whom he now despises. She had been a Malay girl, an orphan benevolently adopted by the adventurous trader Tom Lingard, and Almayer had agreed to marry her at Lingard's suggestion. He had calculated that though it was demeaning to marry a coloured woman, the marriage would win him Lingard's favour and a share in Lingard's fortune – 'And then she may merci-fully die', he reflected. But the fortune has not yet materialised, and the wife has lived on to be a cunning witch-like schemer who opposes him secretly, arranging for his beloved daughter to elope with Dain.

The trading-post which at first had seemed to promise such wealth to Almayer has become a trap, an ambush to his ambitions. The British never arrive, but leave control of the region to the less enter-prising Dutch, and what trade there is in the region goes to his rivals, the shrewd Arabs; and Lingard has travelled to Europe to raise money for his schemes and seems lost without trace. Thus Almayer dreams of an expedition with Dain to find gold – and with gold, freedom. What happens, of course, is a multiple disillusionment for Almayer. The expedition never takes place, because Dain, after a fight with the Dutch authorities, escapes to Bali; and Nina, who has had bitter experience of white people's hypocrisies, elopes with him. Almayer actually helps them to flee, claiming that it would be a disgrace for white men to find his daughter with a Malay. Having lost his daughter and his supposed ally, Almayer burns down his house and lives in the Folly; an opium-smoking Chinaman joins him, and Almayer becomes addicted to the opium; the Folly is renamed 'The House of Heavenly Delight'; and Almayer dies a drug-addict's solitary death. The covert plotter, Abdulla, has won.

Thus in the opening pages of this novel Conrad has introduced the themes that he will pursue in so many later works: 1. The theme of isolation, physical and psychological, in an exotic setting. 2. The theme that men seek opiates for existence, having a capacity for romantic dreams that may tantalise them or lure them on to disaster or defeat. 3. The theme that even where humans appear to be close and interdependent they may be scheming against each other. 4. The theme that no one of the competing nations or races may be essentially worthier than another. Those readers who attribute racial prejudice to Conrad should notice that the crux of *Almayer's Folly* – the moment when a 'happy ending' seems a real possibility – comes when Almayer is tempted to abandon his jealousy and his racial prejudice and to join Nina in her flight with Dain: 'What if he should suddenly take her to his heart, forget his shame, and pain, and anger, and – follow her! What if he changed his heart if not his skin and made her life easier between the two loves.....!' As much as anything, it is racial pride that destroys Almayer. And connoisseurs of leit-motifs will notice that the river which carries Dain and Nina to a new life across the sea is the very river on which Almayer used to stare, dreaming of the gold that lay upstream and which one day might carry him and Nina to a new life across the sea.

The ending of 'An Outpost of Progress', 1897

The Managing Director of the Great Civilizing Company (since we know that civilization follows trade) landed first.....The captain and the engine-driver of the boat followed behind. As they scrambled up the fog thinned, and they could see their Director a good way ahead. Suddenly they saw him start forward, calling to them over his shoulder: – 'Run! Run to the house! I've found one of them. Run, look for the other!'

He had found one of them! And even he, the man of varied and startling experience, was somewhat discomposed by the manner of this finding. He stood and fumbled in his pockets (for a knife) while he faced Kayerts, who was hanging by a leather strap from the cross. He had evidently climbed the grave, which was high and narrow, and after tying the end of the strap to the arm, had swung himself off. His toes were only a couple of inches above the ground; his arms hung stiffly down; he seemed to be standing rigidly at attention, but with one purple cheek playfully posed on the shoulder. And, irreverently, he was putting out a swollen tongue at his Managing Director.

(*TU*, 116–7)

There are obvious connections with *Almayer's Folly*. This time there are two men, not one, in the jungle outpost; the jungle is African and not Bornean; but again, fond hopes and dreams have given way to disillusionment and death.

Kayerts and Carlier had come to their African trading station complacently thinking themselves to be the vanguard of civilisation, bringing 'Quays, and warehouses, and barracks, and – and – billiard rooms. Civilization, my boy, and virtue – and all'; and naturally they had hoped to make a lot of money from trade as well. But although they had begun affably enough, the isolation and their incompetence had told on their nerves; they had connived in slavery and killing in the region (the station was in practice being run by a black, Makola); and eventually the two whites had quarrelled bitterly over a spoonful of sugar. One had chased the other round the hut; there had been a shot; and Kayerts, horrified to discover he had killed Carlier, has now hung himself from a cross. Thus an emissary of Christian civilisation has killed his fellow and died by means of the symbol of Christianity; by a further irony, it is the cross that marks the grave of his white predecessor at the station; and further, it is a cross that had been erected by the Managing Director and put straight and firm by Carlier, the victim of the man who now dangles from it. Notice how a distinctive atmosphere of savage black comedy is created by Conrad's unflinchingly sardonic vividness of phrase: 'one *purple* cheek *playfully posed*'; 'irreverently, he was putting out a *swollen* tongue'. In such phrases, Conrad proves himself to be the great intermediary between the Flaubertian realism of the nineteenth century and the shock-tactics of Modernism in the twentieth century.

The narrator of 'An Outpost of Progress' had earlier pronounced the contemptuous epitaph of Kayerts and Carlier in words which are an indictment of urban civilisation as a whole:

They were two perfectly insignificant and incapable individuals, whose existence is only rendered possible through the high organization of civilized crowds. Few men realize that their life, the very essence of their character, their capabilities and their audacities, are only the expression of their belief in the safety of their surroundings. The courage, the composure, the confidence; the emotions and principles; every great and every insignificant thought belongs not to the individual but to the crowd: to the crowd that believes blindly in the irresistible force of its institutions and of its morals, in the power of its police and of its opinion. But the contact with pure unmitigated savagery, with primitive nature and primitive man, brings sudden and profound trouble into the heart.

(p. 89)

A passage from Heart of Darkness, *1899*

'I came upon a boiler wallowing in the grass, then found a path leading up the hill. It turned aside for the boulders, and also for an undersized railway-truck lying there on its back with its wheels in the air. One was off. The thing looked as dead as the carcass of some animal. I came upon more pieces of decaying machinery, a stack of rusty rails. To the left a clump of trees made a shady spot, where dark things seemed to stir feebly. I blinked, the path was steep. A horn tooted to the right, and I saw the black people run. A heavy and dull detonation shook the ground, a puff of smoke came out of the cliff, and that was all. No change appeared on the face of the rock. They were building a railway. The cliff was not in the way of anything; but this objectless blasting was all the work going on.

'A slight clinking behind me made me turn my head. Six black men advanced in a file, toiling up the path. They walked erect and slow, balancing small baskets full of earth on their heads, and the clink kept time with their footsteps. Black rags were wound round their loins, and the short ends behind waggled to and fro like tails. I could see every rib, the joints of their limbs were like knots in a rope; each had an iron collar on his neck, and all were connected together with a chain whose bights swung between them, rhythmically clinking. Another report from the cliff made me think suddenly of that ship of war I had seen firing into a continent. It was the same kind of ominous voice; but these men could by no stretch of imagination be called enemies. They were called criminals, and the outraged law, like the bursting shells, had come to them, an insoluble mystery from the sea. All their meagre breasts panted together, the violently dilated nostrils quivered, the eyes stared stonily up-hill. They passed me within six inches, without a glance, with that complete, deathlike indifference of unhappy savages. Behind this raw matter one of the reclaimed, the product of the new forces at work, strolled despondently, carrying a rifle by its middle. He had a uniform jacket with one button off, and seeing a white man on the path, hoisted his weapon to his shoulder with alacrity. This was simple prudence, white men being so much alike at a distance that he could not tell who I might be. He was speedily reassured, and with a large, white, rascally grin, and a glance at his charge, seemed to take me into partnership in his exalted trust. After all, I also was a part of the great cause of these high and just proceedings.'

(Y, 63–5)

Marlow has been telling his hearers on the yawl *Nellie* about his journey through the Congo some years before; here he recalls his arrival at the Company's Outer Station. The most obvious and important point to be made about this passage is that it conveys a controlled but intense indignation against racial exploitation and the hypocrisy of the imperialists: there is no doubt of Marlow's sympathy for the exhausted and emaciated blacks of the chain-gang. Conrad had seen actual instances of such ill-treatment during his Congo journey in 1890; and we should not forget that this tale appeared in the year of the Boer War, when British and Afrikaner competed violently for the spoils of Africa. At this time in Britain, the vast majority of Tories, the majority of Liberals, and even a majority of those who deemed themselves Socialists, were pro-imperialist: the Fabians were, and of course Marx and Engels had seen imperialism as a predatory yet progressive phase of history. Such bravely humane writings as Conrad's *Heart of Darkness* and Cunninghame Graham's 'Bloody Niggers' were pioneering works in their forthright criticisms of racial exploitation; and they may, in small but significant ways, have helped to swell the wave of indignation against King Leopold's predatory activities in the Congo: indignation which, increased by Roger Casement's report for Parliament and by E. D. Morel's polemical writings, eventually swayed Leopold to hand the Congo over to the Belgian Government, a move which reduced the more flagrant inhumanities.

The passage quoted has a characteristic ironic contrast. On one side we see instances of the inefficiency, wastefulness and futility of the imperialists' endeavours – objectless blasting, upturned trucks; and on the other side we see the price in human terms of those activities: the emaciated natives of the chain-gang, starving slave-labourers. The juxtaposition makes a telling indictment of the folly, hypocrisy and callousness of the so-called emissaries of progress, the 'pilgrims' who are idolators before ivory.

However, the passage has greater resonance than this. The somewhat surrealistic landscape, in which the boiler is wallowing in the grass like a metal animal from another planet, seems to hint of a future time when all man's technology will be annulled by the non-human environment. Similarly, the depiction of the treatment of the natives leads to big, searching questions: we are led to ask 'Who are the real savages here, the blacks or the Europeans?' This encounter with the chain-gang is just one of the many shocks that Marlow is to experience as he travels on deeper into Africa, deeper towards the Inner Station, deeper into a continent – and into human nature. These shocks force him, and us, to ask repeatedly, 'What, if anything, justifies imperialism? On what does civilisation rest? And what are the foundations of moral conduct?'

Another important feature of this passage is its development of the tale's linguistic theme. Clichés are invoked and ironically undercut. After an account of a futile and ugly muddle of machinery, after a pointless explosion, comes the explanation: 'They were building a railway'. We are shown black slaves: and then comes the official jargon: Marlow notes that 'They were called criminals'. In his attention to the uses and abuses, the seductions, ambiguities and limitations of language, Conrad anticipates an important preoccupation of modernist literature and of twentieth-century philosophy; indeed, the reader of *Heart of Darkness* will be well prepared for Ludwig Wittgenstein's demonstrations that 'our language determines our view of reality, because we see things through it'.

Marlow had observed a French ship conducting 'one of their wars' by shelling 'enemies' (i.e. firing shells into an Africa which contains uncomprehending natives); a debased native is 'one of the reclaimed'; the European 'Workers' are generally destructive and often slothful; Kurtz's victims are 'rebels'; Kurtz's megalomanic depravity is, according to the manager, the 'vigorous action' for which 'the time was not ripe': 'unsound method'. If the Europeans were presented as consciously hypocritical, the tale would be less disturbing, for conscious hypocrisy entails recognition of the truth. But what Marlow notes around him amongst the Europeans is the credited lie, a sincerity in the use of euphemistic jargon – jargon that sanctions destruction and callousness. Conrad seems prophetic when we consider the proliferation of such political euphemisms in this century, whether by the Nazis with their 'final solution of the Jewish problem' (i.e. mass murder) or by those tyrannies which rejoice in such hypocritical titles as 'People's Republic' or 'Democratic Republic'.

Conrad's attitude to language is janiform: he can see it as truth-revealing or truth-concealing. Marlow strives to convey the truth, though he frequently suggests the inability of language to convey the essential: 'Do you see anything? It seems to me I am trying to tell you a dream – making a vain attempt, because no relation of a dream can convey the dream-sensation . . . . .' Kurtz, on the other hand, has a charismatic eloquence which will sway even decent men to admire him; a power to corrupt others, and himself, through words. Another prophetic aspect of *Heart of Darkness* is that through its portrayal of the seductive eloquence of Kurtz, who might have been a successful political leader 'on the popular side', Conrad offers a warning against the kind of demagogy that would eventually bring Hitler to power.

The art of Conrad is an art of ambush. In his works we see protagonists variously ambushed by circumstances; and by his techniques the reader too may be ambushed by the text. In the passage cited we see how Marlow is treated as an accomplice of the exploiters by that native who guards the slaves and who 'with a large, white, rascally grin, and a glance at his charge, seemed to take [Marlow] into partnership in his exalted trust.' After all, Marlow reflects, 'I also was a part of the great cause of these high and just proceedings.' The tale is about complicity. Marlow, as an employee of the company and even by simply being a European with a European's acceptance of ivory commodities, is involved in the exploitation he detests. The tale in its structure has cunningly ambushed the reader so as to make him an accomplice, in addition. It has had not one narrator but two of them. At first, when we begin the tale, we think the patriotic anonymous narrator speaks with authorial force; but his words are undercut by the entry of Marlow, with his 'And this also has been one of the dark places of the earth', and for a while we are uncertain of our bearings. Then, as Marlow's narration takes over, and as we come to terms with his personality, we tend to accept his authority, and thus when he records his fascination by Kurtz we are drawn into a complicated moral entanglement. Again, Marlow had initially allayed the distrust of the British reader by talking of the British empire as a place where you know that some 'real work' is being done; but Marlow's ensuing narrative, by never actually calling the company Belgian or the region the Congo, and by stressing that 'all Europe' – including England – 'contributed to the making of Kurtz', makes it impossible for the British reader to stand smugly aloof from the indictment of imperialism. 'Kurtz had been educated partly in England . . . . . His mother was half-English, his father was half-French.' The tale offers a choice of evils: between the cor-ruption of the flabby Europeans, who exploit the natives callously and thoughtlessly, and the intense corruption of Kurtz, who becomes a savage god, adored by the natives among whom he lives.

Jim's jump: Lord Jim, *1900*

'"With the first hiss of rain, and the first gust of wind, they screamed, 'Jump, George! We'll catch you! Jump!' The ship began a slow plunge; the rain swept over her like a broken sea; my cap flew off my head; my breath was driven back into my throat. I heard as if I had been on the top of a tower another wild screech, 'Geo-o-o-orge! Oh, jump!' She was going down, down, head first under me . . ."

'He raised his hand deliberately to his face, and made picking motions with his fingers as though he had been bothered with cobwebs, and afterwards he looked into the open palm for quite half a second before he blurted out –

'"I had jumped . . ." He checked himself, averted his gaze . . . "It seems," he added.

'His clear blue eyes turned to me with a piteous stare . . . . .'

(pp. 110–1)

The narrator is Marlow; the speaker is Jim. The jump is the jump that has ruined Jim's reputation and brought disgrace to him. He had been chief mate on an over-crowded pilgrim-ship; the ship had hit an obstacle and had begun to sink; the other European officers had lowered a boat alongside and urged a friend, George, to jump in. Instead, Jim leaps; the boat reaches shore; the pilgrim-ship is reported sunk by the captain; but the ship has not sunk. With all its hundreds of Moslem passengers, it has been safely towed to harbour, and now Jim has faced the public disgrace of the inquiry. One great irony is that Jim is an egoistic romantic who has long had dreams of glory for himself, and if he had only stayed on that ship he would be the hero of the hour; but instead, he is branded a coward and a traitor to the seaman's code. Later, in the jungles of Sumatra, he will appear to redeem himself by being a paternalist governor to the natives; but eventually a white brigand, whose life Jim spares, will treacherously kill some of those natives, including the chief's son, and Jim will give his life in atonement to that chief.

The quoted passage is part of a leit-motif or recurrent theme of 'the jump' in the novel. As a cadet on a training-ship, Jim had missed his chance of glory because he had failed to jump when other boys leapt into a cutter to take part in a rescue-operation. But in the pilgrim-ship episode, he *does* jump, and thus misses his chance of glory. The next leap is the one that carries him from captivity in a stockade on his arrival at Patusan, the start of his apparently redemptive adventures there. When Patusan is invaded by the brigand, Gentleman Brown, and Jim faces this murderous opponent, we are told that

'They met, I should think, not very far from the place, perhaps on the very spot, where Jim took the second desperate leap of his life – the leap that landed him into the life of Patusan, into the trust, the love, the confidence of the people.'

And by a telling irony, when Brown is seeking to negotiate favourable terms, he uses metaphors which infallibly though unintentionally remind Jim of Jim's past disgrace:

'"This is as good a jumping-off place for me as another. I am sick of my infernal luck. But it would be too easy. There are my men in the same boat – and, by God, I am not the sort to jump out of trouble and leave them in a d – d lurch."'

There is a clear implication that by these accidental reminders of his guilty past, Jim's negotiating position is weakened and he is softer with Brown than he otherwise would be, thus precipitating the deaths of those native friends; but it is also the case that by letting Brown go, Jim has acted with honour. Typically, the novel invites us to see the difficulty of choosing between an honourable course which may be risky and a practical course which may appear dishonourable.

The passage quoted at the head of this section, the 'I had jumped . . . . . it seems' passage, also focuses another subtlety of the text. The brave side of Jim is there in the frank admission of cowardice, 'I had jumped' – he faces the facts, as he faces the inquiry; and the egoistic, evasive side of Jim, the Jim who seeks an excuse and would blame circumstances for his bad luck, is there in the 'it seems'. That double perspective (was the jump voluntary or involuntary, a decision or a reflex?) characterises so much of the novel, in which Conrad has dramatised brilliantly the disparity between the external view of an action – the view that the Court of Inquiry takes of Jim's leap – and the internal view of it – the entirely different perspective of Jim, moment by moment during the time of crisis. What Conrad explores here was to be the basis of another fine novel by a later novelist (Albert Camus: *L'Etranger* – *The Outsider*): the sense that there is a radical disparity between crucial actions as conventionally, circumstantially, morally perceived, and those actions as actually lived. The recounting of the subjective experience of those fateful moments is so vivid that we share Jim's paralysis, uncertainty, bewilderment and impulsiveness; conventional moral judgements of cowardice or irresponsibility seem inappropriate; we think: 'There, but for the grace of God, go I.' Yet when Jim says: 'There was not the thickness of a sheet of paper between the right and wrong of this affair', Marlow coolly observes, 'How much more did you want?', and we are reminded of the weight of authority and common sense that stands behind those traditional circumstantial moral judgements.

The novel both asserts that Jim was 'one of us' and asks whether he was 'one of us'. The phrase is a leit-motif with many meanings. It means variously: 'a gentleman, as we are', 'a white man', 'a white gentleman', 'a good seaman', 'an ordinary person' and 'a fellow human being'. The phrase echoes the words that God uttered to the angels when Adam ate the forbidden fruit: 'Behold, the man is become as one of us, to know good and evil.' The Biblical text is a reminder that *Lord Jim* is a novel not merely about the moral situation of one particular individual but also about the situation of man generally as moral being, pulled this way by ideals that may frustrate him and that way by realities that may degrade him. Which are truer: the confusing messages of immediate reality or the subsequent 'decodings' by moral rationality?

Three Conradian cruces

A literary crux occurs when a word, phrase, passage or sequence offers extreme difficulty to commentators. Three notorious cruces in Conrad are Kurtz's words, 'The horror! The horror!', in *Heart of Darkness*; Stein's 'Destructive Element' speech in *Lord Jim*; and the relationship between the narrator and Leggatt in 'The Secret Sharer' (*TLAS*). The concept of janiformity enables us to resolve all three problems together.

1   Kurtz's words, 'The horror! The horror!'

These are Mr Kurtz's last words, and Marlow makes much of their significance. Some commentators find them affirmative, others find them nihilistic, others find them obscure. If we look closely at the text, we find that Marlow suggests the following meanings for 'The horror! The horror!': 1. Kurtz is deeming his own past actions horrible, and this is 'a moral victory'. 2. Kurtz deems to be horrible but also desirable the temptations of the jungle: the whisper has 'the strange commingling of desire and hate', and therefore is not a moral victory, after all, it seems. 3. Kurtz deems horrible the inner natures of all mankind: 'no eloquence could have been so withering to one's belief in mankind as his final burst of sincerity', and his stare could 'penetrate all the hearts that beat in the darkness'. 4. Kurtz deems horrible the whole universe: 'that wide and immense stare embracing, condemning, loathing all the universe.....''The horror!'''

Until this point in the tale, Kurtz has been a janiform character: to put it simply, he has been both a hollow man and a full man. Marlow has explicitly called him hollow: 'the wilderness echoed loudly within him because he was hollow at the core'. This Kurtz seems to be the ultimate in a long line of hollow men who, though nominally civilised, lack moral backbone; and the emphasis on his apparent virtues, his idealism, his energy, his eloquence, is to show that even a seeming exception only proves the rule about the vacuity at the heart of civilisation. (The emphasis on his eloquence should remind us of the maxim that empty vessels make most noise.) Yet, on the other hand, Marlow has also presented him as the intense *contrast* to the long line of hollow men: a being who, in contrast to the 'flabby devils', has at least, for all his corruption, lived vividly, violently, spectacularly; and if he has sold his soul, he has at least had a soul to sell. As the end of *Heart of Darkness* approaches, Conrad is under an obvious pressure of convention: the convention that a tale must offer final clarification, final resolution of its mysteries and paradoxes. Now Conrad is happier to generate and dramatise paradoxes than to resolve them: he is resistant to the idea of final simplification. So what he offers is a pseudo-resolution: a dramatic statement by Kurtz which seems to promise that grand *finale* of revelation but which, on closer examination, proves to be itself a compressed paradox, an oxymoron: a statement which mirrors, and does not reduce, the extreme ambiguity of the characterisation.

If we consider the texture of the prose at that climactic point in *Heart of Darkness*, we will find that it is not authoritative. Marlow seems over-insistent, and the elements of contradiction in his analyses of Kurtz's words make him seem rather glibly hyperbolic, if not somewhat hysterical. We may speculate whether Marlow is here the mouthpiece of a Conrad who is under strain, or whether, on the contrary, a cool and lucid Conrad is deploying an over-insistent and rather confused Marlow. Twice previously, Marlow's narrative has been interrupted by sceptical, disgruntled sounds from his audience on the yawl *Nellie*. If Conrad had wished to establish a critical distance between Marlow and himself at this point, he could have done so by means of a further sceptical interruption from

Marlow's hearers. As there is none, it seems to me probable that Marlow's confusion is largely that of Conrad, too.

Although crucial passages like this naturally tend to engross much of the attention of commentators, we should remember that a crucial passage whose prose is rather inflated (as it is in this one of Marlow's) actually contains far less of the moral and imaginative force of a work than does a passage which may be much less problematic but more vivid – such as, for example, the description of the journey down the African coast, the account of the chain-gang, or the account of the grove of death.

2 Stein's 'Destructive Element' speech

In Chapter 20 of *Lord Jim*, Marlow seeks advice about Jim from wise old Stein. Stein utters the oft-quoted words:

> '"A man that is born falls into a dream like a man who falls into the sea. If he tries to climb out into the air as inexperienced people endeavour to do, he drowns – *nicht wahr*? ... No! I tell you! The way is to the destructive element submit yourself, and with the exertions of your hands and feet in the water make the deep, deep sea keep you up. So if you ask me – how to be? .....
>
> In the destructive element immerse..... To follow the dream, and again to follow the dream – and so – *ewig – usque ad finem* ..."'

Most commentators find this passage enigmatic, and some resolve the enigma by claiming that it means 'You should pursue at all costs the goal suggested by your idealism'. This interpretation (according to which, of course, Stein is looking sympathetically on Jim's romantic if egoistic ambitions) is sanctioned mainly by the fact that 'dream' can mean 'romantic goal or ideal'.

It seems to me that in function this passage has some resemblances to the crux of *Heart of Darkness* that we have just considered. Jim, like Kurtz, has been presented in an extremely ambiguous light. He has been shown to be more sensitive, imaginative and idealistic than the average seaman, which seems to suggest that he is better than they; but his daydreams distract him from his immediate duty, his idealism is strongly egoistic, and he is capable of bringing disgrace on himself and his profession. Stein's words, like Kurtz's 'The horror!', provide a memorable, climactic statement which, on close examination, proves to mirror and not to resolve the paradoxes of judgement with which we have been faced.

On the one hand, such words as 'In the destructive element immerse ... To follow the dream..... *ewig – usque ad finem*' sound like a rallying cry to all romantic crusaders. Be a Quixote – charge on – don't count the cost – risk your life. And this notion is encouraged by our recollection that *usque ad finem* was the proud family motto that Bobrowski urged on his nephew, Konrad Korzeniowski. But on the other hand, if we follow Stein's speech closely, this contrasting meaning also emerges: When we are born, we fall into the dream of life as if we were falling into a sea. So we should resemble good swimmers. An inexperienced person, finding himself in the sea, tries to climb up out of it in his panic – and for snatching at the sky, he pays the penalty of drowning in the sea. The sensible person co-operates with the water instead of fighting it; he exploits buoyancy, and lets the water carry him while he swims steadily. Thus he survives. In other words, we should be practical realists, ready to adapt to life and make the most of what it offers; we shouldn't be idealists who try to climb up out of ordinary life towards some transcendental goal.

So Stein's speech resolves itself into the janiform recommendation: Be an idealist, and be a realist instead of an idealist. No wonder Marlow records some bewilderment. It may be noted that the self-contradictory elements in the speech express the character of the speaker, Stein; for he is both a practical man of action and also a brooding philosopher-connoisseur-idealist. A few minutes later he will say of Jim: 'He is a romantic – romantic.....And that is very bad – very bad ... Very good, too'.

To the reader who likes a narrative which proceeds by decisive steps, such paradoxes or oxymorons will seem like waffling evasiveness; but other readers may feel that by such means Conrad usefully focuses – brings into sharp definition – the problems of human nature that the work at large has been exploring.

The ending of *Lord Jim* preserves the enigma. Jim has offered up his life as atonement to the natives who feel he betrayed them; yet in doing so he rejects the pleas of his native mistress and his loyal follower. The narrator says that Jim may have regarded his self-sacrifice as 'an extraordinary success', but adds that we can see him as a man called by 'his exalted egoism':

> He goes away from a living woman to celebrate his pitiless wedding with a shadowy ideal of conduct.....
>
> He is gone, inscrutable at heart, and the poor girl is leading a sort of soundless, inert life in Stein's house. Stein has aged greatly of late. He feels it himself, and says often that he is 'preparing to leave all this; preparing to leave ...' while he waves his hand sadly at his butterflies.

3   The meaning of 'The Secret Sharer'

'The Secret Sharer' is a short but brilliant tale. It is lucid, engrossing, entertaining, exciting. As narrative it is vigorous and dramatic, and the prose style is lean – virtually free from the fatty rhetorical encumbrances that we often encounter in earlier and later Conrad.

The tale is patently a success, yet its moral meaning occasions the widest disagreements among commentators. If we do not strive to impose a unitary explanation on the text, but see it, rather, as an elegantly persuasive dramatisation of moral paradox, we come close to its centre.

A young sea-captain, who has just taken charge of his first command, is surprised one night when a swimmer comes alongside. The swimmer is a fugitive from justice; during a storm he had killed a mutinous crew-man on his own ship. The captain at once feels a certain complicity with the fugitive, Leggatt, whom he physically resembles: 'It was, in the night, as though I had been faced by my own reflection in the depths of a sombre and immense mirror'. Although it entails great psychological strain, he conceals the fugitive in his own quarters during the subsequent days, and eventually, in an extremely dangerous manoeuvre at night, takes his vessel close in to the rocky shore of the island of Koh-Ring; the fugitive dives overboard during this prearranged manoeuvre and swims for shore and freedom.

The combination of exciting, adventurous narrative with extreme moral ambiguity or paradox is a hallmark of Conrad's genius. The tale is persuasive in showing how an apparently decent, likeable, law-abiding captain can almost immediately, as a kind of reflex, let considerations of class, upbringing, nationality and physical likeness – what we may call a fraternal ethic – triumph over both the traditional seaman's and the traditional landsman's ethics, which would demand the handing over of Leggatt to justice. If we sympathise with the captain's view – the view that it is good to risk the loss of a ship and her crew in order to save the life of one man – we find that inevitably we are being beckoned towards the mirror-image of that view, since the life saved is that of Leggatt, who believed that it was good to kill one man in order to save a ship and her crew. The reader's sympathies, if liberal (so that he wishes to give Leggatt a second chance), are forced into alliance with illiberal prejudices (e.g., Leggatt's belief that he was right to kill a 'cur', and could do so again; and the fraternal ethic itself, which is represented as partly a matter of social élitism); while his prejudices, if illiberal, are forced into alliance with liberal sympathies.

The tale offers an elaborate system of mirroring. A mirror can offer a symmetrical likeness of a person before it, preserving relationships on the vertical axis. It can offer a symmetrical contrary, for it reverses relationships on a horizontal axis: when I raise my right hand, my reflection raises his left. It can offer a complement, showing the hat that I am wearing but cannot see without the aid of the mirror. And if I stand between two mirrors, there may be a long recession or spiral of mutually-reflecting images. The kinds of mirroring offered in the tale can be noted in the form of a table, thus:

mirroring	mirrored	
Leggatt:	Hero:	Mirror-relationship:
young (in his twenties);	young (in his twenties);	Likeness
same build as hero;	same build as Leggatt;	Likeness
ex-*Conway* boy;	ex-*Conway* boy;	Likeness
'a stranger on board' –	'the only stranger on board'	Likeness
alienated from crew –	alienated from crew –	Likeness
distrusted by them.	distrusted by them.	Likeness
Kills one man	To save life of one man	Contrast
to avert shipwreck.	risks a shipwreck;	Contrast
	the man is Leggatt.	Recession or spiral.
Elitist ethic	Fraternal ethic	Complement
subordinates seaman's	subordinates seaman's	Likeness
and landsman's.	and landsman's,	Likeness
	and endorses élitist ethic.	Recession or spiral.
The ship is imperilled;	The ship is imperilled;	Likeness
the captain is fearful;	the captain is bold;	Contrast
the first mate is bold.	the first mate is fearful.	Contrast

Such elegant patterning of character, incident and ethic, within a tale with a vivid naturalistic surface and a rapid forward narrative thrust, largely accounts for the lingering fascination with which 'The Secret Sharer' has long been regarded. The narrative thrust derives from the relay-race of questions that emerge: How, exactly, will the hero be tested on this, his first command? What sort of being is the unexpected visitant? How will the captain respond to the news that Leggatt has killed a man? How will he succeed in keeping Leggatt's presence a secret? And, behind all such subordinate problems, the central question: Will there be a disastrous or a happy outcome for the hero and his ship? What makes us read so eagerly is the janiform balance of the suspense-principle: from the start, the evidence to support a prediction of a happy outcome is almost evenly balanced by the evidence to support the prediction of disaster.

(For further discussion of this tale, see Watts: 'The Mirror-Tale': *Critical Quarterly* 19, 1977, 25–37. I discuss literary janiformity in 'Janiform Novels': *English* 24, 1975, 40–9.)

7   Nostromo

Genesis and production

In the 'Author's Note' to *Nostromo*, Conrad says that around 1902 he came upon the memoirs of an American seaman who had once served on a schooner owned by a thief.

> The fellow had actually managed to steal a lighter with silver, and this, it seems, only because he was implicitly trusted by his employers, who must have been singularly poor judges of character.

Conrad reflected on the account of the theft, and:

> It was only when it dawned upon me that the purloiner of the treasure need not necessarily be a confirmed rogue, that he could be even a man of character, an actor and possibly a victim in the changing scenes of a revolution, it was only then that I had the first vision of a twilight country which was to become the province of Sulaco, with its high shadowy Sierra and its misty Campo . . . . .

He was at work on *Nostromo* by the beginning of 1903. Originally he seems to have envisaged it as a short piece – he referred to it as 'a tale in the "Karain" class'; and in May he told Cunninghame Graham that though set 'in Sth America in a Republic I call Costaguana', the work 'is however concerned mostly with Italians',

over page *The beginning of the manuscript of* Nostromo.
Conrad made many revisions, small and large, to the whole text as it evolved via serialisation in T. P.'s Weekly *into the eventual book. In this opening paragraph, 'never been anything more' became 'never been commercially anything more'; 'salt fish and oxhides' became 'ox-hides and indigo'; 'on her three-knot way' was deleted; and 'sombre festoonings [of cloud]' became 'mourning draperies. . . . .'. The change of 'Sulaco seemed to have found an inviolable sanctuary' to 'Sulaco had found an inviolable sanctuary' actually reduces the original ironic precision.*
The first paragraph introduces several important themes: economic evolution; the contrast between human acquisitiveness and nature's serene dignity; and the potential defilement of sanctuary. The emphasis on the calm of the Placid Gulf also prepares us for the episode when Decoud and Nostromo are becalmed in their vessel at night. Thus the opening paragraph of the novel is as deliberate as the concluding one, which so carefully incorporates the phrase 'a mass of solid silver' in the description of the nocturnal sky.

NOSTROMO..

Part First
The Silver of the Mine
~~The Isabels~~

I

Through all the ages of Spanish
rule and for many years afterwards the town of Sulaco (the
luxuriant beauty of the orange gardens bears witness to its antiquity)
had never been anything more
important than a coasting
port with a petty trade in
salt fish and ox hides. The
clumsy ~~gets~~ deep sea galleons
of the conquerors, that, needing
a brisk gale to move at all
would lie helplessly becalmed
where your modern sailing

ship built on clipper lines
forges ahead on her three-
knot way by the mere flapping
of her sails, ~~were~~ had been
barred out of Sulaco by
the ~~calms~~ prevailing calms of
its gulf. Some harbours of
the earth are made difficult
of access by the treachery
of sunken rocks and the
tempestuous character of
their shores: Sulaco seemed
to have found an inviolable
sanctuary from the temptations
of ~~the~~ world in the solemn
hush of the deep Golfo Placido as if within an enormous
semicircular and unroofed
temple open to ~~the sky and~~
~~to~~ the ocean, ~~while~~ its walls of
lofty mountains ~~here~~ remain hidden
under the sombre festoonings of

~~clouds~~

which suggests that originally it dealt centrally with the involvement of Nostromo with Viola and his daughters. As had happened with *Lord Jim*, the tale burgeoned into a novel as Conrad proceeded. Eventually it appeared as a serial in the popular magazine, *T.P.'s Weekly*, between 29 January and 7 October 1904, and in the same October it was published as a book by Harper's (London and New York).

Sources

> Didn't it ever occur to you, my dear Curle, that I knew what I was doing in leaving the facts of my life and even of my tales in the background? Explicitness, my dear fellow, is fatal to the glamour of all artistic work, robbing it of all suggestiveness, destroying all illusion.
>
> (Conrad to Richard Curle, 24 April 1922; *Conrad to a Friend*, ed. Curle, 1928, p. 124)

Richard Curle had written for the *Times Literary Supplement* an account of Conrad's works which emphasised their autobiographical qualities; and Conrad's testy rebuke is partly the response of a proud old man who seeks to guard his privacy and partly the response of a dedicated artist who seeks to avert the danger of a reductive simplification of the works. A list of the source-materials of a literary masterpiece can sometimes appear to 'explain away' that masterpiece, but it may sometimes give the reader a keener eventual sense of the work's imaginative integrity. Any such list has to be ruthlessly selective. A full list would be infinite: it might include such matters as the author's preference for certain syntactical rhythms rather than others, or for certain pictorial lighting-effects in descriptions, for example, and the causes of such preferences. The short lists that follow are conventional in range; I omit from them source-materials in an unconventional sense (e.g. thematic preoccupations and dialectical impulses) which are discussed in the later section.

Personal encounters

The 'Author's Note' tells us that Antonia Avellanos is modelled on Conrad's 'first love' – a proud nationalistic girl who was admired by Conrad and his schoolmates. This may well be the case, though Antonia is partly a familiar fictional type (the noble, ardent and beautiful heroine who suffers stoically), and she owes her name and her emancipated spirit to a girl encountered by E. B. Eastwick and described in his book *Venezuela*.

Conrad's note about Antonia strengthens one's sense that Decoud is based largely on the younger Conrad. We can readily imagine that Decoud's mixture of cynicism, romanticism and patriotism closely resembles Conrad's own, and that the 'idle boulevardier' of Paris has much in common with a former idle boulevardier of Marseilles; and Decoud's suicidal pistol-shot re-echoes in the imagination when we recall that the young Conrad had once put a pistol to his own breast and pulled the trigger.

The 'Author's Note' also explains that Nostromo himself derives partly from the thief described in the source-tale and partly from Dominic Cervoni, the Mediterranean sailor, tough and capable, who was the first mate of the *Saint-Antoine* and with whom Conrad claimed to have attempted gun-running. (The researches of Norman Sherry – *CWW* 163–5 – confirm the historic existence of Dominic, who belonged to 'the Brotherhood of the Coast – a kind of Mafia'.)

The fictional landscape of Costaguana is established with such a convincing richness and seeming knowledgeability of detail that the reader may be surprised to discover that the much-travelled Conrad actually saw very little of the South American continent. Conrad told Cunninghame Graham in 1903: 'I just had a glimpse 25 years ago – a short glance. That is not enough pour bâtir un roman dessus [to build a novel upon].' And to Richard Curle he remarked that he had been ashore for about twelve hours at Puerto Cabello and about two-and-a-half to three days at La Guaira – 'and there were a few hours in a few other places on that dreary coast of Ven[ezue]la'. This was during the *Saint-Antoine* voyage (1876–77), when, according to Jerry Allen (in *The Sea Years of Joseph Conrad*) the vessel carried arms for the conservative rebels against the liberal government in the Colombian Civil War, which was then raging. Her speculation is plausible enough: Conrad hints in the 'Author's Note' to *Victory* that he was engaged in some lawless activity during that voyage.

The topography of Costaguana derives from Conrad's recollections of the Venezuelan coast, perhaps his glimpses of the West Indies to some minor extent, and what he had heard or read of Colombia, Argentina, Chile and other places. He told Graham: 'Costaguana is meant for a S. Am^{can} state in general; thence the mixture of customs and expressions.' As it has both Pacific and Atlantic seaboards and a city called Santa Marta, geographically it resembles Colombia rather more than other South American regions; though the more we sense that Costaguana represents 'a S. Am^{can} state in general', the more we may sense that the novel is about economic imperialism in general, history in general and human nature in general.

Conrad's friend Cunninghame Graham was an authority on South and Central America, having spent many years travelling and working there. He claimed to have seen action, in his youth, with a revolutionary army; certainly he had journeyed through a devastated Paraguay in the aftermath of the war of 1865–70 conducted by the brutal dictator, Francisco Solano López. Graham provided Conrad with anecdotes and recollections (e.g. the '*y dentista*' anecdote of Pt III, Chap. 9), with books by himself, his wife and others, which provided accounts of American life, and with an introduction to Pérez Triana, the Colombian Ambassador.

Norman Sherry (*CWW*, 149) has suggested that Gould is based partly on Cunninghame Graham:

> Both are given Spanish names – Don Roberto, Don Carlos; both are remarkable for their flaming hair and moustaches; both have early family connections with the country in a political sense; both met their wives on the continent of Europe; both wives sketch and both wives went on an exhausting tour of a South American country with their respective husbands.

We might add that Graham, like Gould, was a celebrated equestrian figure and had prospected (for gold if not silver) in ancient mineworkings. On the other hand, some of Graham's political attitudes (his scepticism about economic imperialism and modern 'progress' in general) seem to have been assimilated by the narrator of *Nostromo*.

During a journey through the Paraguayan wilderness in 1873, Graham had been lent a gun by an Italian called Enrico (or Enrique) Clerici, who kept a tavern at Ytapua. Fierce and leonine, this former follower of Garibaldi appears in two of Graham's tales, 'Cruz Alta' and 'The Captive', and is clearly a progenitor of Giorgio Viola in *Nostromo*. (He refers to Garibaldi as 'my saint', and like Viola keeps a picture of this leader on his wall.)

From Conrad's letters (*LCG*, 157–8) we know that Santiago Pérez Triana was used in the book. He was the son of a Liberal President of Colombia who had been ousted during a revolution; and his numerous publications (such as *Down the Orinoco in a Canoe*, 1902, and his contribution to the *Cambridge Modern History*, vol. XII, 1910) show that he was a patriot who looked with sadness on the waste and misrule of Colombia's past and hoped that foreign investment (particularly British) might establish a future of peace and justice. His ideals doubtless contributed to those of Don José Avellanos in the novel. In appearance, however, Pérez Triana was short and stout, and much unlike the ageing, ailing, elder statesman of Costaguana; so it is possible that while he lent his ideas to Avellanos, he lent his body to Don Juste López, the eventual President of independent Sulaco.

Literary sources

1 F. B. Williams (pseudonym of H. E. Hamblen): *On Many Seas: The Life and Exploits of a Yankee Sailor*, 1897. This gave the story of

Nicolo, the silver-thief: the basis for the narrative of Nostromo's theft of silver.

2 G. F. Masterman's *Seven Eventful Years in Paraguay*, 1869. This provided many names of people and places: Don Carlos Decoud, Mitchell, Padre Corbelán, Gould, Barrios, Captain Fidanza, the Blancos, and 'the Cerro Santo Tomás, a bold square mountain' (equivalent to the square San Tomé mountain in *Nostromo*). Conrad's descriptions of Guzmán Bento and Pedrito Montero may derive partly from Masterman's description of the tyrant López. The torturing of Monygham and others by the sadistic priest, Father Berón, was probably suggested by Masterman's account of his own tortures at the hands of Padre Román. The parrot that cries 'Viva Costaguana' in the novel is the offspring of the parrot that cries 'Viva Pedro Segundo' in Masterman; and even the phrase 'Gran bestia!' uttered by Decoud can be found in *Seven Eventful Years*.

3 E. B. Eastwick: *Venezuela*, 1868. This offered various names: Mount Higuerota, Sotillo, Guzmán, Ribera and Amarilla; and its description of Puerto Cabello provided a basis for the description of Sulaco harbour and the Golfo Plácido beyond. More interestingly, Eastwick recalls the 'reigning beauty' of Valencia, Antonia Ribera, a Europeanised, well-educated, emancipated girl with blue eyes and rich brown hair, who is said not to wish to marry anyone but a foreigner: evidently a relative of Antonia Avellanos.

Eastwick also recalls an embarrassing moment at a banquet when the Venezuelan President toasted him with the vulgar words: 'I drink to the gentleman who has brought us thirty thousand pounds.' Conrad magnifies this incident in Pt I, Chap. 8 ('I drink to the health of the man who brings us a million and a half of pounds', says Montero). In Eastwick, there is an account of the Venezuelan army: 'lean old scarecrows and starveling boys not five feet high, the greater number half naked, with huge strips of raw beef twisted round their hats or hanging from their belts.' Conrad, avid for unexpected and therefore vivid detail, pounced on the beef: his version is: 'Emaciated greybeards rode by the side of lean dark youths, marked by all the hardship of campaigning, with strips of raw beef twined round the crowns of their hats.'

4 Other books. Ramón Páez's *Wild Scenes in South America*, 1863, provided descriptions of flora and fauna and anecdotes about General Páez. (Conrad's selective use of this minor source will be discussed in a later section.) Garibaldi's memoirs provided the name Anzani, hints for the character of Hernández, details of Garibaldi's career, and particularly the account of the torture by *strappado* which was the basis for Conrad's description of Hirsch's torture. Anatole France's essay 'Mérimée', as we have noted previously, contributed to the characterisation of Decoud. Cunninghame Graham's *A Vanished Arcadia* and *Hernando de Soto* repeatedly suggested

that modern 'progress' might really entail the despoliation of South America. Lastly, R. F. Burton's *Letters from the Battle-fields of Paraguay* (1870) describes the havoc wrought by the campaigns of the tyrant Francisco Solano López and mentions a Don Juan Decoud, the promising son of a distinguished family, who edits a Liberal newspaper.

5 Newspapers and periodicals. In the decade before the publication of *Nostromo*, Conrad had had work published in the magazines *Cosmopolis*, *Blackwood's* and *The New Review*; he took *The Times* and was an avid reader of *The Saturday Review* (which published material by such acquaintances of his as Graham, Shaw and Wells). Anyone who, as I have done, devotes some time to browsing among those periodicals soon recognises that *Nostromo* emerges from the international news and political debates of the day with the inevitability of a battleship emerging from the clamour and bustle of a war-time shipyard. Imperialism, both martial and economic, was the dominant topic, as Britain found that her power was being challenged by new rivals, particularly by the United States and Germany; and around the turn of the century, Central and South American affairs figured prominently in the news: there was the Spanish-American War, during which Spain lost Cuba and the Philippines, and later there was the United States' intervention in Colombia at the secession of Panama (1903). Of course, the turbulent unrest in the unstable South American republics (and the perils of investing in them) had often enough, during the mid to late nineteenth century, been a topic of regretful comment in the British papers; prominent coverage had been given to the war between Chile, Peru and Bolivia over the Atacama nitrate fields (1879–84), the war mentioned in Pt I, Chap. 6, of *Nostromo* (p. 76). One of the key-notes of the novel is the recurrent phrase 'material interests', and this phrase was a cliché of political debates in the press. On 24 February 1900, for example, the Liberal magazine *The Speaker*, which subsequently published work by Conrad, contained an article by George Russell ('The Revival of Imperialism') which says: 'Today.....We see lust of territory, lust of gold, lust of blood; the idolatry of material interests; the shameless repudiation of all moral appeals.'

Even a small and apparently implausible detail of the plot may possibly have been suggested by a newspaper item. In Pt II, Chap. 8, of the book, the lighter carying the silver, Nostromo, Decoud and Hirsch collides with Sotillo's troop-ship. Hirsch vanishes from the lighter during the collision, and Nostromo thinks he has drowned; but Hirsch reaches shore as a prisoner, having amazingly transferred himself to the larger vessel during the moments of contact. I find that at the end of January 1898 the British ship *Ardoe* collided in the English Channel with the French ship *Burgese Strasbourg*: the *Ardoe* had to be beached to prevent her sinking, and her steward vanished (and was presumed drowned) during the collision; but when the *Burgese Strasbourg* limped into Dunkirk, *The Times* was able to report that 'She had on board the missing steward of the *Ardoe*, who climbed on board the French ship when the two vessels were in contact'. (*Times*, 2 February 1898, p. 7.)

THE TREATMENT OF THE SOURCE-MATERIALS

> It dissolves, diffuses, dissipates, in order to re-create; or where this process is rendered impossible, yet still at all events it struggles to idealize and unify. It is essentially *vital*, even as all objects (*as* objects) are essentially fixed and dead.
>
> (Coleridge on the 'secondary imagination':
> *Biographia Literaria*, Chap. 13)

From the heterogeneous source-materials Conrad derived names and phrases, bits of plot, palettes of 'local colour', historical references, political arguments and thematic motifs. Conrad's creative imagination strove to co-ordinate and unify this material, to heighten its vividness and to charge it with moral significance. His aims were mimetic – to offer an imitation of the life that might be found in a South American state; they were kathartic, for his personal fears and tensions also sought expression; they were dialectical, for he was engaged in a complex debate with his cultural environment; and they were symbolic, for his urge to compress and relate significances generated symbols.

Here is just one instance of Conrad's ability to vivify his source-material. Among his books was Ramón Páez's *Wild Scenes in South America* (Sampson Low, London, 1863), a memoir of South American life with numerous descriptions of the flora and fauna; and I notice that on page 163 Páez writes:

> Less imposing than the preceding [the tiger owl] – although more terrifying in their way – are the *ya acabó* and the *pavita* – two other species of owl considered harbingers of calamity or death, when heard fluttering around a house. The first portends an approaching death among the inmates, and is therefore looked upon with dread even by men who would not flinch at the sight of the most formidable bull or jaguar. Yet that appalling cry, *ya acabó*! *ya acabó*! – it is finished! it is finished! – seems so fraught with evil mystery, that few hear it unmoved.

In Pt III, Chap. 8, of Conrad's novel, *Nostromo*, having swum ashore from the gulf, wonders whether Teresa Viola may be still alive.

> As if in answer to this thought, half of remorse and half of hope, with a soft flutter and oblique flight, a big owl, whose appalling cry: 'Ya-acabó! Ya-acabó! – it is finished; it is finished' – announces calamity and death in the popular belief, drifted vaguely

like a large dark ball across his path. In the downfall of all the realities that made his force, he was affected by the superstition, and shuddered slightly. Signora Teresa must have died, then. It could mean nothing else. The cry of the ill-omened bird, the first sound he was to hear on his return, was a fitting welcome for his betrayed individuality. The unseen powers which he had offended by refusing to bring a priest to a dying woman were lifting up their voice against him. She was dead . . . . . A man betrayed is a man destroyed. Signora Teresa (may God have her soul!) had been right. He had never been taken into account . . . . . The anger of her denunciations appeared to him now majestic with the awfulness of inspiration and of death. For it was not for nothing that the evil bird had uttered its lamentable shriek over his head. She was dead – may God have her soul!

(418–9, 420)

The echoes of phrasing ('appalling cry', 'it is finished!', 'calamity and death') make quite clear that Conrad took the owl from Páez's text. But whereas Páez was simply reporting on the fauna of South America, Conrad incorporates this detail not merely to provide plausible local colour but also as to make varied comment on its context, so that the owl gains symbolic force. The owl's cry suggests to Nostromo that Teresa must be dead; by reminding him of her, it recalls to him Teresa's repeated claims that he was betraying himself by serving Mitchell and Gould; and his increasing sense that she was right is reinforced by guilt, for instead of fetching the priest that the dying woman had begged for, he had served the company by sailing the silver-boat. The emergence of superstitious credulities from beneath his egoistic scepticism is part of that under-mining process which will lead him to let Decoud die and to steal the silver. The owl's ominous cry is one of the many supernatural elements in the narrative – the first of these being introduced in the book's opening pages, with their account of the haunted Punta Mala. Conrad's treatment of source-material tends not only to heighten significance but also to multiply ironies. The bird's 'It is finished!' is taken by Nostromo to refer to Teresa; but it refers too, in a sense, to Nostromo: for now his career, as an honest, untroubled overseer and factotum, is finished forever.

Nostromo *and the meanings of its techniques*

In this discussion, I initially offer some reminders of the book's problematic techniques; next, I discuss the plot, or rather the view of history suggested by a plot-summary; and thirdly, by looking closely at two important passages, I bring together the previous findings. What emerges is a political reading of the novel's techniques which indicates a closer and more constructive relationship between technique and plot than some of the more influential commentators have detected.

Problematic mobility

When we first begin *Nostromo*, one of our strongest impressions is of a bewildering mobility – a kaleidoscopic quality accompanied by an extremity of irony and a conceptual jaggedness. There are constant shifts in perspective: we're shifted from person to person, from area to area, from one time to another; there's a bright vividness and knobbly concreteness of description, yet also a commentary of aloofly sceptical generalisations. At one minute we're down in the thick of the crowd, being jostled against Nostromo's silver saddle-gear, and at the next we're taking a bird's-eye view of events and places, looking far along the coast and out across the Golfo Plácido. There's an epic scope and a solipsistic undertow. What is prominent and solid in one section dissolves and fades in the next. The wheels of the carts aren't simply wooden: they're of solid wood marked with 'the strokes of the axe' – they're *that* solid; yet during the night in the Placid Gulf, the world and the self seem about to dissolve into mere blackness.

Tolstoy's *War and Peace* has comparable scale and scope, a similar desire to relate great to small, public to private and general to particular; but its exposition is relatively smooth and steady, whereas *Nostromo* is jumpy, pouncy, twisting. One of the characteristics of *Nostromo* which clearly differentiates it from previous novels, English and Continental, is an extreme *mobility of viewpoint*. And under that general heading could be listed the following four sub-headings: 1. *Temporal* mobility. There are unexpected juxtapositions of events from different times; and Conrad is fond of delaying our decoding of large and small effects: experiences are thrust at us before we are in a position to comprehend their significance. 2. There is extreme *visual* mobility. As noted, sometimes we are on the ground, sometimes we are taking a mountain's-eye view of events on the plain. 3. There is considerable *narratorial* mobility – mobility between informants. Towards the end of the book, much essential information is provided by Captain Mitchell's address to a visitor, and we have to allow for ways in which the information may be distorted by his personality or falsified by his ignorance. At another point, we are dependent on a letter being written by Decoud; and we have to make similar allowances. It is true that for much of the time we have the guidance of, ostensibly, an omniscient anonymous narrator who sounds much like Conrad; yet at the opening of Chap. 8 in Pt I, this narrator actually identifies himself as a mere character, an anonymous visitor to Costaguana: one of those 'whom business or curiosity took to

Sulaco in these years before the first advent of the railway'. As this narrator soon resumes the customary spectral mobility of most fictional omnisciences (eavesdropping on solitaries, drifting through skulls), we may wonder why Conrad bothered briefly to give him a local habitation and identity. The reason is partly psychological: Conrad, like Eliot in *The Waste Land*, needs to don a mask, however transparent, in order to speak most eloquently. In *Heart of Darkness*, many subversive things are said in the course of Marlow's tale; and Conrad, if criticised for such observations, could always say: 'Look again: the opinions are identified as Marlow's; they are not necessarily mine.'

The fourth kind of mobility is *analogical* mobility, which generates many ironies. This is a common device of novels and longer poems, though *Nostromo* uses it more systematically and searchingly than most. The critic Cleanth Brooks once said that in *The Waste Land* we are repeatedly shown apparent similarities which reveal underlying contrasts, and apparent contrasts which reveal underlying similarities. In *Nostromo* this technique interlinks numerous characters and historical phases. For example: Nostromo and Gould, though outwardly so different from each other, are both corrupted by their possession of silver (or in their possession by it); and Dr Monygham's love for Mrs Gould is compared with a secret store of unlawful treasure, so Monygham is thus linked to the Nostromo he distrusts. Decoud, shortly before his death by pistol-shot, repeatedly thinks of himself as a man suspended by both hands from a tense, thin cord; thus we are reminded of Hirsch, who before his own death by pistol-shot was suspended by both hands from the tense, thin cord of the *strappado*. Don Carlos Gould, the financial king of Sulaco who is so frequently seen as a proudly equestrian figure, is juxtaposed with the equestrian statue of King Carlos IV of Spain, the last of the Spanish emperors of South America: which raises the question of whether, for all the appearances of progress, the old story is being repeated – the story of exploiters and exploited, of overlords and the subjugated, of imperialism whether martial or economic. (As Gould succeeds, so he becomes more stonily statuesque himself; and when he prevails, the old statue of King Carlos is removed as 'an anachronism'.)

A Marxist narrative?

In such ways the techniques throw us about, ambush and exercise us. And when we have survived those ambushes and can look back on *Nostromo*, the main pattern of Costaguana's history emerges clearly enough; and the pattern has some distinctive similarities to that detected in (or imposed on) history by Marxists. We have noted that from 1897 onwards, Conrad's closest literary friendship was with Cunninghame Graham. This celebrated – indeed notorious – campaigner was he whom Engels described as 'Communist, Marxian, advocating the nationalisation of all means of production'. Distinctly relevant to *Nostromo* is the fact that Graham, who had prospected for gold in Spain, had spent several years adventuring in Central and South America; and in his books on South American history (which Conrad read with great pleasure) he had sardonically drawn ironic parallels between the predatory activities of the Spanish conquistadores long ago and the more hypocritically predatory activities of British, European and North American economic imperialists in modern times. Of course, even before Conrad had met Cunninghame Graham, Conrad's writings had displayed some of those features which give that apparently Marxist quality to *Nostromo*. We have seen that from the start, in *Almayer's Folly* and *An Outcast of the Islands*, he had taken a thoroughly sceptical view of human activities: he had distrusted idealistic and pious rhetoric and had been prompt to suggest the power of economic self-interest operating behind a smoke-screen of noble talk. However, it is not coincidental that with the arrival of Cunninghame Graham a new incisiveness enters Conrad's political thought.

In *Nostromo*, numerous aspects of the plot bring Marxism to mind. Firstly, there is the recurrent emphasis on economics as a key to history, with the quest for material gain providing the main structure beneath the cultural superstructure. Secondly, there is the related suggestion that even if men are not the puppets of a method of production ('Your very ideas', said Marx and Engels, 'are the outgrowth of your bourgeois means of production'), in the long run the success of men's schemes depends on the compatibility of those schemes with international economic forces. For example: Decoud has the idea that Sulaco should secede from Costaguana, thus becoming a separate state, and his scheme comes to fulfilment: an individual's imagination seems to have changed history. But his scheme succeeds because, among other reasons, there is a show of force by the United States: we are told that the US warship *Powhattan* was the first to salute the flag of Sulaco; and the reason for the North American show of force is that a lot of North American capital is invested in the Sulaco silver-mine. (The immediate historical precedent for this part of the novel was the secession of Panama from Colombia in 1903, a secession ensured by the arrival of US warships: thus the United States effectively seized control of Panama and its canal. 'What do you think of the Yankee Conquistadores in Panama? Pretty, isn't it?' said Conrad sarcastically to Cunninghame Graham.)

A third feature of *Nostromo* which brings Marxism to mind is the book's emphasis on the ways in which a state's political apparatus can be manipulated in the interests of the wealthy. The best example is provided by Gould's increasing power. Initially, when he plans to re-develop the silver-mine, he says:

'What is wanted here is law, good faith, order, security. Any one can declaim about these things, but I pin my faith to material interests. Only let the material interests once get a firm footing, and they are bound to impose the conditions on which alone they can continue to exist. That's how your money-making is justified here in the face of lawlessness and disorder. It is justified because the security which it demands must be shared with an oppressed people. A better justice will come afterwards. That's your ray of hope.'

(84)

However, in order to get the mine established, Gould has to resort to bribery on such a large scale that it soon looks as though the cheaper option will be to finance a revolution which will bring to power a so-called dictator, Ribiera, who is pledged to serve the cause of the mine and of foreign investors generally. Yet this in turn engenders a further revolution: the Montero brothers, seeking wealth and power for themselves, are able to exploit nationalist feeling against the foreign investors, racial hostility against the whites, and class feeling against the aristocratic land-owning class; Ribiera is overthrown, and Pedro Montero invades the rich province of Sulaco. For a while the fate of the province hangs in the balance, but eventually the Monterist army is repulsed, the independence of Sulaco is assured and the new state seems to prosper. Nevertheless, near the end of the novel, bitter reflections on Gould's initial hopes for a new era of justice are cast by two of the most reliable commentators on events. Dr Monygham says:

'There is no peace and no rest in the development of material interests. They have their law, and their justice. But it is founded on expediency, and is inhuman; it is without rectitude, without the continuity and the force that can be found only in a moral principle. Mrs Gould, the time approaches when all that the Gould concession stands for shall weigh as heavily upon the people as the barbarism, cruelty, and misrule of a few years back.'

(511)

And Mrs Gould accepts his wisdom:

She saw the San Tomé mountain hanging over the Campo, over the whole land, feared, hated, wealthy; more soulless than any tyrant, more pitiless and autocratic than the worst Government; ready to crush innumerable lives in the expansion of its greatness.

(521)

Now it is certainly true that against these oft-quoted pessimistic opinions we have to set, among other things, the optimism of Captain Mitchell. He looks with complacent pride on new Sulaco, with its railways, department stores and clubs; and for him indeed an era of poverty and bloody civil wars seems finally to have been superseded by a tranquil era in which, under parliamentary government, property-owners like himself can look forward to a peaceful retirement enhanced by the income from their shares in the mine, while, in his view, the masses can enjoy peace, security and a steadily-improving material standard of living. However, we have been given numerous indications that the inner stability and composure of Mitchell depend on a certain thickness of skull; he is honest, generous and reliable, but fails to see the inner pattern of events. Near the end of the novel, the political situation in Sulaco is this: the mine-workers have reached a point of class-consciousness; we are told that they are not likely ever again to take up arms to defend the owners. A communist party has developed, and the workers are being urged to rise against the capitalist exploiters. There are predictions of warfare on two fronts. Antonia Avellanos, Bishop Corbelán and the political refugees from inland Costaguana are plotting a further revolution which would annex Costaguana to Sulaco; and meanwhile Hernández, the ex-bandit who had once supported Gould, has offered himself as military leader to the agitators who hope to 'raise the country with the new cry of wealth for the people'.

So far, so Marxist: apparently an exemplary demonstration of the way in which capitalism, emerging from feudalism, re-shapes in its own interests the political institutions of a country, thrives and prospers for a while, but eventually, through the tendency to monopoly and the creation of a vast and discontented work-force, reaches the phase of internal contradiction which ensures its own downfall. But, of course, the novel offers certain complications.

The most obvious complication is provided by the very pejorative presentation of the Marxist agitator who sits by the bedside of the dying Nostromo. (He's a later version of Donkin, who in *The Nigger of the 'Narcissus'* sits at the bedside of the dying negro, waiting to steal his money.) The agitator is 'pale. . . . ., small, frail, blood-thirsty'. He asks Nostromo to bequeath his wealth to the cause, saying 'We want money for our work. The rich must be fought with their own weapons.' Now this seems an eminently practical request: more practical than offering pious prayers for a change of hearts, for an increase in benevolence and brotherly feeling. Yet the silver had been regarded as a weapon by Gould, too; and he had discovered that it was a double-edged weapon, 'dangerous to the wielder'. Who guards the guardian? The novel has offered numerous examples of men's judgements being corrupted by the possession of the silver, or by the prospects of possessing it; and all too often the material means to some imagined good has perverted the end or become an end in itself: Gould had reached the point of preferring to be blown sky-high with his mine rather than let the wealth fall into anyone else's hands. One of the factors which makes the weapon of wealth two-edged and dangerous is the short-sightedness of the wielder. The Marxist looks like being even more short-sighted than Gould, for while sitting at Nostromo's bedside he says: 'You have refused all aid from that doctor. Is he really a dangerous enemy of the people?' The reason why Nostromo has refused all aid from Dr Monygham is primarily guilt: the doctor suspects that Nostromo has stolen the silver, and Nostromo senses the suspicions. An obvious irony implicit in the Marxist's question is the possibility that Dr Monygham, who in the past had suffered crippling torture at the hands of a dictator, may in the future suffer again, at the hands of one who proclaims the liberation of the oppressed. Another and more general implication is that the old story of the manipulation and exploitation of the many by the few may extend a long time into the future: there may be changes of slogans and changes of masters, but the rapacity, the bloodshed and the parasitism will continue.

And this possibility brings us aptly to the next complication, the matter of the time-shifts. One of the most influential commentators on this novel, Jocelyn Baines, has offered this theory to account for the shifts:

> The elimination of progression from one event to another . . . . . has the effect of implying that nothing is ever achieved. By the end of the book we are virtually back where we started; it looks as if the future of Costaguana will be very similar to her past.
>
> (Baines, 301)

'Nothing is ever achieved'. A technical innovation is, according to this theory, translatable into a conservative political recommendation: man should resign himself to the fact that he is incapable of making improvements in his condition. We can test this opinion by looking at two of the most striking examples of the time-shifts in *Nostromo*.

The time-shifts: two examples

The first of these is the presentation of Dictator Ribiera's escape. We first hear of this in Pt I, Chap. 2. We have been introduced to Captain Mitchell, and we eavesdrop on some of his recollections:

> The political atmosphere of the Republic was generally stormy in these days. The fugitive patriots of the defeated party had the knack of turning up again on the coast with half a steamer's load of small arms and ammunition. Such resourcefulness Captain

Mitchell considered as perfectly wonderful in view of their utter destitution at the time of flight. He had observed that 'they never seemed to have enough change about them to pay for their passage ticket out of the country'. And he could speak with knowledge; for on a memorable occasion he had been called upon to save the life of a Dictator, together with the lives of a few Sulaco officials . . . . . belonging to an overturned government. Poor Señor Ribiera (such was the Dictator's name) had come pelting eighty miles over mountain tracks after the lost battle of Socorro, in the hope of outdistancing the fatal news – which, of course, he could not manage to do on a lame mule. The animal, moreover, expired under him at the end of the Alameda, where the military band plays sometimes in the evenings between the revolutions. . . . .

. . . . . As the Dictator was execrated by the populace on account of the severe recruitment law his necessities had compelled him to enforce during the struggle, he stood a good chance of being torn to pieces. Providentially, Nostromo – invaluable fellow – with some Italian workmen, imported to work upon the National Central Railway, was at hand, and managed to snatch him away – for the time at least. Ultimately, Captain Mitchell succeeded in taking everybody off in his own gig to one of the Company's steamers. . . . . To the very last he had been careful to address the ex-Dictator as 'Your Excellency'.

'Sir, I could do no other. The man was down – ghastly, livid, one mass of scratches.'

(11, 12, 14)

And the chapter concludes by telling us how the indispensable Nostromo and his men had dispersed the mob.

Here the person reading the novel for the first time is likely to conclude that that little episode of history is closed. He will regard it as a retrospect, and will assume that the subsequent narrative will take him into the future. He will naturally think that the account of Ribiera's flight has just two simple functions: to set the scene generally by exemplifying the past political turmoil of the region, and to illustrate the characters of Mitchell and Nostromo, who may be important figures in the subsequent tale. Now certainly the information about Nostromo and Mitchell is very useful; but what is deceptive is the impression that the Ribiera incident is past history and finished with. For Chap. 3, the next chapter, instead of taking us forward in time, plunges us back into the middle of the events Mitchell had mentioned, and the narrative as it proceeds gradually spirals *back* in time; so that about a hundred pages after the account of Ribiera's downfall, we are told of the circumstances of his first presidential visit to Sulaco at the inauguration of his régime. Not until Chap. 8 are we shown how his reformist régime had been brought into existence by means of the money of Gould and Holroyd; and we are told:

> He was more pathetic than promising, this first civilian Chief of the State Costaguana had ever known, pronouncing, glass in hand, his simple watchwords of honesty, peace, respect for law, political good faith abroad and at home – the safeguards of national honour.

(119)

Then the narrative slowly spirals forward in time, so that many pages later, in Chap. 7 of Pt II, another character reports as yesterday's occurrence the very event that Mitchell had described at the beginning of the book. Decoud writes: 'The missing President, Ribiera, ... has turned up here. . . . . . riding on a lame mule into the very midst of the street fighting.' (221)

Thus the narrative has reversed the normal sequence and overthrown conventional expectations. What seemed to be preliminary and peripheral proved to be a central event; a passing episode proved to be a retrospect to a time that had yet to be presented in detail. What are the purposes of this deviousness?

Firstly, and fairly trivially, this technique gives an unusual plausibility to the fictional historical events. When one character, near the middle of the novel, reports as yesterday's occurrence an incident that a different character, early in the novel, had reported from a different viewpoint and with a different emphasis, the incident acquires a stereoscopic quality. Secondly, and less trivially, the method gives a radical and tentacular quality to the ironies. If normal chronological narration had been used, we would have learned first about Ribiera's pious hopes at the inaugural banquet and much later about his ludicrous escape on a lame mule, and retrospective ironies would have flickered about the original scene. But the proleptic narration means that because we know from the start about his escape, we become thoroughly sceptical spectators at that banquet. As President-Dictator Ribiera raises his glass, our memories superimpose on his hopeful features the features of a battered fugitive, 'ghastly, livid, one mass of scratches'. The rhetoric at the dinner has an utterly hollow ring, because the context is a mocking echo-chamber to the speech – as mocking as the green parrot which reduces all political discussion to a shriek of 'Viva Costaguana!'

Thirdly, as Baines noted, the sense of history as cyclical and repetitive plays against the sense that history displays a steady evolution. As the narrative impinges on us, Ribiera has his downfall, Ribiera is put into power, Ribiera has his downfall: a cycle. As we rearrange the impinging events to make orthodox narrative sense, Ribiera is established by the financial powers in order to safeguard their interests; he is overthrown; and out of the ensuing turmoil a new independent state emerges which for a time safeguards their interests; a state under President Juste López. In one sense, there is no going back: the modern state cannot be unmade. But in another sense, of which the narrative fluctuations have reminded us, there is a constant recurrence of folly and exploitation, though in varying forms.

Fourthly, and most importantly. The time-shifts and the related dislocations in the narrative have value *as resistances to be overcome*: for in this way they induce a complex moral and political therapy in the reader. Most commentators have failed to notice that there is a curiously close connection between what the novel diagnoses as man's political limitations and what the novel in all its technical richness and deviousness is designed to do. In the 'Author's Note' to *Nostromo*, Conrad says that the book displays 'the passions of men short-sighted in good and evil'. This preface emphasises the moral short-sightedness of men, and the narrative provides numerous examples of that myopia. There's Gould, unable to foresee the ways in which the mine may corrupt his judgement; Mitchell, complacent about the social changes and insensitive to the agonies entailed and the new strife to come; and Ribiera, failing to foresee the brevity of his régime. There are constant misjudgements of one character by another; some people sacrifice present life on the altar of an imagined future; others are blinded to the future by the immediate present. Conrad's oblique method induces in the reader the very flexibility that most of the people in the novel lack, and suffer from lacking. While demonstrating the political infancy of men, the novel embodies its political maturity in techniques which entail for the reader an education in that maturity. The basic structure of *Nostromo*, therefore, resembles that of St Paul's paradox: 'One of themselves, *even* a prophet of their own, said, The Cretians *are* alway liars. . . . . This witness is true.' By delaying the decoding of events, Conrad forces us to share the myopia of his characters; and by provoking the decoding, he provides the therapy which helps us to share his own keen vision.

One of the best commentators on the book, Albert Guerard, has taken a much more dubious and sceptical view of its techniques. He says:

> The first part of *Nostromo* invites and then frustrates the normal objectives of readers to an astonishing degree. A reader's first objective may be to identify with one figure and then use him as a post of observation. But each opportunity – Captain Mitchell, Giorgio Viola, Nostromo, Sir John, Mrs Gould, Charles Gould – is withdrawn almost as soon as offered. . . . . The common reader's notorious general aim – to enter into the book and become one

of its characters – is carefully and austerely baffled. The novelist
. . . . . maliciously chops at his hands.

(CN, 215)

In practice, we can and do decode the scrambled information; we
can and do reconstruct the calendar of historical events into regular
sequence. We falsify the novel's meaning if we over-emphasise either
the initial chronological flux or the deciphered chronological order,
either the contingency or the determinism. A strong patterning of
events emerges, but only after we have experienced the recalcitrance
of events; a clear historical viewpoint is established, but only after
we have been shown the ways in which history may falsify events by
smoothing out the knobbly awkwardness of their impact; and a
bleak and sombre view of man's capacities emerges, but only after
we have had the closest of contacts with the particular needs, drives
and sufferings of a variety of men. *Nostromo* is a fictional history
whose methods cast doubt on the human veracity – the fidelity to
the texture of life – of actual historians. Conrad would have agreed
fully with the spirit of Aristotle's remark, 'Poetry, therefore, is more
philosophical and of higher value than history, for history agglomer-
ates, whereas poetry unifies.' There is a historian in the novel itself
– Don José Avellanos, author of *Fifty Years of Misrule* – and there is
obvious irony in what happens to his work. Martin Decoud says:

> 'Hasn't he seen the sheets of *Fifty Years of Misrule*, which we have
> begun printing on the presses of the *Porvenir*, littering the Plaza,
> floating in the gutters, fired out as wads for trabucos loaded with
> handfuls of type, blown in the wind, trampled in the mud? I have
> seen pages floating upon the very waters of the harbour.'

(235)

Here Decoud sounds like the spokesman of a thoroughly cynical
novelist; so the second example of the time-shifts that I will consider
is provided by the treatment of the death of that speaker, Martin
Decoud; and this will be a way of testing Albert Guerard's claim
that the third part of *Nostromo* is marred by an 'uncertain or uselessly
wavering point of view.' (*CN*, 206.)

At the end of Chap. 8 of Pt II, Nostromo leaves Decoud on the
island, the Great Isabel. A boatload of silver is buried there. The
island offers a refuge to Decoud, because back in Sulaco the invading
forces of Pedrito Montero are seeking to capture him as a political
enemy. Decoud isn't marooned, exactly: Nostromo has said that he
will try to return to the island in a couple of days; and in any case,
Decoud – who has a rowing-boat – hopes to intercept a passing ship.
However, he is left there, and nobody sees him again. Not until
many chapters later, in Chap. 10 of Pt III, do we first hear of Decoud's
death. Years in the future, Captain Mitchell, reminiscing about the

history of Sulaco, takes a visitor into the cathedral and shows him a medallion on the wall. The inscription is 'To the memory of Martin Decoud, his betrothed Antonia Avellanos'; and Mitchell explains that it 'commemorates that unfortunate young gentleman who sailed out with Nostromo on that fatal night'. Later in the same chapter, the narrative at last spirals back through the years to give us a close-up, a full account of Decoud's death.

That account is one of the most important and resonant passages in the whole of Conrad's writings. The setting is the small island unvisited even by sea-birds, surrounded by the serene, silent and oppressive beauty of the Placid Gulf.

> Solitude from mere outward condition of existence becomes very swiftly a state of soul in which the affectations of irony and scepticism have no place. It takes possession of the mind, and drives forth the thought into the exile of utter unbelief. After three days of waiting for the sight of some human face, Decoud caught himself entertaining a doubt of his own individuality. It had merged into the world of cloud and water, of natural forces and forms of nature. In our activity alone do we find the sustaining illusion of an independent existence as against the whole scheme of things of which we form a helpless part.
>
> (497)

After seven days:

> Both his intelligence and his passion were swallowed up easily in this great unbroken solitude of waiting without faith. Sleeplessness had robbed his will of all energy, for he had not slept seven hours in the seven days. His sadness was the sadness of a sceptical mind. He beheld the universe as a succession of incomprehensible images.
>
> (498)

On the eleventh day, like a sleep-walker, waiting for the stretched cord of silence to snap, he weights his pockets with four bars of silver, gets into the rowing-boat and rows for a while towards the setting sun. Then at dawn he draws a revolver and shoots himself.

> The stiffness of the fingers relaxed, and the lover of Antonia Avellanos rolled overboard without having heard the cord of silence snap in the solitude of the Placid Gulf, whose glittering surface remained untroubled by the fall of his body.
>
> (501)

These pages describing the solitude and death of Decoud work potently and memorably, in spite of the fact that there are some narrative implausibilities, and even though Conrad does not let the reflections and actions of Decoud speak for themselves but supplies a great deal of sombrely pessimistic narratorial comment. One implausibility is that Decoud remains on the island when he could have used the rowing-boat to take himself away from that oppressive solitude to somewhere on the coast. Yet, in practice, few readers are troubled by this, because the death of Decoud has a strange inevitability; and few are troubled by the narrator's explicit judgements, even though, out of context, their extreme scepticism would provoke objections. What happens is that both the death and the comments on it form a thematic nexus: they sum up majestically in image and epigram some of the strongest thematic implications of the work, and those implications have been previously pressing on us, subliminally, in a great variety of ways.

When Decoud, close to death, beholds the universe as 'a succession of incomprehensible images', we sense that he may, hideously, be experiencing not a derangement but an insight, an insight into the central meaninglessness of the creation. This possible insight is something that we as novitiate readers of the book have experienced imaginatively every time we have been assailed and bewildered by the time-shifts, which have given both an impressionistic vividness and an initial disruption to events. At first our plight resembled that of the visitor to Costaguana who, on listening to Mitchell's reminiscences, was

> stunned and as it were annihilated mentally by a sudden surfeit of sights, sounds, names, facts, and complicated information imperfectly apprehended. . . . .

(486–7)

Of course, eventually, we have sorted out the images and given comprehensibility to the initially incomprehensible: the decoding, though often frustrated and delayed, has gradually become less difficult. But one of the most important effects of this narrative method of delayed decoding is that the final deciphering never quite erases that initial sense that perhaps the universe, truly perceived, may be recalcitrant before all man's decoding efforts. Conrad had told Cunninghame Graham: 'Life knows us not and we do not know life – we don't know even our own thoughts.' (*LCG*, 65.)

And just as Decoud's sense of radical meaninglessness has been given some imaginative validity by the initial effects of the narrative techniques, so the extreme scepticism of the narrator's commentary does not seem forced or obtrusive, but simply gives explicit crystallisation to what we have sensed often enough already in the course of the narrative's convolutions and abruptnesses. When we are being thrown about from one time and incident to another, we tend to seek sanctuary in the few constant features; and throughout the temporal changes, for all the shifts of action in the foreground, the scenic background has remained constant. Again and again we have been reminded, in appropriately majestic eloquence, of the enduring, impassive, non-human onlookers of events – the Placid Gulf itself, the cool and unchanging snow-capped Cordilleras, and the vastly serene and icy Mount Higuerota. So when the glittering surface of the Placid Gulf remains untroubled by the fall of Decoud's body, this comes as a seemingly inevitable illustration of the narrator's maxim about 'the whole scheme of things of which we form a helpless part'; and that maxim in turn seems the inevitable inference from a wealth of scenic evidence.

As for the *political* implications of that maxim about 'the whole scheme of things', they are not quite what they first seem to be. The easy reading is to say that they are classically conservative: men may come and men may go, but in the long run the Godless non-human environment prevails: in the long run, man is impotent. However, if we remember that *Nostromo* first appeared in 1904, when the European nations were still disputing about their acquisitions in Africa (with France claiming control of Morocco, while the British sought hegemony in Egypt), one implication is clearly anti-imperialistic, for it associates imperial activity by nations with the action which is only a sustaining 'illusion' in individuals.

If Conrad had followed orthodox chronological order, the death of Decoud would have been described long *before* Mitchell's résumé of the subsequent events. The time-shift method enables Conrad to reverse the orthodox order, so that the death-scene follows almost immediately *after* that long complacent monologue of Mitchell about the ostensibly progressive evolution of Sulaco. For Mitchell, a backward province has at last become the treasure-house of the world; in his eyes, history has been progressive; and the story of Sulaco is for him a story with a happy ending. Man has mastered nature, and civilised man has mastered society: so he thinks. And directly after these reflections, thanks to the method of chronological dislocation, Conrad can deploy the most vivid example of man's littleness. With the death of Decoud, the novel's paradoxes reach their culmination. Scepticism is validated in a scene which yet shows the self-destruction of the sceptic. Conrad says in effect, 'Behold the fate of the sceptic – and beware'; yet he also suggests sceptically that men are puppets; and he also proceeds with a survey of nature and history which has olympian power and authority.

One of the best commentaries on the political meaning of *Nostromo* is the essay 'Autocracy and War', which we discussed in an earlier section. There Conrad argued that the governments of states, like individual men, are in moral infancy. Fearing destruction, they react aggressively.

> The idea of ceasing to grow in territory, in strength, in wealth, in influence – in anything but wisdom and self-knowledge – is

odious to them as the omen of an end.....Let us act lest we perish – is the cry.

(NLL, 109)

So there he commends not aggressive action but 'wisdom and self-knowledge': a phrase which, in the essay, may sound suspiciously vague and cloudy. It begs many questions; it needs many examples. But in fact the novel *Nostromo* had answered many of those questions and provided the examples. The wisdom that Conrad had commended in the novel, by implication and through irony, had entailed ample indignation on behalf of the humble, the exploited and the cannon-fodder of history. The wisdom had entailed ample scepticism, about political jargon and rhetoric, about the possibility that a just society could ever be found under conditions of economic imperialism, and about the maturity of man as a political animal. Yet that wisdom had entailed a hope that can be glimpsed in the challenges offered to us by the novel's shifts in time and space, with their therapy for short-sightedness: a hope that some people may work towards maturity by developing and increasing the ability to apply to the present the lessons of the past, to have foresight which does not require the sacrifice of the life of the present, and to test all general doctrines by mobile responsiveness to individual human experience. As Mrs Gould reflects: 'For life to be large and full, it must contain the care of the past and of the future in every passing moment of the present.' (520–1.)

In 'Autocracy and War', Conrad says that it is 'our sympathetic imagination to which alone we can look for the ultimate triumph of concord and justice'. This imagination, he claims, has been a slumbering faculty; and 'direct vision.....or the stimulus of a great art, can alone make it turn and open its eyes heavy with blessed sleep.' When the techniques of *Nostromo* have opened our eyes, we may look on that work not, finally, as 'a succession of incomprehensible images', but rather as the engineer looked on the enormous side of Mount Higuerota,

> thinking that in this sight, as in a piece of inspired music, there could be found together the utmost delicacy of shaded expression and a stupendous magnificence of effect.

(40)

Chronological tables and maps for Nostromo

Introduction

The provision of maps and histories for fictitious lands has certain analogies with the project of the academician of Lagado to extract sunbeams from cucumbers, except that the academician's project was possibly more practical and scientific, and certainly more euphonious. Nevertheless the following observations should be made.

In Tables A and B, events are provided with dates on the basis of their linkage with known historical events, or of internal consistency, or of general plausibility (which is a mixture of the previous criteria). Thus, Gould's grandfather had fought, we are told, at the Battle of Carabobo; and that historical event took place in 1821. Again, at Gould's meeting with Holroyd in San Francisco, Holroyd refers to the long war over the Atacama nitrate fields as though it had reached its completion. The war lasted from 1879 to 1884; so this is one of the reasons for giving their meeting the date 1884, which in turn makes 1890 a probable year for the main action of the novel. During that main action, the text tells us, Gould is thirty; so 1860 thereby becomes the most reasonable date for his birth; and the final stage of the narrative cannot be much earlier than 1900, if Mrs Gould's 'clear vision of the grey hairs on his temples' refers to present fact rather than future vista. Obviously, certain of the dates I have ascribed to events may well be corrigible, just as my tables correct various errors in the earlier chronological lists by H. S. Spatt (*Conradiana* VIII, 1976, pp. 37–46) and Juliet McLauchlan (*Conrad: Nostromo*, Arnold, 1969, pp. 66–7), to which I remain indebted. (I am also indebted to the wise advice of Hans van Marle.)

The critical uses of such partly-conjectural chronologies are various; and my tables may have admirable or pernicious consequences. Pernicious, in the case of readers who merely seek a crib to enable them to strip a text to its paraphrasable plot for their notebooks. Admirable, for those who, rightly, have wrestled with the various resistances to facile comprehension of the plot that *Nostromo* offers (resistances designed to deflect attention from the superficial to the inner meaning of history) but who, perplexed, feel like retiring from the wrestling match: for the chronologies offer a reassurance that the opponent is in fact a wise mentor. If the reader has already formulated his chronologies, comparison of his with mine will entail a re-searching of the text which almost inevitably will bring fresh strengths to light: it is that kind of text.

Much the same account may be made of the maps. To a surprisingly large degree, the topographical references in *Nostromo* are specific and internally consistent. This precision in the establishment of locations encourages us to construct a mental map of the imaginary region, and the mental map in turn clarifies the action. Cartographers of Sulaco are prompted by the textual information that the Great Isabel is 2 miles from the harbour mouth, Hermosa 1 mile; Sulaco 1 mile from the harbour, with Viola's house halfway between them; and that Rincón is 'a short league' (barely 3 miles) from Sulaco, while Sulaco is 3 leagues from the San Tomé mine. Compared with the number of such incentives, the deterrents are few. One deterrent is that the fictional Santa Marta resembles the real Santa Marta (of

Colombia) in being an important city and valley-centre with an Atlantic seaboard, but yet is far southward of its real namesake; a second deterrent is that though Los Hatos seems to be located in a direction east-south-east of the harbour, references on pp. 473 and 363 are anomalous; and a third is that the railhead appears to be both 80 and 180 miles from Sulaco town. (Tillyard postulated *two* railheads, to solve the problem, but the text refers only to one.) That the harbour of Sulaco is both 'oblong' and 'oval' constitutes no navigational hazard.

Previous maps of the Occidental Province are those by E. M. W. Tillyard (*The Epic Strain in the English Novel*, 1958, p. 203) and W. R. Martin (*Conradiana* VIII, 1976, pp. 165–6). Tillyard's has no set scale, places Rincón almost halfway between Sulaco and the mine, and lets the harbour-to-Rincón route through Sulaco have a west-to-east axis, whereas the text strongly indicates a north-to-south or northwest-to-southeast axis. Martin's maps respect this axial indication, but they place Rincón much closer to the mine than the text suggests. Martin also gives a map of the centre of the town of Sulaco. He locates the Intendencia on the east of the Plaza, whereas the text specifies that it faces Higuerota (which, of course, is to the east of the town) and therefore is on the west of the Plaza. Various putative anomalies are discussed by B. Kimpel and T. C. Duncan Eaves in *Modern Philology* 56 (1958), 45–54.

As with the chronological tables, the maps may be pernicious or constructive, depending on how they are used. As cribs, bad; as challenges and incentives, good. To become seduced by such details is to betray the novel; to ignore such details is to insult it. Above all, the very disparity between the linear clarity of the table or map and the rich bombardment of material deployed by the novel may help the reader to define for himself Conrad's methods and purposes.

Conrad's own subsequent comments on his works, in prefaces or letters, were not always reliable. In a letter of 1918 to Edmund Gosse, for example, he said that the main events of *Nostromo* take place in 'the seventh decade' of the nineteenth-century: yet such timing is too early to fit the text. However, the same letter to Gosse (published in the magazine *Thoth*, Syracuse University, Spring 1969) usefully emphasises that 'Sulaco is a synthetic product', a synthesis of many Central and South American regions; and he adds:

> The historical part is an achievement in mosaic too, though, personally, it seems to me much more true than any history I ever learned.

Thus we see how Conrad has again striven to reconcile concrete particularity with potent generality.

Table A   General chronology

Date	Event
16th and 17th centuries	Spanish colonialists develop Sulaco, establishing an ecclesiastical court there. Local trade in ox-hides and indigo. Silver-mine worked by slaves.
1821	Charles Gould's grandfather fights for Bolívar in British regiment at Battle of Carabobo.
1830	San Tomé mine reopens after War of Independence.
1831	Holroyd born.
1840	Monygham born.
1842–62	Giorgio Viola serves under Garibaldi, first at Montevideo, later in Italy.
1850–56	Epoch of civil war in Costaguana; federalism; Sulaco resists union.
1855	Charles Gould's Uncle Harry, President of Sulaco, defeated; shot by order of General Bento.
1856	Guzmán Bento inaugurates his own 'perpetual presidency'. Twelve years of peace begin.
1860	Charles Gould born; Martin Decoud born.
1864	Antonia Avellanos born.
1866	Nostromo born. Don José Avellanos and Dr Monygham arrested.
1867–68	Monygham tortured by Father Berón.
1868	Don José Avellanos pardoned; Bento dies; Monygham released. During the turmoil following Bento's death, the mine-workers kill their English masters; the mine is closed.
1868–74	Three governments come and go; the fourth obliges Gould's father to accept ownership of the mine.
1876	Linda Viola born.
1878	Giselle Viola born.
1884	Gould's father dies; Gould marries Emilia, and they travel to Sulaco; on the way, Gould talks to Holroyd at San Francisco.
1885	Holroyd visits Goulds; Goulds tour Sulaco seeking labour; mine is reopened.
1888	Holroyd and Gould finance revolution to install a compliant government. During the warfare, General Montero aids the Blanco (Conservative) Party. May: Don Vincente Ribiera elected 'President-Dictator'. November: Ribiera inaugurates National Central Railway at Sulaco.
1889	April: Montero rebels, abetted by his brother Pedrito. May: Decoud arrives in Sulaco with new rifles for Barrios.
1890–91	War of Separation which establishes the Occidental Province of Costaguana as the independent State of Sulaco. *See Table B.*
1897	Mitchell takes visitor on tour of Sulaco.

1898	Lighthouse built on Great Isabel.
1899	Mitchell returns to England, having appointed Viola lighthouse-keeper.
1900	Class conflict increasing. Prominent Sulacans (Corbelán, Hernández, Antonia Avellanos) plan war of annexation against Costaguana. Goulds return from European tour. Nostromo killed by Viola. Viola dies.

Table B   Chronology of central events

Date	Event
1888, May	Ribiera's 'dictatorship' begins.
1888, November	Railway inaugurated at Sulaco.
1889, April	General Montero rebels.
1890, April 21	Battle of Socorro: defeated by General Montero, Ribiera flees with Pedrito Montero in pursuit.
1890, April 27	Nostromo negotiates with Hernández on behalf of Blancos.
1890, April 28	General Barrios and his troops embark for Cayta. Decoud learns of Ribiera's defeat. Hernández offers aid.
1890, April 29	5 a.m.: Silver arrives in Sulaco.
1890, May 1	Rioting erupts. Hernández's aid is accepted.
1890, May 2	4 a.m.: Nostromo meets Decoud at *Porvenir* office and promises that the lightermen will support the Europeans.
	6 a.m. – noon: Sulacan authorities shelter at O.S.N. offices. Ribiera rides into the mob and is rescued by Nostromo and railwaymen. Decoud joins defenders of the Amarilla Club. Authorities escape on *Minerva*. Nostromo leads lightermen against mob and reaches Casa Viola. Hernández rides to Los Hatos to receive refugees.
	4 p.m. – 9 p.m.: Gamacho and Fuentes decide to lead the Monterist mob. Barrios reaches Cayta. López and others plan capitulation to Montero. Decoud proposes the secession of Sulaco from Costaguana. Pedrito Montero reaches railhead. Corbelán sets out to join Hernández.
1890, May 3	c. 1 a.m.–6 a.m.: Nostromo brings Decoud to Viola's and goes to fetch doctor for Teresa Viola.
	c. 6 a.m.: Pedrito leaves railhead. c. 7 a.m.: General Sotillo seizes ship at Esmeralda.
	c. 8 p.m.: Decoud writes to his sister from Casa Viola.
	c. 9 p.m.: Lighter sets out across Golfo Plácido. Refugees from Sulaco make for Los Hatos woods.
	c. 11.30 p.m.: Sotillo's vessel collides with lighter.
	11.50: Sotillo enters Sulaco harbour.

1890, May 4	Before dawn, Nostromo and Decoud bury silver on Great Isabel; Nostromo swims ashore as day breaks. Meanwhile Sotillo holds Mitchell and Monygham, releasing Mitchell at dawn. *c.* 7 a.m.: Don Juste asks Gould to welcome Pedrito. 8 a.m.: Pedrito arrives in Sulaco. *c.* 8.30 a.m.: Pedrito orates on the Plaza. *c.* 10–12: Gamacho orates.
	c. 6 p.m. Pedrito's messenger delivers demand to Pepe at mine. Pepe plans march on town. Gould defies Pedrito. *c.* 6.30: Nostromo awakens. Sotillo kills Hirsch. *c.* 7 p.m.: Nostromo and Monygham meet at Custom House: Monygham proposes the ride to Cayta.
1890, May 5	Travelling on the engine to the railhead, Nostromo begins his journey to Cayta to summon Barrios.
1890, May 15	At sunset, Decoud rows westward from the Great Isabel.
1890, May 16	At dawn, Decoud shoots himself.
1890, May 17	Nostromo sees Decoud's boat and rows it to Great Isabel. Barrios reaches Sulaco harbour and attacks Sotillo's ship, saving Monygham; Sotillo is killed. Pepe leads miners into Sulaco via Land Gate, saving Gould. Barrios captures Harbour Gate. Hernández presses from west.
1890, June, *c.* 1	Don Juste López promulgates new constitution; Barrios pursues Pedrito southwards; Gould prepares to leave for mission to San Francisco and Washington.
1891, *c.* May	Costaguana–Sulaco War ended by international naval demonstration in Sulaco harbour: US cruiser *Powhattan* salutes flag of Sulaco. General (now Emperor) Montero assassinated. The Occidental Province has become the Occidental Republic.

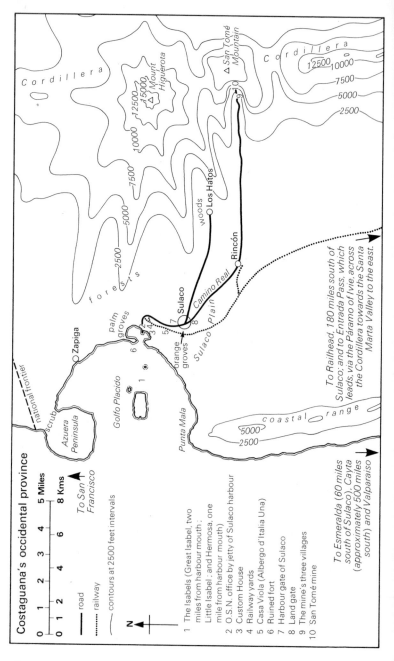

Costaguana's occidental province

road —————
railway ·················
contours at 2500 feet intervals

| Miles | 0 | 1 | 2 | 3 | 4 | 5 |
| Kms | 0 | 2 | 4 | 6 | 8 |

5 Kms / 8 Kms

To San Francisco

N

1 The Isabels (Great Isabel, two miles from harbour mouth; Little Isabel: and Hermosa, one mile from harbour mouth)
2 O.S.N. office by jetty of Sulaco harbour
3 Custom House
4 Railway yards
5 Casa Viola (Albergo d'Italia Una)
6 Ruined fort
7 Harbour gate of Sulaco
8 Land gate
9 The mine's three villages
10 San Tomé mine

To Railhead, 180 miles south of Sulaco; and to Entrada Pass, which leads, via the Páramo of Ivie, across the Cordillera towards the Santa Marta Valley to the east.

To Esmeralda (60 miles south of Sulaco), Cayta (approximately 500 miles south) and Valparaiso

Cordillera
△ San Tomé Mountain
C o r d i l l e r a
12500 10000
7500
5000
2500

Mount Higuerota
15,000 △
12500
15,000
10000

7500
5000
woods
Los Hatos

forests
2500
Rincón
Sulaco Plain
Camino Real

Sulaco
Orange groves
Palm groves
Zapiga
Golfo Placido
Azuera Peninsula
Scrub
national frontier
Punta Mala

c o a s t a l   r a n g e
5000
2500

164

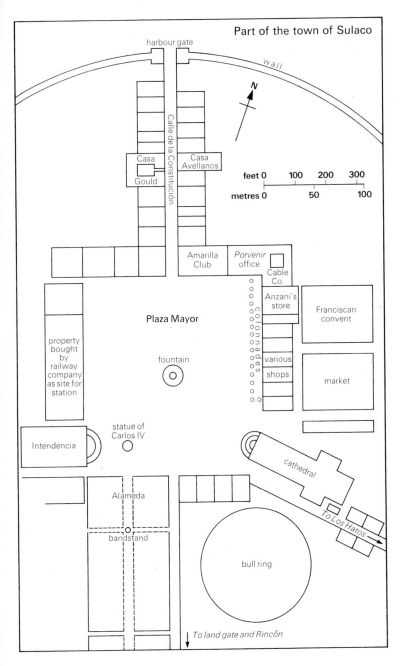

Part of the town of Sulaco

harbour gate

wall

N

Calle de la Constitución

Casa Gould

Casa Avellanos

feet 0   100   200   300

metres 0   50   100

Amarilla Club

Porvenir office

Cable Co.

Anzani's store

Franciscan convent

Plaza Mayor

colonnades

various shops

market

property bought by railway company as site for station

fountain

Intendencia

statue of Carlos IV

cathedral

To Los Hatos

Alameda

bandstand

bull ring

To land gate and Rincón

8 The Conradian Hero

Misgivings

The term 'the Conradian Hero' is very ambiguous. It could refer to a protagonist in the fiction who is conventionally heroic in conduct, or to a synthetic man made of the characteristics of several such people; it could refer to someone who though not conventionally heroic is still the protagonist of the work, the main character (is Kurtz the hero or the villain of *Heart of Darkness*?); to someone who though not the main character still has 'heroic' qualities, or represents some positive values which are important in the fictional discussion. Possibly the term 'a Conradian Hero' could be applied to someone in real life, outside the fiction: to someone like Captain Miłobędzki, for example, the Polish sea-captain, master of the sailing-ship *Dar Pomorza*, a distinguished, courteous, gentlemanly figure (with a scholar's enthusiasm for Conrad's works) who might himself have stepped from Conrad's pages. Again, the term might apply to so many of those self-sacrificing warriors of Poland who, say, in the ruins of Warsaw fought to the death against the Germans, and who were commemorated in Wajda's *Ashes and Diamonds* trilogy for the cinema.

Now what is suggested by these notions of 'Conradian heroes' outside the texts is that Conrad's works cumulatively do imply a model of admirable conduct: it is chivalric, noble and gentlemanly in its combination of courage, dignity and reticence; it is stoical, too, in the readiness to fight against overwhelming odds; and it may be without illusions in its view of man and history. Such an ethical model may be represented by Marlow, or implied by various anonymous narrators, or signalled by such memorable minor characters as the French lieutenant in *Lord Jim*.

But if we look back at the protagonists of the fictions, another reason for the difficulty in talking of 'the Conradian Hero' soon becomes clear. Conrad often likes to work against the grain, to invoke a convention only to question or complicate or subvert it. If he shows an Achilles, his interest lies in the Achilles' heel. Lord Jim looks like a romantic hero – yet he has been partly corrupted by his very dreams of being a romantic hero. The vulnerability of virtue – or its short-sightedness – is one of Conrad's preoccupations; so is his sense of tentacular evil, which sends out a tentacle to grip the seemingly sound and good: his heroes are drawn into complicity with corrupt kindred – Jim with Gentleman Brown, Heyst with Gentleman Jones. And just as Conrad subverts orthodox principles of plot-structure by 'building holes' (ellipses, elisions, perspectival shifts) into his plots, so he is capable of building holes into characterisation by leaving opaque or mysterious those areas which more orthodox writers would fill with ample biographical information.

The manipulations and fracturings of plot give enhanced importance to thematic connections, and the interlinkages established between characters give enhanced importance to the sense of moral and psychological patterning within events, or to a sense of the ironic logic of history. To compare is to contrast; to contrast is to compare. By the networks of connections between characters, Conrad draws attention to individual distinctiveness (and often to human isolation) yet also to ironic likeness and common needs.

Conrad can be a very acute psychologist, but not so much by any profound depiction of an individual's psychology as by his concentration on forces operating variously within particular groupings. Thus in *The Nigger of the 'Narcissus'* we are led to see how difficult it is to distinguish a vicarious self-pity (which divides men) from an altruistic co-operation (which unites): even the wise captain momentarily confuses them, to his cost. In *Heart of Darkness* we are invited to realise the full extent of moral hollowness in 'civilised' men: even the apparently heroic Kurtz proves 'hollow at the core', we are told. In *Nostromo* we are shown how men habitually idealise the material world in which they are ambushed and are tantalised by their own ideals.

Nevertheless, a certain typology clearly emerges from Conrad's works, and I offer it below. Under the headings 'heroes' and 'heroines' I include figures who are protagonists in a narrative and also figures who though not protagonists are important as representatives of values.

A typology

Conrad's heroes

1 The Hamlets (see pp. 70–77). Examples: Decoud (*N*), Heyst (*V*), D'Alcacer (*R*). Civilised, sceptical, reflective, and likely to become immobilised at some point of crisis.

2 The Quixotes (see pp. 70–76). Examples: Lingard of *Almayer's Folly*, *Outcast* and *Rescue*; Captain Anthony in *Chance*. However, all Conrad's active idealists partake of the quixotic: they pursue goals which recede or prove illusory, or succeed only at the price of a kind of monomania which may result in suffering or destruction for themselves or others. This category includes:

The men of egoistic imagination. Examples: Kurtz (*HD*), Jim in *Lord Jim*, Gould in *Nostromo*. Visionaries who may be led to disaster by their vision.

3 The sympathetic narrators. None of Conrad's fictional narrators

(and possibly not even the narrators of some of his non-fictional writings) should automatically be equated with Conrad. But biographically some of the 'I-narrators', generally anonymous ones, stand very close to the author, having had experiences which relate closely to those of the younger Conrad. Examples are the narrators of *The Shadow-Line*, 'Falk', 'The Secret Sharer' and 'A Smile of Fortune': anonymous yet continuous (i.e. interchangeable with each other), recalling past voyages and encounters; fallible but likeable, curious about life, gentlemanly but unconventionally tolerant and broad-minded.

A narrator who is carefully individuated and is more distinct from the author than the foregoing figures is, of course, Marlow. The hero who morally and ontologically (i.e. in fulness of being) is the best of Conrad's characters is probably the Marlow of *Heart of Darkness*, followed closely by the Marlow of *Lord Jim*, at some distance by the Marlow of 'Youth' and at a much greater distance by the Marlow of *Chance*. The Marlow of *HD* and *Jim* is intelligent, sceptical and reflective, but unlike the Hamlets (our Type 1) he is able to respond bravely to crisis after crisis – he is a survivor; he has the imagination of Type 2 but also moral stability, a humane liberalism of outlook; and he has something of the crusading adventurousness of the quixotic type (he rescues Jim, for example, as Lingard had once rescued Willems in *An Outcast*) while preserving a self-critical spirit and a cool grasp of realities. As an ex-*Conway* boy and ex-captain he is also a reasonably prosperous English gentleman of the upper middle class who likes the sound of his own voice and can be patronising; but he remains one of the best friends to be made in English literature: wise, sceptical, open, humane. The Marlow of 'Youth' is rather more sentimental – perhaps slightly the worse for drink; and the Marlow of *Chance* is becoming old, garrulous and waffling, alas.

4 The stalwart workers. Examples: Singleton (*NN*), the boilermaker (*HD*), MacWhirr ('Typhoon'), Don Pepe (*N*), Jörgenson (*R*), and perhaps Davidson (*V*). Not articulate, bright or imaginative, but industrious and utterly reliable: they know their job and stick to it through thick and thin even when others fail.

5 The professional élite. Examples: the French lieutenant in *Lord Jim* (and possibly Brierly and Stein in the same novel), Captain Allistoun in *NN*, the engineer-in-chief in *Nostromo*, and Captain Giles in *The Shadow-Line*. These are the aristocracy of their professions: men of maturity, courage, integrity and wisdom, though they too may be laconic or gnomic in utterance. (Types blend. Peyrol in *The Rover* is a mixture of types 4 and 5, with a dash of the quixotic.)

6 The exotic prince or chieftain. Examples: Dain Maroola in *AF*,

Karain in 'Karain', Dain Waris in *Lord Jim* and Hassim in *The Rescue*. Such men are brown, handsome, noble, brave and apparently virile, though capable of being unmanned by a woman. They may be helped or brought to disaster by the white friends who patronise them. Their natural habitat lies somewhere between the Malay Archipelago of the period 1870–90 and the Hollywood jungle-set of the period 1920–50.

Conrad's heroines

(I use the term loosely to refer both to females who are prominent in a narrative and to females who though not prominent are morally important.)

1 Exotic seductresses. Examples: Nina in *AF*, Aissa in *Outcast*, Kurtz's mistress in *HD*. They are associated with the fecund jungle of which they may seem emanations; potent and with the effect of weakening or incapacitating the man who embraces them, as though primitive nature were taking its revenge on the civilised or as though the dark and feminine were taking its revenge on the white and masculine.

2 Noble idealists. Examples: Kurtz's Intended (*HD*), Antonia (*N*), Natalie Haldin (*UWE*). These are radiant romantic idealists who preserve their faith in the men they love but who are to a large extent ignorant of those men or of the harsh realities of the world.

3 The seemingly subjugated. Examples: Flora Barral in *Chance*, Alice Jacobus ('A Smile of Fortune'), Winnie Verloc in *The Secret Agent*, Lena in *Victory*, Arlette of *The Rover*. These are women with unhappy pasts who are or have been so strongly dominated by men that their inner natures seem to have been crushed or suppressed, but who are yet capable of displaying surprising independence: they may strike back.

4 The Lady Almoners. Examples: Mrs Gould in the later stages of *Nostromo* and Tekla at the end of *Under Western Eyes*. These are the idealistic women who have had disillusioning experience of the world but who still, in their limited sphere, do what they can to make the world a better place.

When Conrad is describing subservient daughters or apparently loyal wives, he frequently notes hidden features which make those females potentially rebellious against their fathers or husbands; as so often, he likes to imply that individuals are largely opaque to each other and that the bonds of solidarity are far weaker than we like to suppose.

We have noted that women of type 1 are often associated with the jungle, dark and fecund; and that women of type 2 are commonly likened to statues, noble and pure. Another peculiarity of Conrad's imagination is that it is sometimes preoccupied by the notion of the symbolic or actual interchangeability of women and wealth. Thus in the first novel, *Almayer's Folly*, as Nina turns more and more from her father to Dain, so Dain's wealth flows into the hidden chest of Mrs Almayer, and the loss of Nina means the end of Almayer's hopes of finding treasure in the hinterland. In *Nostromo*, Gould's love for the silver of the mine gradually supersedes his love for his childless wife, who comes to see him as surrounded by 'a circumvallation' of precious metal; he even sleeps at the mine, with the silver. In 'A Smile of Fortune', the hero finds Alice Jacobus so seductive that to be alone with her he enters into a distasteful business-deal with her father; he loses the girl but unexpectedly makes a big profit. 'I dreamt of a pile of gold in the form of a grave in which a girl was buried, and woke up callous with greed.' Conrad's works may sometimes remind us of Tourneur's aphorism: 'Were't not for gold and women, there would be no damnation.'

9 Conrad's place in literary history

Conrad's earliest works were thematically rich but cumbrous in plotting and inflatedly self-conscious in descriptive style. Then in the period 1897 to 1911, the great period which extends from *The Nigger* to *Under Western Eyes* and includes Conrad's supreme works, *Heart of Darkness* and *Nostromo*, he displays a brilliantly exuberant virtuosity in thought and expression, in concept and technique, which dwarfs the recurrent flaws. From 1911 to 1918 there is a mixed period which includes a great success (*The Shadow-Line*), and some imposing but radically flawed work (*Chance*, with its gratuitously convoluted narrative procedures, and *Victory*, with its ludicrously heavy-handed allegorising). In the final phase there are several novels which look suspiciously like boys' adventure-tales laboriously inflated to elephantine proportions. These are *The Rescue*, *The Arrow of Gold*, *The Rover* and *Suspense*. The decline in his late years can be explained not only by his age but also by what has been termed a 'normalisation' in his outlook. As he aged and became an acclaimed and prosperous figure, so his writing, which had always had a preoccupation with certain very traditional values (loyalty, heroism, fidelity), is no longer concerned to submit those values to baptism by the fires of scepticism and cynism, and the techniques no longer probe and question conventional assumptions.

In his major phase, he was 'ahead of his times', in ideas and techniques; and this was because he was more intelligently and perceptively of his times than most writers then were. In his critical awareness of nineteenth-century preoccupations, he anticipated – often critically – many twentieth-century preoccupations. He was an intermediary between Romantic and Victorian traditions and the innovations of Modernism. He is Romantic in his interest in questing individualism and in his keen responsiveness to the beauty of the natural world in its more useless and dramatic manifestations. He is Victorian in his sense of the burdens of thought in an age when science offers bleak vistas; Victorian in his responsiveness to the magnitude of the imperial adventure, and in the related sense of the importance of an ethic of work and duty among its varied partic-ipants. Yet his sense of individualism can modulate into the Modern-ist's intuition of solipsism; and Modernistic, too, is his sense of the utter absurdity of man in a non-moral universe, his profound scepticism about the value of modern industrial society and its acquisitive imperialisms, and his sense of men as myopic participants in a destructive machine. As Albert Guerard has said, Conrad's view of history 'is sceptical and disillusioned, which for us today must mean true' (*CN*, 177). Even the Modernist's sense of the duplicity, deceptiveness and inadequacy of language is voiced repeatedly by Conrad ('the old, old words, worn thin, defaced'); and in his kaleidoscopic techniques, his mastery of delayed decoding, he clearly and boldly anticipates the experimentation which was to burgeon in poetry and the novel almost a generation after *Heart of Darkness*.

Naturally, then, Conrad has had a rich and varied influence on subsequent writers. The paradox of the virtue of evil, so vividly dramatised in *Heart of Darkness*, was developed further by both T. S. Eliot and Graham Greene. The paradox, which stems both from orthodox Roman Catholic theology and from the Romantic emphasis on the value of intensity, is that it is better to be intensely evil than to be mediocre or secularly good. In the intensity of his corruption, Kurtz has a stature denied to the mediocre figures around him. This paradox is at the heart of *The Waste Land*, and Eliot indicated his debt by alluding in the poem to the tale's opening and, more famously, by choosing a passage culminating in Kurtz's words 'The horror!' as the original epigraph to the poem. The same theme is developed in 'The Hollow Men', with its Conradian epigraph. Graham Greene's *Brighton Rock* also exploits the paradox of the virtue of evil, but Greene's greatest debt is probably to *The Secret Agent*: for Greeneland, that seedy, vulgar, tawdry urban territory, has clear affinities with the base, murky, slimy London of Conrad's novel. (Conrad himself briefly enters *It's a Battlefield*.)

The Conradian theme that loyalty may entail treachery has been extensively developed by Greene, as we are reminded by the epigraph, from *Victory*, which heads his late novel *The Human Factor*: 'I only know that he who forms a tie is lost. The germ of corruption has entered into his soul.' This theme was present in his early works, for example *The Man Within* and *The Name of Action*; and he has said that at that period, Conrad's influence on him was 'too great and too disastrous': 'Never again, I swore, would I read a novel of Conrad's – a vow I kept for more than a quarter of a century, until I found myself with *Heart of Darkness* in a small paddle boat travelling up a Congo tributary in 1959 . . . . . ' (*A Sort of Life*, 1971, p. 208). Conrad's range is emphasised by the fact that novelists as diverse as V. S. Naipaul and John le Carré have acknowledged his potent influence.

Continental writers who have admired Conrad include Thomas Mann and André Gide. Mann's enthusiasm for *The Secret Agent* in particular and Conrad's outlook in general has been published in *Past Masters and Other Papers* (1933), in which he concludes:

Conrad's objectivity may seem cool; but it is a passion – a passion for freedom . . . . . His intellectual message will be for those among us who believe – in opposition to the views of the large majority – that the idea of freedom has a rôle to play in Europe that is not yet played out.

André Gide had visited and corresponded with the ageing Conrad, and later claimed: 'He was the only one of my elders that I loved and knew.' Gide supervised the translation into French of various works of Conrad, and himself was responsible for the translation of *Typhoon*; while his *Voyage au Congo* is dedicated to Conrad and discusses *Heart of Darkness*. The journals show that Gide was particularly fascinated by *Lord Jim* and its demonstration that a momentary and apparently involuntary act can engage the whole subsequent lifetime: Gide's idea of the 'motiveless' or wilfully immoral act (*l'acte gratuit*) in *Les Caves du Vatican* offers a contrast. And in his obituary tribute to Conrad, Gide wrote:

> Nobody had lived more savagely than Conrad; nobody had then submitted life to so patient, sensitive, and wise a transmutation into art.

In the United States, the three major novelists of this century, Ernest Hemingway, Scott Fitzgerald and William Faulkner, all admired and were influenced by Conrad. In 1924 Hemingway declared that though Eliot was now more fashionable than Conrad,

> If I knew that by grinding Mr Eliot into a fine dry powder and sprinkling that powder over Mr Conrad's grave Mr Conrad would shortly appear, looking very annoyed at the forced return and commence writing, I would leave for London early tomorrow morning with a sausage-grinder.
>
> (*Transatlantic Review*, II, 341–2)

There is kinship between Conrad's Singleton and Hemingway's Santiago (in *The Old Man and the Sea*): an ethic of stoic endurance in the face of an environment which may be either serenely neutral or ruthlessly hostile. Both writers look with sympathy on the reticent courage of simple men, battered by life, who persevere without illusions. In the case of Scott Fitzgerald, there is no doubt that Nick Carraway, the partly-critical, largely-fascinated observer of the great Gatsby, owes much to Conrad's Marlow and his ambivalent relationships to Kurtz and Jim; and furthermore Fitzgerald once remarked that the Preface to *The Nigger of the 'Narcissus'* afforded him 'the greatest "credo" in my life'. As for William Faulkner, it has often been observed that his narrative convolutions and obliquities may have been prompted by Conrad's. An American critic writes:

> The slighter *Chance*, rather than *Lord Jim* or *Nostromo*, anticipates the full Faulknerian extension of the impressionistic method. The amount of meditative comment screening the naked scene, the

degree and amount of interposition, gives Marlow at times the very accent and rhythm of a Faulknerian overriding voice.

(*CN*, 267)

When Faulkner was awarded the Nobel Prize, his speech of acceptance was based upon (and vainly attempted to surpass) the humanism of Conrad's essay 'Henry James'.

And finally, it is appropriate that the author of *Heart of Darkness* should now be helping black writers in the emergent nations of Africa. A good instance is provided by the celebrated Kenyan novelist, James Ngugi, whose *A Grain of Wheat* (1967) is a bold adaptation to modern African politics of the themes and dramatic situations of *Under Western Eyes*. Conrad had indicated that a Russian revolution would merely restore old tyranny under a new name; Ngugi makes much the same judgement of black rule in post-imperial Kenya – and his scepticism has perhaps been vindicated by the fact that since I began this book he has been arrested by the Kenyan police and held in jail without trial.

Conrad's outlook, though complex, was unbalanced: it generally inclined towards pessimism. In domestic matters, it is easy to see that he often made drastic and limiting exclusions: there are many happinesses which are real and good and which he omits. In large-scale political matters, however, his outlook has proved alarmingly wise. The most telling vindication of Conrad's genius has been provided by the follies and brutalities of twentieth-century history.

Part Three
Reference Section

A list of symbolic or allegoric names in Conrad's fiction

Some commentators, more skilled as anagrammatists than as critics, have found a plethora of symbolic names in Conrad. An American commentator remarks, for example, that Holroyd (*N*) is 'a kind of God figure. (The temptation to point out the similarity of Holroyd to *Holy rōd* is overwhelming.)' So I must emphasise, yet again, that common sense is right: the prevailing mode of Conrad's fiction is a realistic one in which the vast majority of proper names used have the arbitrariness and inconsequentiality of real life. However, just as Conrad's fiction from time to time generates the allusiveness of symbolism or allegory, so among the proper names we from time to time encounter one which has unusual significance. The fictional context always makes this significance evident: indeed, on several occasions Conrad makes punning jokes to emphasise the fact.

ALMA/MAGDALEN/LENA (*V*). That the heroine of *Victory* should have not one but three names, and all of them allusive, is a sign of a major fault in this novel – it is heavy-handedly allegoric. *Alma* is both a Spanish and an Italian noun meaning soul; it is a Latin adjective meaning kind or nourishing. These connotations are vaguely appropriate to her role as would-be helpmeet to Heyst and as a force of love and life in the world assailed by the force of hate and death represented by Gentleman Jones. *Magdalen* is the name of the Biblical 'fallen woman', and is appropriate to a heroine whose working life has threatened her with possible prostitution and who now feels intermittently sinful in living with Heyst as his devoted mistress. *Lena* is the name bestowed by Heyst: perhaps as an abbreviation of Magdalen; more likely as an abbreviation of Helena, for the plot of the novel has occasional parodic resemblances to the story of Helen of Troy, who, abducted by Paris to be his mistress, occasioned the siege of Troy and the burning of its 'topless towers'. The abduction of Alma by Heyst results in the invasion of his island, a battle, and the conflagration in which Heyst perishes. (The legend of Helen of Troy had been discussed at the beginning of *The Rescue*, which itself has certain parodic echoes of the legend.)

GENTLEMAN BROWN (*Lord Jim*) and GENTLEMAN JONES (*V*). Shelley's phrase, 'The Devil is a gentleman', partly explains the sobriquet of these rather melodramatic villains. (Gentleman Brown owes a little to Marlowe's *Tamburlaine* too.) Jones is described as 'an insolent spectre on leave from Hades', and we are clearly invited to identify him with Lucifer in the following passage, which makes a joke of the point:

> 'Having been ejected, he said, from his proper social sphere because he had refused to conform to certain usual conventions, he was a rebel now, and was coming and going up and down the earth.....I told him that I had heard that sort of story about somebody else before. His grin is really ghastly.....'

KURTZ (*HD*). In the Congo, Conrad had met a dying trader with the German name Klein, which means 'small'. *Kurz* is German for 'short', and Marlow emphasises the ironic appropriateness of this in its adaptation as a surname:

> 'Kurtz – that means 'short' in German – don't it? Well, the name was as true as everything else in his life – and death. He looked at least seven feet long.'

LEGGATT ('The Secret Sharer'). The name is homophonous with 'legate', meaning an envoy from some foreign power. Intermittently and faintly, the tale invokes the possibility that he is a supernatural visitant. The ladder is so providentially left alongside for him; the captain is able to conceal him because the suite of rooms has in plan the shape of an L, we are told – L for Leggatt; and he departs by swimming for the looming mass which has been likened several times to the gate of Erebus, the entrance to Hades.

NARCISSUS (*NN*). Conrad had actually served on a ship with this name; but his decision to preserve the name in the novel makes excellent thematic sense. Narcissus, in classical mythology, fell in love with a beautiful form, not realising that it was his own reflection: his apparent love for another was unwitting self-love. At the heart of the novel *The Nigger of the 'Narcissus'* is the distinction between (*a*) unsentimental solidarity, which binds men to each other and to the ship in bonds of co-operative labour (the ethic of the captain and Singleton), and (*b*) sentimental pseudo-solidarity, the apparent altruism which divides the crew, leads to near-mutiny and imperils the ship. (The latter ethic is generated and fostered by Jimmy, abetted by Donkin.) The narrator emphasises that the sympathy expressed by some of the crew for Wait is in reality a vicarious self-pity. The spectacle of a dying man reminds them that they too must die; they comfort him because they secretly wish to be comforted themselves. 'The latent egoism of tenderness to suffering appeared in the developing anxiety not to see him die.' 'Latent egoism': they are sliding towards ethical narcissism. Even Captain Allistoun is briefly tainted when, feeling pity for Jimmy, he brusquely orders him back to his cabin: and this act precipitates the near-mutiny. (Like 'The Secret Sharer', *The Nigger* is ethically a more spartan and severe work than the majority of commentators wish to recognise.)

NIKITA/NECATOR (*UWE*). *Necator*, Latin for 'killer', is an appropriate pun on the Russian name Nikita (Nick), given the character's sadistic nature. In the tale 'Because of the Dollars' (*Within the Tides*) a similarly ruthless character has the name Fector, which derives from the Latin *interfector*, meaning 'slayer'.

NOSTROMO. *Nostromo* is Italian for 'bosun', and this character was indeed a bosun on his arrival in Sulaco; but the main ironies surrounding his name depend on the more obvious fact that Nostromo is an abbreviation of the Italian phrase *nostro uomo*: our man. The text says that the name derived from 'Captain Mitchell's mispronunciation' – presumably of the phrase. Linda complains that it is no true Christian name – 'no name either for man or beast'; and Teresa Viola says: 'People.....have given you a silly name – and nothing besides – in exchange for your soul and body'. Clearly the name emphasises his identity as one who prides himself on his public utility as general factotum, though it becomes increasingly ironic as his egotism becomes more rebellious; and there is heavy irony when, having betrayed his trust, he assumes the new name, Captain Fidanza: for *fidanza* is Italian for 'trust'.

Nostromo's Christian name, Gian' Battista (John-the-Baptist), has an irony which the text underlines. John the Baptist prepared the way for Jesus Christ and was thus the inaugurator of the Christian era; Nostromo prepares the way for the control of Sulaco by the economic imperialists and is thus an inaugurator of its capitalist era. Decoud calls him 'this active usher-in of the material implements for our progress'.

RANSOME (*SL*). His uncanny 'grace', both of movement and of nature, is stressed; self-sacrificingly, he helps the guilty captain to bring the apparently accursed ship safely to harbour. As the name is homophonous with 'ransom', it is a mnemonic of Jesus Christ, whom the Bible several times calls the ransom of mankind; and in the context provided by the tale's hints of metaphysical evil, there is aptness in the occasional fleeting suggestions of a Christ-like aura about Ransome. The narrator makes a joke of the homophone when he remarks of Ransome: 'He was a priceless man altogether'.

RAZUMOV (*UWE*). The name derives from the Russian noun *pazym*, pronounced ráhzoom, which has the same root as the English word 'reason' and means 'mind' or 'intellect'. 'Razumov' may thus be translated as 'Son of Reason' and is a name appropriate to a dedicated student whose parentage is unknown to the public. 'The word Razumov was the mere label of a solitary individuality.' *Under Western*

Eyes is variously indebted to Dostoyevsky's *Crime and Punishment* (notwithstanding Conrad's avowed hostility to that writer), and the name may have been suggested by that of Raskolnikov's friend Razumikhin.

SINGLETON (*NN*). The character was based on a seaman called Sullivan, and Sullivan was the name Conrad used in the manuscript; but he changed it to Singleton, presumably because he preferred a name with connotations of 'uniqueness', 'simplicity' and 'integrity'. (In the novel, Singleton is the lone survivor of the older generation of simple, reliable seamen; and in a letter to Graham, Conrad remarks that he is 'simple and great like an elemental force'.) In his 'singleness' of character he contrasts with the duplicity of the ambiguous James Wait.

WAIT (*NN*). The narrative exploits various connotations of this name. When shouted, the name is ambiguous, for it sounds like a command. Thus, at its first utterance, Wait brings confusion – and a challenge, for the mate has the impression that a stranger is daring to tell him to interrupt the roll-call. ('Mr Baker advanced intrepidly. "Who are you? How dare you ...?" he began.') This makes a splendidly symbolic opening to *The Nigger of the 'Narcissus'*, portending the bewilderment and near-mutiny that Jimmy will engender during the voyage. The word 'wait' can be a noun meaning 'a delay', and the ship appropriately makes increasingly slow progress until his death, upon which the vessel spurts for home. 'Wait' is, in addition, homophonous with 'weight' – a burden; and the novel clearly exploits this sense, too. When the ship is blown over on its side during the storm, the side which is downwards is the one on which Wait is trapped in his cabin, as though the vessel were weighed down by him; and when his corpse, after waiting, lingering even in death on the plank, at last slides into the sea, 'The ship rolled as if relieved of an unfair burden'.

It should be emphasised that the dominant conventions of Conradian fiction are secular and realistic. Although Conrad creates symbolic and allegoric levels of meaning, he always provides natural explanations of seemingly supernatural occurrences. For example: Jimmy's body lingers on the plank until Belfast shouts 'Go!' at it, whereupon it goes; but the natural explanation of the delay is that a nail had been sticking up from the plank and had caught the shroud, and the natural explanation of the movement is that Belfast had touched the corpse with his fingers, giving it the nudge needed to free it. (And the nail had been sticking up because the carpenter had lost many of his tools overboard when the men had hurled them out in their desperate struggle to rescue Jimmy during the tempest; so the ironies and implications are intricate.)

Biographical list

MAX BEERBOHM (1872–1956). Essayist, parodist and caricaturist, knighted in 1939. His parody of Conrad in *A Christmas Garland* constitutes the most clever criticism of the early (pre-1897) Conradian style. Conrad wrote: 'I have lived long enough to see ['The Lagoon'] most agreeably guyed by Mr Max Beerbohm in a volume of parodies entitled *A Christmas Garland*, where I found myself in very good company. I was immensely gratified. I began to believe in my public existence.' (*TU*. p. vi.)

TADEUSZ BOBROWSKI (1829–94). The rich uncle who became Conrad's guardian after the early deaths of Conrad's parents. Pompous but shrewd, responsible and fair-minded. To his records and published reminiscences we owe much of our knowledge of Conrad's family and upbringing.

THOMAS CARLYLE (1795–1881). Scottish-born historian and social-political polemicist whose works include *Sartor Resartus*, *The French Revolution* and *Heroes and Hero-Worship*. Conrad knew some of his writings and may have been influenced by their emphasis on salvation by work rather than by reflection.

FRÉDÉRIC CHOPIN (1810–49). The Polish composer and pianist. Conrad in late years would summon John Powell to play compositions by Chopin to him – compositions which often, in their romantic virtuosity and plangent melancholy, have affinities with the relatively lyrical parts of Conrad's writings.

CONRAD, JESSIE (1873–1936), née Jessie George, a typist, who married Conrad at a Register Office in 1896 and subsequently bore him two sons, Borys and John. He wrote a preface to her *Handbook of Cookery for a Small House* (1923). After his death she published *Personal Recollections of Joseph Conrad*, *Joseph Conrad as I Knew Him* and *Joseph Conrad and His Circle*.

STEPHEN CRANE (1871–1900). The American reporter and author whose most celebrated work, *The Red Badge of Courage*, appeared in 1895. He was introduced to Conrad in 1897 and the two became good friends. Conrad was interested in his vivid descriptive techniques ('He is *the only* impressionist and *only* an impressionist'), and *The Red Badge* may perhaps have influenced *The Nigger of the 'Narcissus'*. Conrad wrote:

Crane dealt in his book with the psychology of the mass – the army; while I – in mine – had been dealing with the same subject on a much smaller scale and in more specialized conditions – the crew of a merchant ship, brought to the test of what I may venture to call the moral problem of conduct.

(*LE*, 95)

R. B. CUNNINGHAME GRAHAM (1852–1936). Scottish aristocrat, traveller, adventurer, pioneer socialist, public orator, notorious MP, and prolific author of tales, essays, biographies and histories. A close friend of Conrad's for many years, he supplied material for *Nostromo*. He appears as Saranoff in Shaw's *Arms and the Man*, as Mr Courtier in Galsworthy's *The Patrician*, and as Mr X in Conrad's 'The Informer' (*A Set of Six*).

CHARLES DARWIN (1809–82). The naturalist whose *The Origin of Species* (1859) gave the stamp of scientific authority to the widespread Victorian belief in ruthless competition as a means to progress. The sense of a wastefully predatory nature is particularly important in Conrad's earlier tales and novels.

ALPHONSE DAUDET (1840–97). Author of tales and novels; probably best remembered for *Lettres de mon moulin* (*Letters from My Windmill*). Rather surprisingly, in view of its sentimentality, Conrad had an early enthusiasm for his work; but in 'Alphonse Daudet' (*NLL*) the enthusiasm was firmly qualified: 'Daudet, a man as naïvely clear, honest and vibrating as the sunshine of his native land; that regrettably undiscriminating sunshine. . . . .'

CHARLES DICKENS (1812–70). From childhood onwards, Conrad was familiar with Dickens's novels; and the grotesque characterisations and nightmarish depictions of urban squalor in such works as *Bleak House* anticipate effects in *The Secret Agent*. Conrad may also perhaps have learnt from Dickens's bold command of leit-motifs and symbolic detail.

FYODOR DOSTOYEVSKY (1822–81). Conrad purported to regard this great Russian novelist as a mad barbarian ('the grimacing, haunted creature' who offers 'fierce mouthings from prehistoric ages'), but *Under Western Eyes* is variously indebted to Dostoyevsky's masterpiece, *Crime and Punishment*.

JACOB EPSTEIN (1880–1959). The creator of stark, powerful and often controversial works of sculpture. His bust of Conrad and his reminiscences of the sittings (in *Let There Be Sculpture*) form a sombre record of the aged writer.

GUSTAVE FLAUBERT (1821–80). French novelist and story-writer of priestly dedication who in *L'Education sentimentale*, *Madame Bovary* and *Trois contes* (which Conrad admired) strove for a coolly objective portrayal of life's ironies and human fallibilities.

ANATOLE FRANCE (1844–1922). Pen name of Jacques Anatole Thibault: a cool, drily ironic writer whose most successful work was the anti-clerical satire, *L'Ile des pengouins* (*Penguin Island*). His essay on Prosper Mérimée was one of the sources of *Nostromo*. Conrad praised him in two reviews (republished in *NLL*).

SIGMUND FREUD (1856–1939). The father of modern psycho-analysis, whose theories have prompted various approaches to Conrad – part of Albert Guerard's *Conrad the Novelist* and much of Bernard Meyer's *Joseph Conrad: A Psychoanalytic Biography*. Conrad used to speak scornfully of Freud, no doubt foreseeing that psycho-analytic approaches to literature tend to be reductive, for they exaggerate its subjectivity and neglect its objective truth-value.

EDWARD GARNETT (1868–1939). The publisher's reader and literary critic who encouraged and publicised Conrad (and Cunninghame Graham, W. H. Hudson, D. H. Lawrence and others). A sceptical romantic, he valued vividly heterodox writings. His wife Constance, by her labours as a lucid translator, brought the works of Chekhov, Turgenev and Dostoyevsky before the British public.

ANDRÉ GIDE (1869–1951). French novelist and critic who corresponded with the ageing Conrad and undertook the translation of *Typhoon* into French. His tribute to Conrad was published in *La Nouvelle Revue Française* in December 1924.

FORD MADOX HUEFFER, subsequently Ford Madox Ford (1873–1939). Novelist, critic, editor and raconteur. His best novel is generally thought to be *The Good Soldier*, 1915. He collaborated with Conrad between 1898 and 1910 (*The Inheritors*, *Romance*, 'The Nature of a Crime') and he has left lively if unreliable reminiscences of Conrad in *Return to Yesterday* and *Joseph Conrad: A Personal Remembrance*.

HENRY JAMES (1843–1916). Prolific American-born novelist who settled in England and took British nationality in 1915; a writer capable of great subtlety who in his later work became vapidly prolix. In its slow pace and elaborate narratorial deviousness, *Chance* is probably the most Jamesian of Conrad's novels. Ironically, it was in an essay so vapid as to be obscure that James criticised *Chance* for prolixity: 'It places Mr Conrad absolutely alone as a votary of the way to do a thing that shall make it undergo most doing.' ('The New Novel', 1914.) Conrad's tribute to James, whom he terms 'the historian of fine consciences', is in *NLL*.

LORD KELVIN, formerly William Thompson (1824–1907). British physicist and inventor. His second law of thermodynamics, the law of entropy, when popularised created a pervasive nightmare in the imaginations of writers of the late nineteenth century: the nightmare in which the sun cools and dies and all life becomes extinct on a dark earth. Numerous passages in Conrad's letters, essays and fictions express this idea.

RUDYARD KIPLING (1865–1936). The prolific and highly successful writer of short stories, novels and poems: a patriot who celebrated the British Empire, amplifying the imperialistic fervour around the turn of the century, and who preached a gospel of martial virility. He corresponded briefly with Conrad, who respected his techniques but distrusted his outlook. Conrad's 'An Outpost of Progress' can be seen as a critical riposte to such tales by Kipling as 'At the End of the Passage'.

APOLLO KORZENIOWSKI (1820–63). Polish writer, translator, patriot, and father of Joseph Conrad.

D. H. LAWRENCE (1885–1930). The greatest novelist of the generation after Conrad's. The characterisation of Gerald Crich in *Women in Love* may owe something to that of Charles Gould in *Nostromo*; but the two authors were antagonistic. Whereas Conrad sensed the universe to be essentially dead, Lawrence believed it to be essentially vital. Hence Lawrence jeered at Conrad as one of the 'Writers among the Ruins': 'Snivel in a wet hanky like Lord Jim.' In Conrad's opinion (as recalled by Epstein), 'Lawrence had started well, but had gone wrong. "Filth. Nothing but obscenities."'

DR JOHN MACINTYRE (1857–1928). The pioneer radiologist who in 1898, as a party entertainment, demonstrated his X-ray machine to Conrad, thus prompting *The Inheritors*. (See LCG, 107–8.)

GUY DE MAUPASSANT (1850–93). Author of numerous sceptical, realistic and ironic tales and novels. Conrad particularly admired his *Pierre et Jean* and *Bel-Ami*, and was influenced by the essay 'Le Roman'.

ADAM MICKIEWICZ (1798–1855). The greatest of Polish poets, author of the epic *Pan Tadeusz* and of the verse-dramas *Konrad Wallenrod* and *Dziady*. All of these are fervently patriotic; the last two centre on patriotic Konrads. In *Pan Tadeusz*, Jacek Soplica (like Lord Jim later) atones by subsequent heroism for former disgrace.

MARGUERITE PORADOWSKA (1848–1937). A Frenchwoman who married a distant cousin of Conrad's and had an intense correspondence with Conrad during the 1890s. That she was a prize-winning writer of tales and novels (though now they are held in low esteem) doubtless encouraged him to persevere with *Almayer's Folly*.

BERTRAND RUSSELL, 3rd Earl (1872–1970). The philosopher, logician and polemicist. He met Conrad in 1912 and had a brief yet memorable friendship with him, vividly described in Russell's *Portraits from Memory* and *Autobiography*, vol. 1. Russell named his eldest son John Conrad (the name of his friend's younger son) and his youngest Conrad.

IVAN TURGENEV (1818–83). Russian fiction-writer and essayist to whom Conrad pays tribute in *NLL*. Conrad particularly liked *A Sportsman's Sketches* (originally intending his own *Mirror of the Sea* to be in the spirit of that work); the essay 'Hamlet and Don Quixote' offers a proleptic commentary on Conrad's ideas of character; and *Rudin* and 'Enough' may have contributed some elements to *Lord Jim*. Conrad saw Turgenev as a civilised, liberal and humane contrast to Dostoyevsky.

RICHARD WAGNER (1813–83). The German composer whose innovatory operas and music-dramas were a potent cultural influence in the late nineteenth and early twentieth centuries. Conrad remarked that *Almayer's Folly* 'ends with a long *solo* for Almayer which is almost as long as Tristan's in Wagner' (*LMP*, 68); and the heroine of 'Freya of the Seven Isles' likes to 'play fierce Wagner music in the flicker of blinding flashes'. It may be coincidental that both Wagner's *Ring* cycle and Conrad's *Nostromo* have the theme that treasure confers both power and a curse, causing dissension and treachery while destroying love.

ALFRED RUSSEL WALLACE (1823–1913). The British naturalist, traveller and evolutionist. Richard Curle once wrote that Conrad 'loved old memoirs and travels – and I think Wallace's *Malay Archipelago* was his favourite bedside book.' Details from *The Malay Archipelago* help to provide local colour for *Lord Jim* and *The Rescue*.

H. G. WELLS (1866–1946). Writer of novels, tales, essays and histories, whose virtuosity in science fiction brought him great popular success. His unstable, initially warm, friendship with Conrad began when he reviewed *An Outcast of the Islands* in 1895: 'Only greatness could make books of which the detailed workmanship was so copiously bad, so well worth reading, so convincing, and so stimulating.' Wells's *The Time Machine* and *The War of the Worlds* may have had some slight influence on *Heart of Darkness* and *The Inheritors*. Eventually, the two writers disagreed strongly. Conrad said: 'The difference between us, Wells, is fundamental. You don't care for humanity but think they are to be improved. I love humanity but know they are not.' And in *Boon*, Wells jeered at 'the florid mental gestures of a Conrad': 'Conrad "writes". And it shows.'

BRUNO WINAWER (1883–1944). Polish author of short stories and comedies; Conrad helped him by translating his play *Księga Hioba* into English as *The Book of Job* in 1921. This was Conrad's sole translation of a literary text.

Gazetteer

Si itinerarium requiris, circumspice: If you seek his gazetteer, read
Conrad. In his odysseys he traversed far more of the earth's surface
than the majority of writers, and in his works he rendered vividly –
and charged with his own distinctive patterns of significance –
locations as far apart as South America and Bangkok, Cracow and
Stanley Falls, Geneva and Sydney, Borneo and the South Downs.
The more effectively the location, when taken over into a work of
art, is charged with significance, the more defiantly neutral the
factual location may seem when we encounter it – like a familiar
yet coldly untenanted dwelling.

POLAND However, as I have briefly indicated in this book, a visit
to Poland may do more to illuminate Conrad than may the reading
of a hundred commentaries. It is in any case good to be reminded
at first hand of the sufferings, heroism and faith of the Polish people,
in a land which has pagan government and is yet the homeland of
Pope John Paul II. For those who seek there localities with strong
Conradian associations, Cracow is poignantly rich: there is St
Mary's Church with its 'unequal massive towers', busy Florian
Street where Conrad stayed, and the Rakowicki Cemetery, where
the grave of his father proclaims Apollo Korzeniowski 'the victim
of Muscovite tyranny'.

ENGLAND In England, most of Conrad's former dwellings survive,
though they remain in private hands – there is as yet no 'Conrad
home' converted to a museum. If you walk through the rather dingy
and refuse-strewn streets to the rear of Victoria Station, you can
soon come to 17 Gillingham Street (the ground floor is a shop)
where Conrad had lodgings and wrote *An Outcast of the Islands*.
Further down towards the Thames, there still remains much of
Bessborough Gardens, that imposing array of lofty terraces opening
on to the Embankment at Vauxhall Bridge: here Conrad began
his first novel.

Admirers of *The Secret Agent* may care to test their own abilities as
literary detectives by endeavouring to retrace Verloc's route to the
Russian Embassy: page 265 of Gustav Morf's *The Polish Shades and
Ghosts of Joseph Conrad* offers an itinerary; and the pilgrim who retraces
Stevie's fateful progress across Greenwich Park uphill towards the
Observatory will find himself rewarded with pleasant vistas and
close proximity to the National Maritime Museum.
Places outside London. Ivy Walls in Essex, the first house that Conrad

occupied after his honeymoon, has been bulldozed. Pent Farm, Postling, near Hythe, which was his next house and the most famous of his dwellings (he lived there from 1898 to 1907) remains; though, according to Borys Conrad, the original farm buildings have gone, as has the outside lavatory which could accommodate two adults and a child. At Bishopsbourne, near Canterbury, is Oswalds, the large house in which Conrad resided from 1919 until his death. (This and other homes of Conrad are described in Borys Conrad's pamphlet, *Joseph Conrad's Homes in Kent*, available from the Joseph Conrad Society.) Conrad's grave at Canterbury is in the public cemetery on Westgate Court Avenue.

THE VOYAGES   For discussions of the voyages to the West Indies and South America, which may have contributed to *Nostromo*, of the Congo journey, the background to *Heart of Darkness*, and of the Eastern voyages (Bangkok, Singapore, the Sunda Straits, Borneo, etc.) which contributed to the South-East Asian novels and so many of the sea tales, see variously: Jocelyn Baines: *Joseph Conrad*; Jerry Allen: *The Sea Years of Joseph Conrad*; and Norman Sherry: *Conrad's Eastern World* and *Conrad's Western World*.

Further reading

Large bibliographies

T. G. Ehrsam, *A Bibliography of Joseph Conrad*, Metuchen, New Jersey:
Scarecrow Press, 1969.
Bruce Teets and Helmut E. Gerber, *Joseph Conrad: An Annotated
Bibliography of Writings about Him*, De Kalb, Illinois: Illinois Uni-
versity Press, 1971.

Editions of Conrad's works

The J. M. Dent Collected Edition (London, 1946–55) became,
through accessibility and frequent citation by commentators, perhaps
the nearest approach to a 'standard' edition, though it lacked *The
Inheritors*. Conrad's major works and some of the minor works are
available in Penguin. The American Norton editions of *Heart of
Darkness* and *Lord Jim* have abundant paraphernalia. Cambridge
University Press is now producing a scholarly edition of the whole
canon.

Editions of Conrad's letters

G. Jean-Aubry, *Joseph Conrad: Life and Letters*, London: Heinemann,
1927.
Letters from Conrad, 1895 to 1924, edited by Edward Garnett, London:
Nonesuch, 1928.
Letters of Joseph Conrad to Marguerite Poradowska, 1890–1920, tr. and
ed. J. A. Gee and P. J. Sturm, New Haven: Yale UP, 1940.
Conrad's Polish Background, ed. Z. Najder, London: Oxford UP, 1964.
Joseph Conrad's Letters to R. B. Cunninghame Graham, ed. Cedric Watts,
London: Cambridge UP, 1969.

Biographies

Jocelyn Baines, *Joseph Conrad: A Critical Biography*, London: Weiden-
feld and Nicolson, 1960. During the 1960s this became the standard
biography of Conrad.
Norman Sherry, *Conrad and His World*, London: Thames & Hudson,
1972. Perhaps the best introductory biography: concise and amply
illustrated.

Reminiscences

Ford Madox Ford, *Joseph Conrad: A Personal Remembrance*, London: Duckworth, 1924.

Jessie Conrad, *Joseph Conrad as I Knew Him*, London: Heinemann, 1926.

Bertrand Russell, *The Autobiography of Bertrand Russell, 1872–1914*, London: Allen & Unwin, 1967, pp. 207–10.

Criticism

H. G. Wells and Edward Garnett: early reviews of Conrad, reprinted in *Conrad: The Critical Heritage*, ed. N. Sherry, London: Routledge & Kegan Paul, 1973.

Max Beerbohm, '"The Feast" by J-s-ph C-nr-d' in *A Christmas Garland*, London: Heinemann, 1912.

F. R. Leavis, *The Great Tradition*, London: Chatto & Windus, 1948.

Douglas Hewitt, *Conrad: A Reassessment*, Cambridge: Bowes & Bowes, 1952.

Thomas Moser, *Joseph Conrad: Achievement and Decline*, Cambridge, Mass.: Harvard UP, 1957.

Albert Guerard, *Conrad the Novelist*, Cambridge, Mass.: Harvard UP, 1958.

The Art of Joseph Conrad: A Critical Symposium, ed. R. W. Stallman, East Lansing: Michigan State UP, 1960.

Eloise Knapp Hay, *The Political Novels of Joseph Conrad*, Chicago and London: Chicago UP, 1963.

Avrom Fleishman, *Conrad's Politics*, Baltimore: The Johns Hopkins Press, 1967.

Cedric Watts, *Conrad's 'Heart of Darkness': A Critical and Contextual Discussion*, Milan: Mursia International, 1977.

Educational tape or cassette

Laurence Lerner and Cedric Watts, *Conrad*, London: Sussex Tapes, 1972.

Recommended films of Conrad's works

An Outcast of the Islands, dir. Carol Reed, 1952.
The Shadow-Line, dir. Andrzej Wajda, 1976.
The Duellists, dir. Ridley Scott, 1977.

Periodicals devoted to Conrad

Conradiana, quarterly: published by Texas Tech. University.

Joseph Conrad Today, newsletter of the Joseph Conrad Society of America.
The Journal of the Joseph Conrad Society (UK).

General Index

Absurdist techniques:
  115–17
Adowa (ship): 30
Allen, Grant: 39
Allen, Jerry: 138, 186
Apocalypse Now (film): 45
Arnold, Matthew: 59;
  'Dover Beach', 51, 52–3
Austria: 9, 57
Ayer, A. J.: 83

Baines, Jocelyn: *Joseph
  Conrad*: 41, 103, 186, 187;
  quoted, 150
Baird, Tadeusz: *Jutro*, 45
Bangkok: 26
Baudelaire, Charles: 98,
  102
Beckett, Samuel: 68, 70
Beerbohm, Max: 49, 180;
  'The Feast' quoted, 84
Belgian Congo: 27–8, 61–2
Bennett, Richard Rodney:
  45
Bentley, Edmund: 57
Bergson, Henri: 78
Blackwood's Magazine: 64
Boethius: 102
Borneo: 26
Bowen, Elizabeth: 45
Brooke, Sir James: 65–6
Brooks, Cleanth: 146
Browne, Sir Thomas: 102
Burton, Richard F.: 142
Butler, Samuel: 78–9;
  Life and Habit quoted, 79

Caine, Hall: 39
Calderón de la Barca,
  Pedro: 84
Camus, Albert: 68, 70, 116,
  129
Canterbury: 43
Carlyle, Thomas: 59, 109,
  180
Carré, John le: 172
Casement, Roger: 125
Cervoni, César: 20
Cervoni, Dominic: 20
Chaucer, Geoffrey: 102
Chekhov, Anton: 69, 72
Chesson, W. H.: 30
Chopin, Frédéric: 8, 180
Christianity: 51–4
Clerici, Enrico: 140
Coleridge, S. T.: quoted,
  143; 'Ancyent Marinere',
  106–8

Congo River: 27–8
Conrad, Borys: 35, 41, 51–2
Conrad, Jessie: 35, 38, 180;
  Personal Recollections
  quoted, 50–51
Conrad, John: 35
Conradiana: 45
Cooper, James Fenimore:
  18
Corelli, Marie: 39
Cosmopolis: 63–4
Cousin, Victor: 96
Cracow (Kraków): 16, 17,
  41, 185
Crane, Stephen: 35, 180–1
Crimean War: 24
Cunninghame Graham,
  R. B.: 31, 35, 36, 51, 52,
  59–60, 61, 74, 80, 81,
  116, 125, 139–40, 141–2,
  147, 181
Curle, Richard: 138, 139

Darwin, Charles: 53, 88–
  91, 91–2, 98, 181; *Origin
  of Species* quoted, 88–9, 91
Davies, W. H.: 31
Daudet, Alphonse: 181
Delestang, M. and Mme.: 20
Dickens, Charles: 12, 48,
  59, 108–9, 181; *Bleak
  House*, 20, 108, 181
Don Quixote: 17, 18, 70–6
Dostoyevsky, Fyodor: 69,
  181; *Crime and Punishment*,
  179; *Notes from Under-
  ground*, 70, 72
The Duellists (film): 45
Duke of Sutherland (ship): 23

Eastwick, E. B.: *Venezuela*,
  138, 141
Eichmann, Adolf: 92
Eliot, George: 48, 59
Eliot, T. S.: 'The Hollow
  Men', 172; *The Waste
  Land*, 51, 146, 172
Ellis, Captain: 26
Engels, Friedrich: 125, 147
Epstein, Jacob: 43, 181

Faulkner, William: 173–4
Fitzgerald, F. Scott: 173
Flaubert, Gustave: 104–5,
  181; *Madame Bovary*, 104-
  5
Ford, Ford Madox: 35, 39–
  40, 182; *Joseph Conrad*

quoted, 23
Forster, E. M.: 44
France, Anatole: 106, 141,
  182
Frazer, Sir James: quoted,
  86
Frederick the Great: 9
Frétigny (sculptor): 21
Freud, Sigmund: 91–3, 182

Galsworthy, John: 30,
  31, 35, 112
Garibaldi, Giuseppe: 141
Garnett, Edward: 30–1, 32,
  35, 52, 182
Gaskell, Elizabeth: 59
Gautier, Théophile: 96
Germany: 9
Ghetto Uprising: 9
Gide, André: 173, 182
Goncharov, I. A.: 69
Greene, Graham: 172
Guerard, Albert J.: *Conrad
  the Novelist*, 46–7, 92,
  153–4, 171–2, 173–4

Hamblen, H. E.: *On Many
  Seas*, 140–1
Hardy, Thomas: 50, 105
Hemingway, Ernest: 173
Henley, W. E.: 57
Hitler, Adolf: 9, 12, 126
Hudson, W. H.: 31
Hueffer, Ford Madox (later
  Ford Madox Ford): 35,
  39–40, 182; *Joseph Conrad*
  quoted, 23
Hugo, Victor: 12, 16, 102
Hugues, Clovis: 20
Hume, David: *Treatise of
  Human Nature* quoted, 83
Hunt, G. W.: 63
Huysmans, J. -K.: 98
Huxley, T. H.: 53

Jacques, E. H.: 30
James, Henry: 35, 182
James, William: *Principles
  of Psychology*, 92
Janiformity: 7–8, 46–7, 59
Jeddah (ship): 26
Joyce, James: 97

Keats, John: 96
Kelvin, Lord: 54, 86, 182–3
Kierkegaard, S.: 78
Kipling, Rudyard: 33, 34,
  35, 57, 183